PIONEER DAYS IN UPPER CANADA

PIONEER DAYS IN UPPER CANADA

By
EDWIN C. GUILLET

UNIVERSITY OF TORONTO PRESS

CONTENTS

CHAPTER I

The Pioneer Home

"The orders of architecture baffle all description: every one builds his cottage or house according to his fancy, and it is not a difficult thing, in passing through the country, to tell what nation the natives of the houses 'hail from,' if we are aware of any of the whims and conceits that characterize them."

JOHN MacTAGGART (1829).[1]

THE first homes in Ontario were those erected along the Detroit River by several hundred disbanded French soldiers, who were settled there in the last forty years of the French period. Their *côtes*, or long, straggling villages, resembled in appearance the settlements along the St. Lawrence in Quebec. The *habitants'* cottages were low buildings with steep roofs, projecting eaves, and, as a general rule, dormer-windows. Sometimes they were built of logs, sometimes of rough stone if it were readily available, but in either case it was usual to cover the outer walls with pine boards which, when whitewashed, gave the cottages a neat and pleasing appearance. A windmill, or a cross, was quite frequently attached to the chimney of the house. An observer described the French-Canadian's home as "a little house with verandahs all round, few windows and few fancies; everything done with an air of humble comfort."[2] Barns were built of rougher materials, usually logs, while root-houses and bake-ovens were constructed of rocks and clay. The home of the *habitant* had from one to three rooms on the ground floor, and the high-pitched roof provided a loft which was reached by a ladder and used as a sleeping-room. As in other pioneer homes, the floors were commonly made of timbers smoothed off with the axe, but the French often partly covered them with hand-woven rugs. Like those in Quebec, the Detroit River settlements were under the control of seigneurs, who lived in manor-houses varying but little, except in size, from the homes of the peasants.

The first English-speaking settlers in Upper Canada

[1]John MacTaggart: *Three Years in Canada.* 1829. Vol. I, p. 308.
[2]*Ibid.*, pp. 310-11.

were almost entirely United Empire Loyalists, about 5000 in number. Most of the Loyalists came to Canada without worldly goods, their possessions having been either destroyed or confiscated by the revolutionists, or proving impossible to carry with them on their long and laborious trek to their new home in the wilderness. As they reached the government depots at Halifax and St. John in the Maritimes, Sorel, Chambly, Yamachiche, Cornwall and Kingston in the St. Lawrence region, and Niagara and Detroit in the west, they received their "location tickets," supplies and rations, and proceeded to their lots at the first opportunity. A considerable number of German mercenaries who had fought for George III in the Revolutionary War came to Canada at the same time and under the same circumstances as the Loyalists.

Those approaching Canada from the east were conveyed by bateaux up the St. Lawrence, proceeding in brigades of twenty or more. The head of each family held a location ticket, describing the general position of his future land, and as the bateaux were laboriously worked up the rapids the occupants eagerly scanned the wild shores, comparing their appearance with the well-developed farms that they had left behind in order to remain British. Many of the Loyalists were soldiers, and almost every family had a military tent, capable of accommodating eight or ten persons in a very crowded manner. Each night the tent was pitched on the shore, and in the morning the monotonous voyage continued. When they had reached their location it was often necessary to remain encamped for some time, while the surveyors completed their division of the land into lots; and as the tents would not accommodate all, some had to sleep beneath the trees. In some instances the summer had passed before the first "drawings" of land were made; this delay greatly increased the hardship of the first winter in the woods.

At last the surveyor, with his map in front of him, checked off each lot as its number was drawn from a hat. The officers received their lots first, usually the best locations along the waterfront, while the private soldiers and civilians drew theirs from the "back township" locations. Occasionally lots were exchanged so that old comrades in

Ensign James Peachey

ENCAMPMENT OF LOYALISTS AT NEW JOHNSTOWN (CORNWALL), JUNE 6, 1784

A LOCATION TICKET, 1816

BEGINNING A HOME

the same regiment might be near-neighbours. The families, or sometimes the men only, then proceeded to their lot, carrying the tent, such tools and supplies as they had been issued, and a few days' rations. It was often a difficult matter to identify the boundaries of their land, for the forests were full of matted undergrowth and fallen trees, and the undrained swamps and bridgeless streams presented still more formidable difficulties; but the tent was pitched and camp meals were cooked, while a suitable spot was chosen for the shanty after a general idea of the lay-out of the land had been obtained.

Co-operation among settlers was a prominent feature from the first; neighbours helped one another in erecting their crude log shanties, the more difficult of construction because the short-handled ship-axes in general use were but little heavier than hatchets, and only a few other tools of use in the work were available. The log shanty was constructed in the same manner in the later pioneer periods as in Loyalist days; it might be as large as twenty by fifteen feet, but it was very often considerably smaller. The usual shanty was about ten feet long, eight feet wide and six feet high, with the roof sloping to the back, where the wall was frequently not more than four feet high. Round logs, often of basswood or pine, formed the walls. Under the base-logs large rocks were placed for support, and the logs were roughly notched at the corners so that they would fit into one another.

When the log walls had been run up to the desired height the rafters were set in position and the shanty roofed in. The slanting roof was sometimes composed of thick slabs of basswood overlapping one another; other settlers used strips of elm bark about four feet long and two feet wide, placed in overlapping layers and fastened by withes to the poles; while another variety of roof consisted of small hollowed basswood logs laid like tile. When the rude house had been completed, the appearance of its interior varied with the possessions of the owner, and his efforts to make it homelike. Thomas Need's shanty is an example of the success of a bachelor in making his home in the backwoods comfortable, even if crude.

"The next few days were occupied in building a shanty,

or rude hut. . . . It consisted of one apartment, 14 feet by 12 feet in the clear, and contained in the way of furniture a camp bedstead, a chest of drawers, and a well-filled book-case; it had also the somewhat unusual luxury of a chimney, pegs for the suspension of guns and fishing implements, and shelves for my scanty kitchen utensils: a hole in the planks served to admit light, and air found free entrance through numberless cracks and crevices; such as it was, however, it served my purpose well; and when the evening closed I used to light my lamp and sit down to my books with a great feeling of comfort. Several of the classics, which on their shelves at Oxford were rather looked at than into, were now treated with the attention they deserve; and in the solitude of the Bush it was no light pleasure to re-peruse scenes and passages, every one of which was pregnant with some cherished association of school or college."[3]

The roof was usually improved at a later date. Need wrote in his journal on August 7, 1833: "The original roof of my shanty being only of rude logs, I thought it expedient to new-roof it entirely, after the most approved fashion, with thin pieces of deal cut into squares like slate."[4] This roof of cedar, though evidently considered an advanced type, was not satisfactory, for three months later Need states that the rain came through it in many places owing to the laths being warped by the sun. He expected that the rain would restore the roof to its original condition; but "meanwhile the house was a perfect vapour bath".[5]

After a shanty was built the ends of the logs were sawn off, and the cracks chinked with wedge-shaped pieces of wood and plastered with clay inside and out, moss often being used temporarily where clay was unobtainable. Not a nail or screw was used in the construction of these shanties, which were commonly of one room only; though occasionally a partition was later erected at the centre. There was no cellar or foundation, but sometimes a small excavation was made, which was reached by a trap-door and a short ladder. A hole in the roof formed the first exit for the smoke from the open fire in the centre of the room. Before winter set

[3]Thomas Need: *Six Years in the Bush.* 1838. pp. 58-9.
[4]*Ibid.*, p. 70.   [5]*Ibid.*, p. 79.

in an effort was sometimes made to construct a fireplace at one side of the shanty, though many a pioneer family lived for several years without one. Samuel Strickland found that "four thick slabs of limestone, placed upright in one corner of the shanty with clay well packed behind them to keep the fire off the logs, answered very well for a chimney, with a hole cut through the roof directly above to vent the smoke."[6]

The log house was an elaboration of the shanty. The usual building was about twenty feet long, eighteen feet wide and from nine to twelve feet high, and its construction was similar to that of the shanty. White oak or white pine was frequently used for the walls of the log house, and the logs were morticed at the ends and finished as in the shanty, the holes between them being "stubbed" or chinked with chips, moss and mud; where the materials were available, a better job was done by the use of a plaster made of clay mixed with lime or sand. Many an early settler burned limestone during a logging bee in order to secure sufficient lime for this purpose.

It was not usually possible to complete one's home before occupation, and many a house remained in an unfinished condition for two or three years. Those who wished their home to have a finished appearance spent many days hewing down the logs on the inside walls. A log house could not be erected too high or the logs might decay and fall in, but both shanty and log house were occasionally raised a few feet in later years to create a small loft or up-stairs bedroom, quite often used as a sleeping-room for the children; this loft was approached by a ladder, often from the outside.

The roof of the log house was usually of a more permanent nature than that of the shanty, though the bark of the pine, spruce, oak, elm or ash could easily be peeled from the trees in summer and used as a temporary covering, to be replaced as soon as possible by a better roof. The hollowed slab or half-log of the basswood formed a common roof, the convex form of one piece overlapping the edges of the concave forms of the slabs on either side. Shingles

[6]Samuel Strickland: *Twenty-seven Years in Canada West*. 1853. Vol. I, p. 92.

of split pine, cedar or spruce, often made by hand, were used in place of the cruder roof whenever they were available.

In a log house a large fireplace was usually erected. The foundation was of stone, and flat stones formed the hearth. The chimney consisted of a framework of small sticks, two or three inches in diameter, laid in the form of a hollow rectangle, and well plastered inside and out with clay mixed with straw. The wood in these chimneys sometimes caught fire when frost had prevented the clay from becoming hard. On that account ladders were occasionally built on the roofs of log houses, near the chimneys, to enable fires to be put out quickly. Many chimneys were poorly built, and some of the smoke found its way out through holes in the roof or walls.

A variation from the usual construction of chimneys was observed by a traveller in western Upper Canada in the early thirties: "On the boundary of the Huron Tract, next to the London District, we passed a negro settlement. The houses of the coloured people appeared of a particular construction, having the chimney-stack on the outside of the log house, and which stack is composed of thin, sawn timber, placed horizontally and mixed with clay."[7]

The fireplace of the pioneer home was usually a huge affair, eight feet or more wide, and provided the only means of heating and cooking in most early houses; in the earliest pioneer period it also furnished the chief method of lighting the house during the long winter evenings. An effort was made to keep the fire always burning, for it was not easy to strike a light in the days before the lucifer match came into common use, which was many years after 1829, when it was invented. When the fire went out, live embers were sometimes carried from the nearest neighbour's, but this was no easier than striking a light. The huge back-logs which burned slowly in the fireplace were sometimes so large that they had to be drawn into the house by oxen.

The floor of the pioneer home varied with the period and with the economic condition of the settler. In Loyalist times the floor was sometimes merely the hard earth. Sawn lumber was then very scarce, and few settlers were fortunate enough to be able to procure boards. Bark,

[7]Patrick Shirreff: *A Tour through North America*. 1835. p. 178.

and boards sawn by hand with a whip-saw were sometimes used for flooring, but more usually it was made
of timbers roughly squared with axe or adze. Split
logs, called puncheons, three or four inches in thickness,
often composed the floor of early homes in the Niagara
district. Most floors were very rough, for the unseasoned
wood soon warped; consequently it was usual to relay them
after the wood had dried. To clean these crude floors
sand and plenty of hot water, applied with a heavy splint
broom and a mop, was found to be quite satisfactory. Those
who painted their floors were considered to be imitating
the "Yankee" fashion. The most prosperous settlers, particularly the residents of towns and villages, used carpets
to cover the inequalities of the flooring.

Crude substitutes for doors and windows were used
where milled lumber was not available. As a general rule
the openings were sawn or chopped out after the house
had been raised. Some settlers used the laborious whip-
saw to obtain a few boards for a door, while others split
them roughly with a broad-axe. Pioneers are known to
have used a blanket to cover the doorway until something
better was available. Some log houses were built without
windows, the construction of the house being easier when
they were left out; while in many cases the doorway and
the cracks in the walls were considered to let in more than
enough cold air in winter. It was not unusual for settlers
to bore holes in the wall to provide a little additional light
and air, while wooden pegs fixed in similar holes provided
a place to hang utensils and clothing.

Hinges and locks of doors and windows were made of
wood. The wooden latch of the door was on the inside,
and could be lifted from outside by a leather latch-string
passing through a hole a few inches above; this string
might be pulled in at night, but as a general rule it was
left out, and the old saying "the latch-string is always out"
signified the hospitality of our pioneer settlers. The ingenuity which characterised many of those who set up a
home in the wilderness is well exemplified by the methods
which one settler used to construct and hang the door of
his log house:

"A man and his wife, with two children, moved into the

Township of Ops, into a dense forest, eight miles from the nearest settler. For months he chopped away at the forest trees, all alone, and succeeded at length in making a clearing in the forest, and erecting a log house for himself and his family. The logs were peeled and notched at the ends, and laid up squarely, each tier making the house the diameter of a log higher. A hole was cut through for a doorway, and another for a window. To form a door he split some thin slabs from a straight-grained cedar, and pinned them with wooden pins to cross slats.

"The most ingenious parts of the construction, however, were the hinges. Iron hinges he had not, and could not get. With the auger he bored a hole through the end of a square piece of wood, and sharpening the other end with his axe he then bored a hole into one of the logs of the house, constituting in part a door-jamb, and drove the piece of wood into this hole. This formed the top part of the hinge, and the bottom part was fashioned in exactly the same way. Now to the door, in like manner, he fastened two pegs of wood with holes bored through their ends. Placing the ends of the hinges above one another they presented the four ends with holes leading through them, the one above the other. Next he made a long pin with his handy jack-knife, leaving a run at one end of it, and making it long enough to reach from the top to the lower hinge. Through the holes at the ends of the hinge this long pin was placed, and thus the door was hung."[8]

The log house had seldom more than one window, and often had none at all. Until a sash could be obtained, or a rough one made with a jack-knife, a blanket, or a wooden shutter fitted in grooves, covered the opening. From four to six panes of glass, usually seven inches by nine, were inserted in the sash by the Loyalists, for glass and putty were issued to most of them. Some settlers, however, used oiled paper in their windows until glass could be procured; while others preferred to stuff waste material such as old clothes into the opening, rather than use the very brittle American glass which was often all that was available.

Such were the log houses of the pioneers, rude homes in which many of the first generation passed the rest of

[8]Thomas Conant: *Upper Canada Sketches*. 1898. pp. 59-61.

THE OLD CREDIT MISSION, 1837

School   Council-House   Church   Peter
                                                                 Jones'
                                                                 Study

SIR JOHN A. MACDONALD'S BOYHOOD HOME
Located west of Kingston, four miles north of Adolphustown

From Geikie's *Life in the Woods*

OUR HOME IN THE WOODS

"Dens of dirt and misery which would be shamed by an English pig-sty."—Susanna Moodie

J. E. Loughlin

INTERIOR OF A SETTLER'S HOME IN 1812

their lives; structures which were commonly raised in one day at the expense of a few gallons of whisky for the refreshment of those who came to help. But the average log house was neither a thing of beauty nor a joy forever. Mrs. Moodie's indictment of the emigration propaganda of the times does not mince words:

"In 1830 the great tide of emigration flowed westward. Canada became the great landmark for the rich in hope and poor in purse. Public newspapers and private letters teemed with the unheard-of advantages to be derived from a settlement in the highly-favoured region . . . . They talked of log houses to be raised in a single day, by the generous exertions of friends and neighbours, but they never ventured upon a picture of the disgusting scenes of riot and low debauchery exhibited during the raising, or upon a description of the dwellings when raised—dens of dirt and misery, which would, in many instances, be shamed by an English pig-sty."[9]

The extreme hardship of living under such conditions cannot easily be imagined. Many families were so disheartened at the prospect that they would have returned to the Old Land immediately if that had been within the realm of possibility. Instead of the meadows and lanes which the Englishman loved there were unending forests and swampy trails through the bush. The great loneliness which most settlers felt, but bravely suppressed in the hope of better days to come, is shown in the plaintive lament of an anonymous resident of Otonabee Township.

MY HAME

"I canna ca' this forest hame,
  It is nae hame to me;
Ilk tree is suthern to my heart,
  And unco to my e'e.

If I cou'd see the bonny broom
  On ilka sandy know';
Or the whins in a' their gowden pride,
  That on the green hill grow:

[9]Susanna Moodie: *Roughing It in the Bush.* 1852. Introduction to the 3rd Edition, 1854.

If I cou'd see the primrose bloom,
In Nora's hazel glen;
And hear the linties chirp and sing,
Far frae the haunts o' men:

If I cou'd see the rising sun
Glint owre the dewy corn;
And the tunefu' lavrocks in the sky
Proclaim the coming morn:

If I cou'd see the daisy spread
Its wee flowers owre the lee;
Or the heather scent the mountain breeze,
And the ivy climb the tree:

If I cou'd see the lane' kirk yard,
Whar' frien's lye side by side:
And think that I cou'd lay my banes
Beside them when I died:

Then might I think this forest hame,
And in it live and dee;
Nor feel regret at my heart's core,
My native land for thee."[10]

As settlement spread in later years into "the wild lands" of the older counties, and to the vast unopened territories back from the lakes, the log house continued to be the pioneer home of the settler. Conditions under which it was raised were not usually as primitive as in earlier times. Some settlers were able to hire workmen to build their houses, though the "raising bee" was much more usual. In organized emigrations arrangements were sometimes made to have the log shanties for the incoming settlers constructed before their arrival. The Irish emigrants brought out to Peterborough County in 1825 by the Hon. Peter Robinson had their houses built at the expense of the government by men hired for that purpose, and the cost per house was only $10. Captain Basil Hall, an English traveller who investigated conditions in this settlement two years later, describes these log huts (to build which two men were

[10]*Cobourg Star*, December 27, 1831.

sufficient to cut down the trees and erect the entire house in two days) as about twenty feet by twelve, and seven feet high. The roof of each was made of logs split into four lengths and hollowed out; they overlapped like tiles, "so that each alternate log formed a gutter or channel to carry off the rain".[11] The openings between the logs in the walls were filled with mud and moss; sometimes the house had a window, sometimes not. While these homes were mere shanties, yet the hardship of settling in the new land was mitigated to the extent that the bewildered settler had at least a roof over his head when he began the great adventure in the backwoods of Canada.

The temporary homes of these Irish settlers when they first arrived at Scott's Plains (Peterborough) were even more primitive than the log shanty. Immediately upon their arrival they set to work upon the construction of "rude huts or wigwams, composed of slabs, bark, or the branches of trees, and sods, to shelter them from the weather during the interval which must elapse before they could be located upon their lands in the neighbouring townships".[12] The five log buildings which Peter Robinson erected to serve as his headquarters were of a comparatively advanced type, with square gables and shingled roofs. The logs of the walls and partitions were hewed to a level surface in the interior of the buildings, and, considered as a whole, they were long regarded "as first class houses, and models of taste and perfection in the youthful town".[13]

In some districts Building Societies were established as joint-stock companies; these lent money to settlers on the security of their lands, and enabled many a man to erect or improve his home.[14] Most emigrants, however, continued to come individually and unassisted, and constructed their

[11]Basil Hall: *Travels in North America in the Years 1827 and 1828.* 1829. Vol. I, p. 292.

[12]Thomas Poole: *Early Settlement of Peterborough and Peterborough County.* 1867. p. 5.

[13]*Ibid.*, p. 16.

[14]In the Douglas Library, Queen's University, Kingston, is a pamphlet, published in 1847, descriptive of the Kingston Building Society. An account of the Newcastle District Building Society, including lists of shareholders and members, may be found in E. C. Guillet: *Cobourg*, in the *Cobourg Sentinel-Star*, July 28, 1932.

log homes with the help of their neighbours. As Walter Riddell puts it:

"A settler would come in and either draw or buy a lot, chop down a few large trees and put up a shanty, covering it with bark or split basswood logs. Leaving for a short time, he would come back bringing his wife with him, the young couple having taken their wedding jaunt over a blazed track through the woods, carrying all their worldly possessions on their backs, making their bed of cedar or hemlock boughs, setting themselves down in the forest to subdue the wilderness and by patient industry and persever-ance hew out a home."[15]

Those whose means enabled them to hire workmen might have a house erected at no great expense, for a book pub-lished in 1822 says that the cost to an immigrant "for build-ing a log house, with a shade for his oxen, and pig-stie" was only £7 10s. ($30); and it is further stated that "for this sum his house may have two apartments, a stone chimney and hearth, and two glazed sash windows".[16]

While the initial hardships of pioneer life were some-times not as severe as in the Loyalist period, yet they were often very great. The Reids and Stewarts were settlers of an excellent type who received land in Peterborough County and arrived on their lots in 1823. A mason had been hired to construct chimneys, but the frost prevented the comple-tion of the work, and the Reid family lived all winter in "merely a shed or hut made of logs, and roofed with slabs hollowed out of logs to turn the wet; the shanty was quite open at one side, and in front was a great log fire".[17] The snow during that winter was from three to four feet deep, but "the little children, from two years old and upwards, sat around the fire, heavy snow falling all the time; . . . . yet they were never so healthy or so lively".[18]

Even in houses of improved type and construction the cold was often very intense. Mrs. Traill describes how cold it was in her home during the winter of 1833: "The mercury

[15]Walter Riddell: *Historical Sketch of the Township of Hamilton.* 1897. p. 7.
[16]Charles Fothergill: *A Sketch of the Present State of Canada.* 1823. p. 57.
[17]Thomas Stewart to Basil Hall, quoted in Hall, *op. cit.,* Vol. I, p. 313,
[18]*Ibid.*

was down to twenty-five degrees in the house; abroad it it was much lower. The sensation of cold early in the morning was very painful, producing an involuntary shuddering, and an almost convulsive feeling in the chest. Our breaths were congealed in hoar-frost on the sheets and blankets. Everything we touched of metal seemed to freeze our fingers."[19]

Owing to the poor means of heating the homes, the cold was felt in town houses almost as much. From the days of early settlement many of the homes of Kingston were of limestone because of the abundance of it in the vicinity; but even in these houses, and others of the better types in the towns, water commonly froze in one's bedroom during the night. Letters of a century ago contain frequent references to the coldness of the houses in winter; and even those who had stoves had difficulty in their erection and management. The letters between Ann Macaulay in Kingston and her son, John, in Toronto, contain many allusions to stove pipes, the buying of wood, the use of candles because of the dearness of oil, and other related matters. John Macaulay wrote to his mother in November, 1837: "We live in a very airy house. The wind almost blows through it;"[20] his mother, referring to the previous winter, wrote: "If I may judge by the quantity of ashes, I burnt an immensity of wood, for in February I was obliged to take out 12 bushels as the ash-house was quite full, which never happened since I kept house."[21]

From time to time improvements to the log house were made by the more enterprising settlers: perhaps a coat of whitewash was applied (paint was very scarce); later on a verandah or stoop might be added, with vines growing up the posts to soften the rough appearance of the home. The average house in Upper Canada, however, was still of a poor type when compared with the homes in Britain and the United States in the same period; this accounts in a large measure for travellers' descriptions of "the miserable

[19]Catherine Traill: *The Backwoods of Canada*. 1836. Edition of 1929, p. 161.
[20]Macaulay Papers; John Macaulay to Ann Macaulay, November 22, 1837. (Archives of Ontario).
[21]*Ibid.*; Ann Macaulay to John Macaulay, November 6, 1837.

log houses" to be found in all parts of the province. The appearance of every farmhouse varied, however, with the energy, thrift and natural abilities of the owner.

Nationality played an important part in the type and general appearance of the home. Dutch settlers were particularly fond of stoops; while Americans who could afford them preferred large, white frame houses with green blinds for the windows, like the fine old "Colonial" home of the United States. These houses are somewhat jocularly described by a writer in the early thirties as "painted white, with nine windows and a door in front, seven windows in either gable, and a semi-circular one above all, almost at the top of the angle of the roof, the blinds painted green, the chimney-stalks highly ornamented, and also the fanlight at the door. . . . . It is almost needless for me to say that this is the mansion of Jonathan, or the U. E. Loyalist from the United States."[22]

The liking for frame houses was not, however, restricted to settlers of American origin. As Dr. Dunlop said: "When a man gets on a little in the world, he builds a frame house, weather-boarded outside, and lathed and plastered within."[23] Frame houses usually cost from $1000 to $2500, but it was difficult to make them air-tight, and consequently some people objected to them because they were "as hot as an oven in summer, and as cold as an open shed in winter."[24] In 1823 a traveller visited Johnson's Inn, near the site of the present town of Barrie. He describes the inn, as "a clap-boarded house, square in shape and rather large, standing upon a gravelly bank close to the lake. It contained a good kitchen, three or four sleeping-rooms, partly in the roof, two good parlours, and a bed-chamber for guests of quality. I have had worse at the best hotels in Washington."[25] He observed, however, that "so new was the wood when the house was put together, or so hot are the summers in Kempenfeldt Bay, that it had shrunk most grievously. The kitchen and parlour might

[22]MacTaggart, op. cit., Vol. I, pp. 309-10.
[23]William Dunlop: Statistical Sketches of Upper Canada. 1832. p. 108.
[24]Ibid., p. 109.
[25]J. J. Bigsby: The Shoe and Canoe, or Pictures of Travel in the Canadas. 1850. Vol. II, p. 71.

Anne Langton

TWO INTERIOR VIEWS OF JOHN LANGTON'S "BACHELOR"
ESTABLISHMENT, STURGEON LAKE, 1833

Reproduced by Courtesy of Mrs. Andrew Doole   Mary Adams

THE PRESTON HOMESTEAD NEAR LAKEFIELD
A typical "second" or "third" home, after prosperity had rewarded
the toil of the pioneer

THE DECEW STONE HOUSE, NIAGARA, AS IT APPEARED IN 1903
The headquarters of Fitzgibbon before the Battle of Beaver Dams

almost be called parts of a cage, so well were they ven-
tilated".[26]

Some of the Irish settlers, on the other hand, varied
the log shanty until it was similar to the homes in common
use in rural Ireland. The chief characteristic was the high
earth embankment against the walls of a low house, which
sometimes gave it the appearance of a cave in a hillside. A
Scotchman who was in charge of public works at Bytown
(Ottawa) in the late twenties, states that the Irish labourers
often lived in mud cabins. Perhaps his nationality caused
him to be somewhat prejudiced against the Irish, but there
would seem to be considerable truth in his description. He
says: "At Bytown on the Ottawa they burrow into the
sand hills; smoke is seen to issue out of holes which are
opened to answer the purpose of chimneys."[27]

The "common", or unimproved log house was seldom, if
ever, comfortable, though it was often made to last the
longer because it was exempt from the taxation imposed
upon the more advanced types. As late as 1834 the
assessors classed almost twenty-three *per cent.* of the homes
in Upper Canada as log cabins, though two years earlier
Mrs. Traill observed that there were very few houses of
this type in the settlements along the St. Lawrence and on
the main road north from Cobourg towards Peterborough,[28]
though a large part of the latter district had been settled
less than ten years. In fact a traveller who was particularly familiar with the settlements in the vicinity of Perth
noticed as early as 1821 that clap-board homes were "the
mode now most prevalent, both in town and country."[29]

Some log houses, even those built as first homes, showed
interesting variations in architecture usually lacking in
homes of the type. On the shores of Pigeon Lake, Peterborough County, a few English settlers of some wealth
built log houses of various fancy shapes, but without much
practical utility. Samuel Strickland, settled near Peterborough, describes a fine log home that he erected in 1826
as "of elm-logs, 36 feet long by 24 feet wide, which I divided

[26]*Ibid.*, p. 70.
[27]MacTaggart, *op. cit.*, Vol. II, p. 243.
[28]Traill, *op. cit.*, p. 80.
[29]John McDonald: *Narrative of a Voyage to Quebec, and Journey
   from thence to New Lanark, Upper Canada.* 1823. p. 21

into three rooms on the ground floor, besides an entrance-hall and staircase and three bedrooms upstairs."[30] He tells how he made by hand the pine shingles for its roof. When Strickland was living in Goderich (1829) as an employee of the Canada Company he constructed his house "with cherry-logs neatly counter-hewed both inside and out, the interstices between the logs being nicely painted with mortar."[31]

He was not a lover of log houses, however, in spite of the fact that those which he constructed were much superior to the usual home of the pioneer settler. Like his sisters, Mrs. Traill and Mrs. Moodie, he had been accustomed to a home of better type, and to this general objection were added other considerations which grew out of his experience:

"If I were commencing life again in the woods, I would not build anything of logs except a shanty or a pig-sty; for experience has plainly told me that log buildings are the dirtiest, most inconvenient, and the dearest when everything is taken into consideration. As soon as the settler is ready to build, let him put up a good frame, roughcast, or stone house, if he can possibly raise the means, as stone, timber and lime cost nothing but the labour of collecting and carrying the materials. When I say that they cost nothing I mean that no cash is required for these articles, as they can be prepared by the exertion of the family. Two or three years should be spent in preparing and collecting materials, so that your timber may be perfectly seasoned before you commence building. With the addition of from a hundred to a hundred and fifty pounds in money to the raw material a good substantial and comfortable dwelling can be completed."[32]

Homes of squared logs, clap-board, roughcast, stucco, stone or brick, many of them large and almost palatial, gradually replaced the more primitive type, and one may still see old log houses used as sheds, while the improved second home stands near by. Houses and barns of squared logs are still quite common in the outlying parts of Old Ontario, while many log houses of the more primitive type are now (1932) being erected in Northern Ontario by

[30]Strickland, *op. cit.*, Vol. I, p. 98.
[31]*Ibid.*, Vol. I, p. 263.   [32]*Ibid.*, Vol. I, pp. 170-1.

families aided by the government in a period of severe economic depression.

Colonel Thomas Talbot's first residence was a log hut. Mrs. Anna Jameson thus describes the fiery Colonel's second home at Port Talbot:

"It is a long wooden building, chiefly of rough logs, with a covered porch running along the south side. . . . The interior of the house contains several comfortable lodging-rooms, and one really handsome one, the dining-room. There is a large kitchen with a tremendously hospitable chimney, and underground are cellars for storing wine, milk and provisions. Around the house stand a vast variety of outbuildings of all imaginable shapes and sizes, and disposed without the slightest regard to order or symmetry. One of these is the very log hut which the Colonel erected for shelter when he 'sat down in the bush' four-and-thirty years ago, and which he is naturally unwilling to remove. Many of these outbuildings are to shelter the geese and poultry, of which he rears an innumerable quantity."[33]

Brick buildings were long a luxury in the province generally, though in certain districts where brick clay was readily available such homes became common when prosperity rewarded the toil of the pioneer. One of the first brick buildings in Upper Canada was the home erected in 1790 by Colonel James Bâby; around this mansion, long used as a fur-trading post, grew the village of Sandwich. The foundation of the building was of stone, and the wood used in its construction was of walnut. Another very early brick building was Captain Myers' house, erected on the brow of the hill at Myers' Creek (Belleville) about 1794; the bricks for this home were made in Sydney Township, five miles east of Trenton.

In the early eighteen-thirties travellers observed that the homes of Upper Canada were improving. Joseph Pickering, writing in 1832 from Port Talbot, refers to "new frame and brick houses and other buildings rising up everywhere".[34] Patrick Shirreff noticed "that the houses of the

[33]Anna Jameson: *Winter Studies and Summer Rambles in Canada.* 1838. Vol. II, pp. 195-6.
[34]Joseph Pickering to Effingham Wilson, March 21, 1832. See Joseph Pickering: *Inquiries of an Emigrant* 1831. Preface to the 4th Edition, 1832, p. x.

French along the banks of the Detroit River and Lake St. Clair were "generally brick, and occasionally frame, but seldom with the stone basement of the lower province. . . . On some parts of the River Detroit, Lake St. Clair, and on the Thames, many people reside literally amongst water, passing to and from their houses on planks."[35]   At the western end of Lake Erie and along the Thames, he found, however, that wood was almost the only building material: "The dwelling-houses and farm-offices are of the shabbiest kind, and only two brick houses were seen in a distance of twenty-seven miles, passing from Amherstburg round Lake Erie."[36]

Fortune frequently smiled upon the inhabitants of the towns somewhat earlier.   The Parliament Buildings of York, erected in 1796-7, were largely of brick, and by the eighteen-twenties many similar structures had been built.   Thomas Hamilton, a visitor to York in the early thirties, observed that brick was in common use, though the Government House was of wood, which he considered "a singular circumstance".[37]   Brockville had a number of brick buildings in 1821, and in several other towns, such as Cobourg and London, the same material was being used a few years later in building stores or homes; the brick farmhouse, however, was unusual until the fifties and sixties.   Many of the fine old mansions which may be seen throughout the rural districts of Old Ontario date from the era of prosperity ushered in by the Crimean War, a period of "good times" further intensified as a result of the Reciprocity Treaty and the American Civil War.

The erection of stone houses depended almost entirely upon the availability of the material.   One of the first stone homes in Upper Canada was erected by Colonel John Macdonell at Glengarry Point soon after the first Loyalist settlement along the shores of the St. Lawrence. The limestone buildings of Kingston and Bytown (Ottawa) resulted from a disposition to use readily available materials, and throughout the province many a "second" or

[35]Shirreff, *op. cit.*, pp. 209-10.   [36]*Ibid.*, p. 212.
[37]Thomas Hamilton: *Men and Manners in America.* 1833. Vol. II, p. 335.

"third" home was constructed of stones cleared from the fields.

The architectural design of the later houses and the appearance of their exterior and interior were almost as variable as their occupants. The influence of economic status, of taste, and of nationality predominated in the planning of the home. Dr. Dunlop describes the evolution of the house from the log-hovel to the brick mansion, and states that the history of any settlement could be read in the buildings and farmyard. This old-timer, always a hater of innovations, suggests that a well-built log house was good enough for him:

"The original shanty, or log-hovel, which sheltered the family when they first arrived on their wild lot, still remains, but has been degraded into a piggery; the more substantial log house, which held out the weather during the first years of their sojourn, has, with the increase of their wealth, become a chapel of ease to the stable or cow-house; and the glaring and staring bright-red brick house is brought forward close upon the road, that the frame dwelling, which at one time the proprietor looked upon as the very acme of his ambition, may at once serve as a kitchen to, and be concealed by its more aspiring and aristocratic successor."[38]

Most of the first settlers in "The Queen's Bush," as 2,000,000 acres of land near Lake Huron and Georgian Bay was commonly called, suffered hardships at the middle of the eighteenth century varying but little from those of the earlier periods. Mrs. Cook, who settled in the fifties in Bruce County, recalled that "the shanty to which we went had a bark roof, and this roof leaked so badly that when it rained my husband had to hold an umbrella over us when we were in bed".[39] The floors of this home were made of such lumber as drifted ashore from passing vessels. The first settlers in Beaver Valley, near Meaford, in the same period, erected houses of two stories, but they contained but one room on each floor, and the upper chamber was reached by a ladder.

[38]Dunlop, *op. cit.*, p. 109.
[39]Reminiscences of Mrs. Cook, quoted in W. L. Smith: *Pioneers of Old Ontario*, 1923. p. 261.

Although an orderly appearance certainly adds to any home, yet economic conditions in the early days were such that many a settler was too poor to spend much time or money improving his home. Those who judged by the exterior only, as travellers usually did, might have been agreeably surprised by the neatness of the interior. Home is, after all, more than logs or bricks: it is neat or slovenly in its appearance, pleasant or unpleasant in its atmosphere, in proportion to the effort of its inhabitants to make it so. The attractiveness of the interior of the home depends largely upon house furnishings, which are outside the scope of this chapter; but the appearance of the fireplace, as a permanent feature of most pioneer homes, is of interest here. Occasional American stoves were to be found in Upper Canada even before the War of 1812, but the open fireplace long remained the usual means of heating the home, although gradually superseded by outdoor bake-oven or by stove for cooking purposes.

The method of constructing the fireplace and chimney among the Loyalists has already been described; in later settlements there were variations. The pioneers of the Ottawa Valley proceeded as follows:

"If a stone could be found large enough to stand on the ground against the wall, it was set up; if not, a piece of thin wall was built with stones and blue clay mortar to keep the fire from the logs or wall of the building. Then two crooked cedars were got and the ends pointed or thinned to drive into the chinks between the logs on each side of the stone work. The other ends were pinned to the beam across the house, about four feet in from the end wall. Cedars were cut the length for these laths from one side to the other. The first lath was laid in a good bed of clay mortar on the stonework on the back. Then the cedars, flatted a little on their upper side, had a bed of mortar laid on, and laths cut laid on them across the lath on the back; some of them were nailed in the end to the crooked cedars, laid in plenty of mortar. When they reached to the level of the highest ends of these crooked cedars, with the three sides, or back and two sides, they laid a lath in mortar on the beam and formed the fourth side.

"So they built the chimney, which they called a fireplace till they got above the scoops. The substitute they made for hair in the mortar was cut straw or beaver-meadow hay, cut with the axe on a block, sometimes pounded to make it more pliable. The back was kept straight with the house wall, but the other three sides were drawn in so that from five or six feet wide at the bottom it would end in three by two feet at the top. The mortar was laid to give three-quarters of an inch on the inside of the laths, and made smooth to be safe. They often caught fire but a cup of water thrown against it generally extinguished it."[40]

In the later fireplaces brick or stone often replaced the clay-and-wood chimneys of earlier times, though where bricks were not available the old method had still to be used. Some distance up the chimney there was usually placed a cross-bar of iron or wood, and from this hung the chains to which were attached the pots and kettles used in cooking. "The hanging of the crane" was the sign of the establishment of a new home, and was sometimes the occasion of a celebration. The crane was fitted with hooks for the kettles and pots, which swung back and forth as required. Field stones were often used to place the wood upon, though in later days iron or fancy brass "dogs", sometimes known as andirons, were common. Among the implements, some of which were found in every fire-place, were the hand-bellows, tongs, a long-handled shovel, frying-pan and a variety of iron pots. Kettles of various sizes, but usually about two feet in diameter, were used for the baking of bread; these kettles had an iron lid, and coals were placed above and below while the bread was being baked.

Although its use in cooking came to an end with the introduction of stoves, yet the hearth has remained the symbol of home. The cheerful atmosphere of the open fire, enhanced, perhaps, by the chirp of the cricket, has made it the rallying-centre of the family. Many were the uses to which the fireplace was put: squashes were hung near it to prevent their being frozen, and guns to keep free from rust; in front, on poles suspended by cords from the ceiling, were placed chunks of beef or venison and

[40]J. L. Gourlay: *History of the Ottawa Valley.* 1896. pp. 47-8.

strings of apples; sometimes meat was hung to dry inside the chimney, too far away from the fire to be roasted but not so far up that it would be blackened by smoke. Mrs. Catharine Traill's description of the second home of her friend, Mrs. Thomas Stewart, one of the first settlers in Douro Township, Peterborough County, shows us how delightful the fireplace and its surroundings might be made:

"Though so many years have elapsed since those days, I can recall as a vivid picture the family group at Auburn in the primitive log house. The father occupied one side of the ample hearth from which the huge pile of blazing logs cast broad lights and shadows on the walls and rafters where all sorts of guns, pistols, fishing-rods, paddles and models of canoes and small river craft were arranged, not without taste for artistic effect. Indian bows and arrows, and sundry skins of small, furred, native animals, claws of bears, and wings and talons of eagles, hawks and herons were fastened on the walls, while the head of a noble deer with branching antlers supported other trophies of the hunter's skill.

"The broad mantel-piece held curious fossils, specimens of rocks and crystals gathered from the limestone boulders, with flint arrows and spear-heads and fragments of pottery of ancient Indian manufacture. By a small work-table, relic of other days, might be seen the dear mistress of the household with her three daughters, each busily plying needle or knitting-pins; while on the warm fur rugs, basking in idle enjoyment of the warmth, the younger children and two noble dogs, one, that now rare animal, an Irish grey-hound, a privileged personage; the other a fine water-dog of good breed and appearance. Close by, an Indian cradle held a sleeping infant. . . . Mr. Stewart was then an honourable member of the Upper House of Legislative Council; he lived to see much change in the then densely-wooded township where his was almost the first dwelling raised, and where he had heard the sound of the chopper's axe awakening the echoes of those lonely, forest-crowned banks of the rushing Otonabee."[41]

[41]Catharine Traill to Eleanor Dunlop, quoted in 2nd Edition, 1902, pp. 144-5, of Frances Stewart: *Our Forest Home.* 1889.

THE REMAINS OF AN EARLY STONE FIREPLACE

FIREPLACE AND FURNISHINGS, 1813

AN OLD BREAD OVEN

KITCHEN UTENSILS IN 1813

CHAPTER II

FOODS AND COOKING

"Very merry at, before, and after dinner, and the more for that my dinner was great, and most neatly dressed by our own only maid. We had a fricasee of rabbits and chickens, a leg of mutton boiled, three carps in a dish, a great dish of a side of lamb, a dish of roasted pigeons, a dish of four lobsters, three tarts, a lamprey pie (a most rare pie!), a dish of anchovies, good wine of several sorts, and all things mighty noble and to my great content."

The Diary of Samuel Pepys, April 4, 1663.

SHAKESPEARE'S lines,

"Now good digestion wait on appetite,

And health on both,"

would hardly have been applicable to many foods in common use in pioneer days had it not been for the hard work which was essential in a new settlement. Certainly the foods were often of such coarse ingredients, and the meals so lacking in variety, "the spice of life", that they would seldom whet a modern appetite, much less be conducive to health. In considering the foods of other times it must be recognized, however, that, as in our day, nationality and economic status are the deciding factors in the meals of the various classes of people which make up a nation.

The first inhabitants of Upper Canada, apart from the Indians, were the garrisons at the forts, and the soldier's usual food of bully beef, pea soup and hard tack is too well-known to require much description here; there was, however, a considerable amount of salt pork eaten by the soldiers in Canada, and they varied their diet by netting large numbers of whitefish, salmon, sturgeon and other species then so plentiful in our lakes and rivers, and by shooting wild fowl such as ducks, turkeys and pigeons, and a large variety of game—deer, raccoons and rabbits, among others.

Governor Simcoe told a traveller that the commissariat had often to depend upon flour from London and salt meat from Ireland, for there was not much excess production of wheat or meat in Canada at that period.[1] That this was

[1] La Rochefoucauld-Liancourt quoted in William Canniff: *History of the Settlement of Upper Canada*. 1869. p. 204.

not always the case is shown by La Rochefoucauld-Liancourt's investigations in the summer of 1795; he learned
that pork, peas and wheat were being exported in considerable quantities from the vicinity of Kingston, and that
some of the wheat was ground in Montreal and the flour
sent back to Upper Canada.[2] Even fifty years later, however, a traveller found that "quantities of salted provisions
are still imported for the consumption of the soldiers."[3]

It was usual for the authorities to advertise in the
Gazette in order to give local merchants a chance to fur-
nish the supplies. On March 1, 1798, John McGill, government agent, advertised for "flour and peas, wanted at Fort
George, for the supply of His Majesty's forces in Upper
Canada". It was stipulated that the produce must be
packed in casks, and "warranted to keep good and sound
for twelve months after delivery".[4]

The food of the Indians, *voyageurs* and lumbermen in
early times was much coarser than that of the first settlers.
The Indians were accustomed to live largely on the fruits
of the chase, though some of them grew pumpkins, maize
and tobacco. In later years contact with the white man
added large quantities of rum, brandy and whisky to their
diet, and made other changes. One of their main dishes in
the early part of the nineteenth century was a sort of stew
made up principally of lumps of venison and potatoes, but
including anything else of an edible nature that they happened to have. Another type of "Irish stew" common
among the Indians was made up of rice, beaver and partridge, boiled with a little pounded corn.

The early Indian, French, and Scottish *voyageurs* of the
North-West and Hudson's Bay Companies subsisted during
their arduous expeditions into the Far West largely on bear
grease and coarse cornmeal, with the addition of game and
fish. Salt pork, peas and biscuits usually formed the main
food of the "Goers and Comers" who covered the route from
Montreal to the Grand Portage at Fort William; they were
consequently called "Pork-eaters" by their much hardier

[2]Duc de la Rochefoucauld-Liancourt: *Travels through the United
    States of North America.* 1799. Vol 1, pp. 280-1.
[3]Anna Jameson: *Winter Sketches and Summer Rambles in Canada.*
    1838. Vol. I, pp. 267-8.
[4]*Upper Canada Gazette*, March 1, 1798.

brethren in the interior. The French-Canadian bateaumen on the St. Lawrence and the lakes similarly ate raw pork and hard biscuit, which they appear to have enjoyed. Before setting out in the morning they would eat pea soup, and tobacco seemed almost a food to them, for they smoked a considerable part of every day. The food of the lumbermen varied but little from that of the settlers; but the manner of eating customary among them, as among *voyageurs*, bateaumen, and Indians, was uncouth, meals being considered as a necessity which should be completed as quickly and as easily as possible.

A notable exception to the coarse food which was the usual fare of the fur trader was the luxurious banquet sometimes provided on special occasions for high officials at the main posts. Many a grand dinner took place, for example, at the North-West Company's post at Fort William, where eastern and western traders met. Here, in an immense wooden building, was held the annual meeting. The partners from Montreal always eclipsed in importance their brethren from the interior posts, and the proceedings were conducted with a grandeur which recalls the days of feudalism.

It is recorded that "grave and weighty councils were alternated by huge feasts and revels, like some of the old feasts described in Highland castles. The tables in the great banqueting room groaned under the weight of game of all kinds; of venison from the woods and fish from the lakes, with hunters' delicacies, such as buffaloes' tongues and beavers' tails; and various luxuries from Montreal, all served up by experienced cooks brought for the purpose. There was no stint of generous wine, for it was a hard-drinking period, a time of loyal toasts and bacchanalian songs, and brimming bumpers.

"While the chiefs thus revelled in hall, and made the rafters resound with bursts of loyalty and old Scottish songs, chanted in voices cracked and sharpened by the northern blast, their merriment was echoed and prolonged by a mongrel legion of retainers, Canadian *voyageurs*, half-breeds, Indian hunters, and vagabond hangers-on, who feasted sumptuously without, on the crumbs that fell from their table, and made the welkin ring with old French ditties, mingled with Indian yelps and yellings".[5]

Upon their arrival in Upper Canada, the Loyalists, who, apart from a few hundred French on the Detroit, were the first permanent settlers of importance, were supplied by the government with rations, consisting of "flour, pork, and a limited quantity of beef, a very little butter, and as little salt".[6] The rations were continued for three years as a general rule; but, as their discontinuance unfortunately coincided with the bad harvests of 1788-9, it resulted that there was intense suffering among most of the inhabitants of Upper Canada, and especially among the settlers who had been unable to establish themselves firmly upon the land, and who were consequently ill-prepared for a period of scarcity. The hardships of "the famine year" and the straits to which the people were reduced, will be described separately,[7] but it may be said here that hundreds of families lived for months on such materials as soup from beef bones, bran, boiled green grain, and the herbs, roots, bark and berries to be found in the woods; many, particularly children, died from malnutrition. Game might have been more extensively used as food but for the fact that powder and arms were scarce at that time; while fish quickly became distasteful when eaten too frequently.

In ordinary times, however, the Loyalists had plenty to eat. Beef and mutton were long scarce since feed for farm animals was often unobtainable; but salt pork, relieved by fish and game, provided plenty of meat. In preparing pork the hams and shoulders of the carcass were usually smoked, and the rest preserved in strong brine. The smoke-house was generally used in April, when the best pieces of the meat were carefully washed and hung. A smudge of beach or maple sticks was then built upon the floor beneath, and the door tightly closed. After several days' smoking, the meat would keep for months, even through the heat of summer. In some localities a bee was held for butchering, and everything from the killing of the animals to the making of sausage was finished in one day.

[5]Washington Irving: *Astoria.* 18?. p. 25.
[6]Canniff, *op. cit.,* p. 184.
[7]See Section III, Chapter III.

To grind wheat into flour was a matter of great difficulty in early times. Before the first mills were built by the government, and long after in the case of those settlers who lived remote from them, a crude type of hand-mill, or a hominy-block, supplied a very coarse wheat flour, sometimes called "samp", from which an equally coarse bread was made. As such flour contained all the bran it was, no doubt, healthful; but it was not highly valued at the time if the "precious stone flour" from the mill could be obtained.

The bread was usually baked in kettles in the fireplace, though in after years a clay bake-oven was usually erected, either in the wall near the fireplace or outside the home under the same roof as the smoke-house. The kettles had an iron lid, and hot coals were placed above and below while the bread was being baked. An early settler said that she had "never tasted better bread than some which was baked in the old iron pots;"[8] but others with less experience frequently found that a beautiful brown crust was merely the "goodly outside" covering an interior of putty. Similar kettles were used for the boiling of corn, and for cooking pork and potatoes, which formed an important part of each of the three meals of the day. A popular dish similarly prepared was composed of game or fowl cut into small pieces and baked in a deep dish, with a heavy crust.

The bake-kettle was superseded by the reflector, which was "an oblong box of bright tin enclosed on all sides but one. It was placed on the hearth with the open side next a bed of glowing coals. In it were placed the tins of dough raised a few inches from the bottom so the heat could circulate freely about the loaves. The upper part of the reflector was adjustable, to enable the housewife to inspect the contents".[9]

The reflector was sometimes used for roasting, but a roaster was kept where the family could afford it. This utensil is described as "smaller than the reflector and constructed in a similar manner; and, running from end to end through the centre, was a small iron bar, one end of

[8]Reminiscences of Mrs. Walter Riddell, in the *Farmer's Sun*, August 4, 1898.
[9]W. S. Herrington: *Pioneer Life on the Bay of Quinté*. (In Lennox and Addington Historical Society, *Papers and Records*, Vol. VI, p. 12).

which terminated in a small handle or crank. This bar, called a spit, was run through the piece of meat, and, by turning the handle from time to time, the meat was revolved and every portion of the surface was in turn brought next the fire. The drippings from the meat were caught in a dripping-pan placed underneath for the purpose. These drippings were used for basting the roasting meat, and this was done with a long-handled basting spoon through an opening in the back, which could be closed at will".[10]

Cornmeal was extensively used among the pioneers, for corn was easier to grind than wheat. Porridge was made of the meal, and plenty of maple sugar eaten with it. For supper the hardened porridge was often cut in slices and fried; while cornmeal and buckwheat griddle cakes, eaten with wild honey, were frequently made, as was also Johnny cake, except in those ultra-loyal sections where an American dish was considered disloyal. Corn flour, sifted through a fine cloth, was made into a sweet, light bread, considered by many to be much superior to Johnny cake. Wild rice, highly prized by the Indians, is another grain which was considerably used by the Loyalists.

Tea was long too expensive to be a common drink, so a number of substitutes were used, such as hemlock, sassafras and a Canadian plant which now goes by the name of New Jersey tea. Many of the men preferred whisky or rum, which were for many years consumed in large quantities at meals and elsewhere. Maple sugar was in common use, though some of the wealthier settlers purchased the coarse, brown Muscovado sugar from merchants.

The restricted diet ordinarily available led many an inventive housewife to attempt special dishes. Some recipes were of British, others of French, German, American or Dutch origin. For example, "pumpkin loaf" consisted of boiled pumpkin and cornmeal baked into loaves and eaten hot with butter. Among other special dishes was the Dutch pot pie, often a popular dish at bees. Butter and milk were not always the common foods that one might suppose, for the scarcity of feed before turnips were grown, and the severity of the winters, prevented many a farmer from keeping cattle all the year round. In early times the

[10]*Ibid.*

use of butter, which was often of poor quality, was sometimes restricted to adults, while the children dipped their
bread into ham gravy.

Pies of wild fruits, and cakes of various kinds were
made when finer flour was available. Apples were not
commonly used in early times, but wild strawberries, raspberries, gooseberries, cranberries, blackberries, blueberries
and many other varieties grew in profusion near at hand and
were largely used. Greens from the woods supplied the general lack of vegetables, which were but little grown in the
early pioneer period. Until about the middle of the nineteenth century the tomato was considered poisonous, but its
beauty led to its being hung up in the house as a "love apple".
In general the Loyalists lived in plenty as far as food was
concerned; the reminiscences of early settlers are filled
with references to the huge quantities of game, fish, berries,
nuts, and other "natural blessings" that they found everywhere provided for their use by the bounty of Providence.

The only inhabitants of Upper Canada in Loyalist times
who were frequently able to enjoy the finer products of
the culinary art were the officers of the army, higher government officials, and occasional wealthy merchants. These
classes were located largely at Kingston, Niagara, Detroit
and, a few years later, at York. Governor Simcoe's wife
gives us in her diary a number of examples of the niceties
of cooking, and also describes several foods not generally
used by the less-privileged sections of the population. The
Simcoes had a cook-stove, at that time very rare in Canada,
and much less pork was used at their table, and more eggs,
veal, beef, fish and game. Racoon and porcupine meat,
boiled black squirrel, wild turkeys, ducks, and roasted
wild pigeons are among the variations in food referred
to in her diary.[11]

In summer, however, Mrs. Simcoe preferred to eat
chiefly vegetables and fruits, and she found that most people did the same, except that a little salt pork was usually
used in addition. In August and September large quantities
of boiled or roasted Indian corn provided the main part
of the dinner.[12] It is noted concerning the use of wild

[11]*Diary of Mrs. John Graves Simcoe*, March 10, 1793.
[12]*Ibid.*, August 31, 1795.

pigeons, then to be obtained in such profusion, that some of
the settlers in the Western District salted down the wings
and breasts in barrels for later use, "and at any time they
are good to eat after being soaked."[13]

The Simcoes were very fond of fish and a number of
varieties appeared on their table. Mrs. Simcoe describes the
Lake Ontario whitefish as "exquisitely good. We all think
them better than any other fresh or salt-water fish. They
are so rich that sauce is seldom eaten with them". As to
the method of cooking them she says: "They are usually
boiled, or set before the fire in a pan with a few spoonfuls
of water and an anchovy, which is a very good way of
dressing them".[14] Another fish sometimes used was the
sturgeon,[15] much coarser than whitefish, but better than
sea sturgeon. They were often as large as six feet in length,
and the manner of preparing them for the table is thus
described: "Cooks who know how to dress parts of them,
cutting away all that is oily and strong, make excellent
dishes from sturgeon, such as mock turtle soup, veal cutlets,
etc., and it is very good roasted with bread crumbs."[16]
Herrings were also used, Mrs. Simcoe noting that on a
bateau trip to Quebec she carried "tea, cold tongue and fowl,
and herrings".[17] At a ball at Niagara "some small tortoises,
cut up and dressed like oysters in scollop shells," were
served at supper, and were pronounced very good.[18]

Bread and cakes were, of course, commonly used by the
wealthier classes, and it is stated by Mrs. Simcoe that
American bakers made the best.[19] A Moravian woman
brought her a loaf of bread "so peculiarly good" that she
enquired the recipe, and learned that "it was made with
rennet and whey, without yeast or water, and baked in

---

[13]*Ibid.*
[14]*Ibid.*, November 4, 1792.
[15]Sturgeon Lake is thought to have received its name not because
    sturgeon were caught there, but from the fact that a tribe of
    Indians removed thither from Niagara, where they had been
    accustomed to engage in fishing. There are, however, early
    references to sturgeon as being found in the Trent Lakes.
    See, for example, the *Methodist Magazine*, 1828, p. 74. (Quoted
    supra, p. 61).
[16]Simcoe, *op. cit.*, November 4, 1792.
[17]*Ibid.*, September 21, 1794.
[18]*Ibid.*, April 23, 1793.
[19]*Ibid.*, August 6, 1793.

wicker or straw baskets. . . . The bread was as light as possible, and rich, like cake". [20]

The Governor's wife never tired of experimenting in the use of wild plants. The dried leaves of the tree known as the balm of Gilead were found to be "good in pea soup, or forced (*i.e.* ground) meat".[21] Wild asparagus was used, and a number of herbs as greens. Tea was commonly drunk at meals, as were also wines, which the richer classes were able to import. Wild grapes were sometimes made into wine, as well as into vinegar. Sometimes Mrs. Simcoe gathered the flowers of the sumach "and poured boiling water upon them, which tastes like lemonade; it has a very astringent, hard taste".[22] Coffee made of peas is referred to as used by some of the settlers nearby. Maple sugar was in common use, though imported sugar was available, and some was made from the sap of the black walnut.

Mrs. Simcoe was particularly interested in the variety of wild fruits which then grew in such profusion. The Indians were very fond of fruit and often brought fine samples to the Governor. On one occasion they gave him "cranberries as large as cherries, and as good", and stated that the best of them grew under water.[23] The Indians supplied the Simcoes with chestnuts also, "which they roast in a manner that makes them párticularly good".[24] Thomas Talbot once brought Mrs. Simcoe "a cake of dried hurtle-berries made by the Indians, which was like Irwin's patent black currant lozenges, but tastes of smoke".[25] May-apples, "a great luxury",[26] were sometimes preserved, and black whortleberries, larger than those of England, were found to make "as good puddings as Levant currants".[27]

The cultivation of peach and cherry trees had already been commenced at Niagara in 1793, and the Simcoes had "thirty large cherry trees behind the house, and three standard peach trees, which supplied us last autumn for tarts and desserts, besides the numbers the young men ate. My share was trifling compared to theirs, and I eat thirty in a day. They were very small and high-flavoured. When

[20]*Ibid.*, August 31, 1795.
[21]*Ibid.*, July 21, 1793.
[22]*Ibid.*, September 8, 1795.
[23]*Ibid.*, April 26, 1793.
[24]*Ibid.*
[25]*Ibid.*, November 4, 1792.
[26]*Ibid.*, August 31, 1795.
[27]*Ibid.*, August 7, 1794.

tired of eating them raw, Mr. Talbot roasted them, and they were very good".[28]   Among other fruits enjoyed by the Simcoes were wild strawberries, raspberries, plums, and water-melons, the cultivation of which had been introduced from the United States.   While the grapefruit was almost unknown in Canada until the end of the nineteenth century, and has come into common use only in recent years, Mrs. Simcoe notes in her diary that she "received some shaddocks, a species of orange, from the West Indies, which I considered excellent fruit."[29]

It may be assumed that foods similar to those described by Mrs. Simcoe were used by the official classes in Kingston, Niagara, Detroit and York, and by a few of the wealthier inhabitants in other settlements.   Duties of officials commonly ended about 2 p.m. and dinner was served at three.   An ordinary meal at York is described by Joseph Willcocks in his diary, under date of October 6, 1800: "We had for dinner a salmon, a fillet of veal, a pair of roast fowl and a bread pudding."[30]   On another occasion he ate "roast pork, sassauges, black Puddings, soup, corned beef and pancakes."[31]   On Christmas Day, 1800, he enjoyed a heavy repast of "soup, roast beef, boiled pork, a turkey, plum pudding and mince pies". [32]

Other inhabitants of the few villages scattered over Upper Canada at the opening of the century ate meals as variable in quality and variety as the economic and social status of families.   It is noticeable, however, that the English custom of serving a variety of meats, together with rich batter puddings and pies for dessert, was followed by the residents of both urban and rural districts insofar as their means enabled them to do so.   In the rural settlements, however, the time of meals varied with the circumstances of the various seasons; in summer it was customary to work an hour or so after daybreak, and then have breakfast; while dinner generally occurred at noon, and supper at dark.   Needless to say there was no comparison in table

[28]*Ibid.*, July 2, 1793.
[29]*Ibid.*, August 6, 1792. The original name of the fruit was given in honour of a sea captain who was among the first Europeans to observe it growing and obtain samples.
[30]*Diary of Joseph Willcocks*, October 6, 1800.
[31]*Ibid.*, February 11, 1802.
[32]*Ibid.*, December 25, 1800.

J. Henry Sandham, R.C.A.

HUNTERS RETURNING WITH THEIR SPOIL

Royal Ontario Museum   George Catlin

INDIAN STALKING DEER

J. Gillespie

DUNDAS, CANADA WEST, IN 1848

From Bigsby's *The Shoe and Canoe*, 1850   J. J. Bigsby

ANDREW'S TAVERN, ABOVE BROCKVILLE

manners and ways of eating between the inhabitants of the
rural districts and those of the official class in the towns,
where dinner and supper were frequently served and eaten
in style. At Niagara the Simcoes followed the custom among
British governors of having a regimental band play during
meals, though it may be said that the bands of that day
bear little comparison in the matter of size or musical ability
with those of to-day.

Prices of tea, sugar and other luxuries were very high at
the commencement of the century. Pierce & Co.'s general
store in York advertised tea in 1799 at from 8s. to 19s. per
lb.; loaf sugar 3s. 9d. per lb.; and raisins and figs 3s. per
lb.[33] In 1802 Quetton St. George & Co. offered for
sale nutmegs, cinnamon, cloves and mace, butter, cheese,
chestnuts, hickory and black walnuts and cranberries.[34]
The excessive cost of transport by bateau and schooner kept
the prices of all imported goods at such a height that the
average citizen was precluded from purchasing them.

The meals at inns and wayside taverns were as variable
as the establishments and their proprietors. In the very
early period of settlement one was lucky to get a good meal
at any tavern. Carey's Inn, near Gananoque, was well-
known in the seventeen-nineties, but it was accessible only
by open boat. Joel Stone, founder of Gananoque, lived with
Carey for some time. The food which was provided was
obtained with difficulty, for we learn that "no bread could
be obtained except hard biscuits. For Mr. Stone and for
travellers they kept a kind called King's biscuit, while for
the others they provided navy biscuit. They kept two cows
and exchanged the milk with the bateaumen for biscuit,
and exchanged the latter again with the Indians for fish,
venison, game and wild fruit."[35]

British travellers in Upper Canada usually expected
much more than they were served at inns. In 1816 Lieutenant Francis Hall stopped at a tavern near Dundas and
called loudly for veal or pork chops, but all the pork had
been salted and no other meat was available, so bread with

[33]*Upper Canada Gazette*, July 13, 1799.
[34]*Ibid.*, December 11, 1802.
[35]Judge McDonald of Brockville quoted in J. Ross Robertson (Ed):
    The Diary of Mrs. John Graves Simcoe. 1911. p. 106.

cheese or butter was the menu.[36] In 1826 Joseph Pickering paid 1s 6d., New York Currency (about 19 cents), for breakfast at Umstead's Tavern, Talbot Street, and states that the meal was, "as usual, fried beef or pork, pickles and preserves, tea-cakes and butter".[37] Beer, cider and whisky were common drinks in taverns as well as homes, but cider would not keep long enough to be used all the year round.

In 1827 Captain Basil Hall and his wife came unexpectedly upon an inn some miles east of the Grand River; but the innkeeper was unaccustomed to visitors and had to forage for some time before an old hen was killed and some bacon, eggs and bread discovered for the entertainment of the guests.[38] Samuel Strickland stopped in 1828 at a German tavern, Sebach's, on the Huron Road; but the best he could get for supper was "a piece of dirty-looking Indian meal-bread, and a large cake of beef tallow, and, to wash down this elegant repast, a dish of crust coffee without either milk or sugar".[39]

In 1833, when Patrick Shirreff crossed into Upper Canada at Niagara after travelling in the United States, he was struck with the comparative crudeness of conditions on this side of the line. While he was one of those travellers who found more to find fault with than to praise, yet his opinions are certainly the same as almost anyone would express today if he were transplanted into the conditions which obtained in pioneer Upper Canada. Shirreff found the taverns objectionable because of the vulgar company as well as the poor food. He observed that "the bar-rooms of the hotels were filled with swearing, tipsy people," and that the butter served at meals, "instead of being, as in the States, hardened by means of ice, was an unclean liquid".[40]

At Richmond Hill Shirreff was served a dinner "of roast beef alone, so tough that my friend remarked that the animal must have died in the yoke from distress. Human

[36]Francis Hall: *Travels in Canada and the United States in 1816-17.* 1818. p. 211.

[37]Joseph Pickering: *Inquiries of an Emigrant.* 1831. November 3, 1826.

[38]Basil Hall: *Travels in America in 1827 and 1828.* 1829. Vol. I, p. 239.

[39]Samuel Strickland: *Twenty-seven Years in Canada West.* 1853. Vol I, p. 251.

[40]Patrick Shirreff: *A Tour through North America.* 1835. p. 94.

teeth could make little impression upon it, and I satisfied
hunger with bad bread and water."[41]   At the best hotel in
Goderich he was fortunate (?) enough to participate in a
"family dinner", the principal part of which was "a tureen
full of Scotch broth, with a tea-cup for a divider, and, from
the shortness of the handle, the fingers of the server were
immersed in stirring up the liquid.   The entertainment
was poor enough, and cost the moderate sum of sixpence
sterling".[42]   Between Amherstburg and Sandwich he had
breakfast at a small inn with a French sign; the fare consisted of "poor green tea, bad butter and worse bread".[43]

Mrs. Anna Jameson was similarly impressed by tavern
meals.   At an inn at Beamsville she was served a breakfast
of bad tea, "buttered toast, *i.e.*, fried bread steeped in
melted butter, and fruit preserved in molasses—to all which
I shall get used in time—I must try, at least".   The supper
meal at the same tavern is described as "the travellers' fare
in Canada", and consisted of "venison-steaks, and fried fish,
coffee, hot cakes, cheese, and whisky punch".[44]   Another
traveller noted that it was advisable to carry one's own provisions when visiting remote districts, for "split fowl and
leathery ham" was the usual fare at out-of-the-way inns.[45]

The standard of deportment at tavern meals was based
upon the rush and bustle of the American rather than the
stolid placidity and formality of the Englishman.   At most
pretentious inns a loud bell or horn was sounded a half
hour before, and at meal times, whereupon everyone rushed
into the dining-room and spent ten minutes or so eating his
food as rapidly as he could, without style or ceremony but
with great noise.   The fact that everyone sat at the same
table, irrespective of social position, was a source of great
annoyance to most English travellers; while to be surrounded by rustic labourers who used their knives as spoons
was not conducive to the enjoyment of meals.   In those
days it was customary to lay most of the blame for such
conduct upon the democratic Americans, who were considered by the average Englishman to be the source of all
evil.

[41]*Ibid.*, p. 106.   [42]*Ibid.*, p. 173.   [43]*Ibid.*, p. 198.
[44]Jameson, *op. cit.*, Vol. I, p.77.
[45]J. J. Bigsby: *The Shoe and Canoe, or Pictures of Travel in the
      Canadas.* 1850. Vol. II, p. 72.

Thomas Need, an Oxford graduate who lived for some years in the wilds of Verulam Township, Victoria County, and was the founder of the village of Bobcaygeon, gives an excellent description of tavern meals in Cobourg in 1832. The breakfast bell was sounded at 7.30 and repeated at 8 o'clock, whereupon there was "a general rush from all parts of the house and the neighbouring stores. . . . Instantly the work of destruction commenced—plates rattled—cups and saucers flew about, and knives and forks found their way indifferently into their owners' mouths or the various dishes on the table. There was little talking and less ceremony,— 'I say Miss' (to the lady in waiting) 'please some tea'—or, 'I say Mister', (to me) 'some steak, I guess I likes it pretty rawish', being the extent of both .

"The meal was composed of tea, coffee, toast, and bread, and the never-failing buckwheat cakes, with a variety of sweetmeats, crowned with a *pièce de résistance* in the shape of a huge greasy dish of beef steaks and onions. . . . The company was of a motley description, Yankees and emigrants, washed and unwashed, storekeepers, travellers, and farmers. . . . Ten minutes sufficed for the dispatch of the meal; after which, each and all retired in silence and haste as they had entered, stopping, however, as they passed the bar, for the never-failing dram and cigar, which concludes the business".

At dinner the host of the inn occupied the head of the table and "dealt out a 'Benjamin's mess' to each hungry expectant: puddings and creams succeeded the substantials, which were conveyed to the mouths of the different guests with frightful rapidity on the blades of sharp, dirty knives. I ventured to ask for a spoon, a request which only drew from 'Miss' a disdainful toss of the head, accompanied by the exclamation of 'My! If the man be'ent wanting a spoon now!' There was no conversation; and as soon as nature was satisfied the dinner-bolters severally rose from the table and quitted the room".[46]

In addition to the general faults everyone had his own pet objection to tavern meals: "Tiger" Dunlop, for example, disliked "everything deluged with grease and butter", as he found customary in the taverns in and

[46]Thomas Need: *Six Years in the Bush*. 1838. pp. 34-5.

near London. He blamed such methods of cooking upon the Dutch, and the type of meal led him to write humorous recipes, of which the following is a delicious sample:

"To dress beef steak:—Cut the steak about ¼ inch thick, wash it well in a tub of water, wringing it from time to time after the manner of a dish-clout; put a pound of fresh butter in a frying pan, (hog's lard will dò, but butter is more esteemed), and when it boils put in the steak, turning and peppering it for about a quarter of an hour; then put it into a deep dish, and pour the oil over it till it floats, and so serve it."[47]

These examples of tavern meals must be taken as the worst that might be expected, rather than necessarily the usual fare; for people tend to emphasize their unfortunate experiences, and perhaps occasionally to mention the best, rather than to describe the commonplace. The average tavern meal was somewhere between these extremes, varying, as it does at the present day, with the efforts of the cooks and proprietors to provide good service. But it is quite evident that those who had to patronize taverns, either for meals or lodging, were subjected to many annoyances of which the food was often one of the least.

For grand events, however, the innkeeper or caterer in the towns could rise nobly to the occasion and provide a sumptuous repast. When the inaugural train ran over the Cobourg and Peterborough Railroad on December 29, 1854, a grand banquet was served in the town hall of Peterborough. The viands provided by Perkins, the caterer, are described as "of the most *recherché* description, comprising fresh cod from Boston, venison from the backwoods, and in fact all the substantials and delicacies of the season. As to the wines they were of the best and costliest kinds. In a word the entertainment was got up in the most artistic style—regardless of expense, and reflected great credit on the liberality of the Peterborough gentlemen".[48]

The period of pioneer life in the vast regions at the rear of the early Loyalist settlements lasted from about 1800 to the middle of the century, and well beyond in the case of the northerly sections of Old Ontario. The back

[47]William Dunlop: *Statistical Sketches of Upper Canada.* 1832. p. 56.
[48]*Cobourg Star*, January 10, 1855.

townships of the earliest-settled counties along the St. Lawrence, the Bay of Quinté, Lake Ontario, the Niagara River and Lake Erie, were gradually filled up, often by the children of the first settlers; while further north, "the backwoods" or "the bush" received an ever-increasing number of immigrants. In living conditions these new settlements differed but little from those of Loyalist days; though hardships were sometimes less intense, they were usually very great. While the foods and the methods of cooking were in some respects similar to those of the earlier period yet there were many variations; a complete account will, therefore, be of value, even though at the risk of some repetition.

There was always great difficulty, except in winter, in transporting supplies and provisions from "the front". Pork and flour in barrels were easiest carried, and consequently remained the staple foods. A 200-pound barrel of pork was usually worth about $20, and a barrel of flour of 186 pounds varied in price from $7 to $12. In many districts food was frequently scarce, and the threat of famine was always real. In 1835 and 1836 the harvests were particularly bad, prices were as much as five times the usual level, provisions were hard to obtain even for cash, and many people experienced want comparable to the "hungry year" of Loyalist days; but even in ordinary years the pioneer farmer often found it hard to supply his family with food.

A settler in the vicinity of Peterborough in the early twenties describes the scarcity of provisions during the first year of settlement; he states that it often happened that there were not sufficient provisions to supply his family and workmen for the next day. "I have gone out", he says, "with my ox-team and a man to forage, and after travelling an entire day returned with a couple of sheep that had not a pound of fat on them, a little pork and a few fowls."[49] When flour was not available, cakes were made out of plain bran, and Indian corn was boiled, and these foods, with salt pork and pease soup, made up the meals for both adults and children. The Stewarts used wild plants as

[49]Thomas Stewart to Basil Hall, April 21, 1828; quoted in Basil Hall, *op. cit.*, Vol. I, p. 317.

greens, while hemlock "tea" and burned Indian corn "coffee" were the substitutes for the real articles, which were too expensive. No milk was available during the first winter, as cattle could not be kept over because of the scarcity of winter feed; the lack of this important food was particularly hard upon the young children of the family, who could not readily accustom themselves to coarse meals.

The importance of a knowledge of foods and methods of cooking among immigrants may be gauged from the fact that almost all "Guides to Emigrants", though written largely by men, include considerable advice and a number of recipes for their information. Many of these booklets on emigration are more idealistic than practical, and their suggestion of the bounty of nature and the extreme kindness of neighbours called forth the indignation of such settlers as Mrs. Traill and Mrs. Moodie, who did not misrepresent the truth in their accounts of pioneer life.

The general foundation of settlers' meals was made up of pork, flour, potatoes and corn. Those who had not plenty of bread and potatoes were unfortunate, for starchy foods enabled one to eat quantities of salt pork. In summer a considerable amount of beef and other meats could be substituted by the more prosperous settlers; but many ate pork all the year round, attempting to vary it by making pork pies or other dishes.

When it became possible to keep cattle over the winter, buttermilk and cheese were common foods, and the abundance of game and fish made them readily available for the table whenever the settler had time to engage in sport. Some young men, like those referred to by Mrs. Moodie, "considered hunting and fishing as the sole aim and object of life";[50] but other settlers, who were too busy to hunt, traded pork or flour to the Indians in return for venison, fish, ducks, partridges, and other small game.

In new settlements, even after the middle of the nineteenth century, wheat had sometimes to be ground in a coffee- or pepper-mill, or by an improvised grindstone mill. The first settlers in Smith Township, Peterborough County, in 1818, roasted or boiled wheat to make it easier to grind,

[50]Susanna Moodie: *Roughing It in the Bush*. 1852. Edition of 1923, p. 305.

while some parents even chewed the grain in order to make it soft enough for their children to eat.

Bread was generally made from wheat flour, but corn, rye and buckwheat were sometimes used. After a settler had become fairly well established, he might buy a cook-stove, or at least build a bake-oven. This was commonly erected on a large stump, and consisted of brick, stone or clay, with a roof of bark logs or slabs to protect it from the rain and wind. A fire was built in the oven, and when it was hot the ashes were removed and the loaves put in to bake. There was no way for moisture to escape and consequently bread made in bake-kettles or ovens was frequently partially steamed. Some early settlers in Peterborough County kneaded the dough and baked the bread in a rather remarkable manner:

"A portion of a trunk of a basswood tree about three feet long and two feet in diameter was split in two halves through the centre. One of these was hollowed out as smoothly as possible, to be used as a kneading-trough. About three pounds of flour, with enough water to wet it thoroughly, was put into this and well kneaded. It was then flattened out and placed in a round long-handled pan, the front of which was held before the fire by means of a string attached to the end of the handle, while live coals were placed beneath and behind it."[51]

When wet weather set in it was found preferable "to roll up the wet flour in lumps about the size of a potato. These were put in holes scraped in the hot ashes, and covered also with hot ashes and then coals, so as to cause them to bake without being burned. This was found more palatable than that baked in the pan, and, in the absence of better, was highly esteemed".[52]

When the wheat had to be ground in a coffee-mill, the flour seldom made good bread, but usually "coarse and black".[53] Most settlers, however, managed to get fairly good milled flour, even if they tramped thirty miles for it. Women often mixed boiled potatoes, or cornmeal, with the wheat flour, partly to improve the flavour of the bread,

[51]Thomas Poole: *Early Settlement of Peterborough and Peterborough County.* 1867. p. 173.
[52]*Ibid.*
[53]Frances Stewart: *Our Forest Home.* 1889. 2nd Edition, 1902, p. 86.

but largely to save flour. The usual yeast was made from boiled hops, but "barm" composed of salt, flour and warm water, or milk, fermented, was employed in some districts; while if nothing better was available "bran leavings" was used to save those who ate the bread from indigestion.

Among other home-made products besides yeast were molasses, vinegar, gelatine, cider, beer, and sometimes whisky, though it was more usual to purchase the whisky from local distilleries, of which there were always plenty. Baking soda was not infrequently made from the lye of burnt corn-cobs, though settlers who lived near towns were able to buy such ingredients from merchants, some of whom manufactured for sale a good quality of yeast, vinegar, and other products of the kind.

Pumpkins were put to many uses as food, as well as providing excellent feed for cattle. They made good pies when boiled and mixed with eggs, milk and spices, sugar not usually being added. Some housewives sliced pumpkins and dried them for winter use, while many also made molasses from them, the recipe which Mrs. Stewart used being as follows: "It is cut into pieces, boiled till pulpy, then the juice is pressed out and boiled till it is thick and dark-coloured like treacle; it tastes rather acid and rather sweet; I think it very bad."[54] This type of molasses was sometimes called "punkin sass" by Americans. Pumpkin soup was another variation of this valuable food, which was the more used since other fruits and vegetables were not common among the rural inhabitants, for most of them had not time to spend in the care of gardens, even if the seeds had been readily available.

In later years apples replaced pumpkin in pies to a considerable extent. A paring bee produced large numbers of strings of dried apples, and these were suspended from the ceiling of kitchen or attic. After they were perfectly dry they might be packed in boxes or paper bags, and when needed for pies, puddings or tarts they were boiled with sugar. Samuel Strickland describes a similar method of preserving other fruits at small cost in a day when glass jars and even stone crocks were scarce:

"Plums, raspberries and strawberries are boiled with a

[54]*Ibid.*, p. 61.

small quantity of sugar, and spread about half an inch thick on sheets of paper, to dry in the sun. This will be accomplished in a few days; after which the papers are rolled up, tied, and hung up in a dry place for use. When wanted for tarts these dried fruits are taken from the paper and boiled with a little more sugar, which restores the fruit to its former size and shape. Our ladies make jams and jellies after the orthodox European fashion."[55]

With reference to the pickling of vegetables Mrs. Traill wrote:

"The great want of spring vegetables renders pickles a valuable addition to the table at the season when potatoes have become unfit and distasteful. If you have been fortunate in your maple-vinegar, a store of pickled cucumbers, beans, cabbages, etc., may be made during the latter part of the summer; but if the vinegar should not be fit at that time, there are two expedients: one is to make a good brine of boiled salt and water, into which throw your cucumbers, etc. . . . Another plan, and I have heard it much commended, is putting the cucumbers into a mixture of whisky and water, which in time turns to a fine vinegar, and preserves the colour and crispness of the vegetable; while the vinegar is apt to make them soft, especially if poured on boiling hot, as is the usual practice".[56]

Turnips, a luxury in early days, were grown quite extensively by some of the more progressive settlers in the thirties and forties, but their introduction had been recent, and few knew how to cultivate them properly. The Hon. Asa Burnham, an early settler near Cobourg, stated that in 1842 he and a few others first raised them in that neighbourhood: "I thought hoeing and cultivating them would rip them all up, but they turned out a fine crop. I stored them, but covered them up too warmly, so that they all rotted. I soon learned by experience how they should be treated".[57]

The experience of Mr. Burnham, who was one of the most progressive farmers in the province, is typical of that

[55]Strickland, *op. cit.*, Vol. II, pp. 296-7.
[56]Catharine Traill: *The Backwoods of Canada*. 1836. Edition of 1929, pp. 355-6.
[57]Speech at St. Andrew's Society Dinner, November 30, 1864. *Cobourg Sentinel*, December 10, 1864.

of many a settler who attempted to introduce the cultivation of fruits and vegetables. For many years they were little grown except in the Niagara District, "the Garden of Canada", and along the Detroit River, where the French settlers had orchards in the early seventeen-nineties which supplied even Niagara with apples and cider. In both of these districts melons, peaches, cherries and apples were being cultivated before the commencement of the nineteenth century, while vegetables such as onions, cucumbers, celery and cabbage were soon afterwards commonly grown.

In other districts progressive settlers, like Thomas Need in Victoria County, and the Traills and Stewarts in Peterborough County, grew melons, lettuce and cabbage, and various root crops, which they were able to keep through the winter. Those whose means made possible the hiring of servants, often spent considerable time in horticulture, which enabled them to revive pleasant memories of their gardens in Britain. In July, 1833, Thomas Need noted in his journal that he was occupied chiefly "in the garden, in which I sowed the seeds of cucumber, melon, lettuce, parsley, endive, mustard and turnip. I also planted potatoes for seed next year, and picked out cabbages and broccoli".[53]

Gooseberries, raspberries, strawberries and currants were grown from plants imported from England, but they were seldom as good as those grown in the Old Country. Most settlers, of course, were satisfied to gather the wild fruits, of which the grape was, perhaps, most extensively used. In the early sixties the cultivation of the grape was being investigated by the government with a view to its development, and the vineyards of the Niagara district were the result. Many settlers who had orchards paid but little attention to them, sometimes leaving the fruit to the pigs; but a few men made a name for themselves and conferred a benefit upon humanity by their care of the wild fruit trees. John McIntosh, an early settler in Dundas County, transplanted a number of wild apple trees in 1796, and one of them lived to allow grafts to be distributed throughout the province, the McIntosh Red earning the reputation of being one of the best apples.

[53]Need, *op. cit.*, p. 66.

Drinks varied with the locality, and the preference of individuals. Whisky, beer, cider, buttermilk, tea and coffee were commonly used at meals; while among special beverages was spruce beer, a popular summer drink in York during the early years of the town's history. Coffee was harder to obtain than tea, and burnt corn sometimes provided a substitute. Tea, chiefly green, was widely used, but, though it cost on an average about $1 a pound, it was frequently neither of good quality, nor well made; one traveller considered that some she was served at a tavern tasted "for all the world like musty hay".[59] Maple sugar sweetened it, if any sugar at all was used, and some people added whisky or brandy to make "bush tea" more palatable.

The duty on tea led to a great deal of smuggling. Merchants not infrequently imported one or two chests from Great Britain, with the custom-house mark on them, and then kept filling them up with smuggled American tea. A traveller was told in 1824 that "of every fifteen pounds sold, thirteen were smuggled"; and that one merchant in Niagara was known to have annually smuggled 500 to 1,000 chests of tea into the province.[60]

Those who were unable to purchase the real thing used hemlock, peppermint, "New Jersey tea", sweet balm and other herbs to make a beverage often quite palatable. A traveller familiar with the settlements in the vicinity of New Lanark and Perth in the early eighteen-twenties gives a somewhat detailed account of these substitutes:

"Different kinds of herbs are produced in the woods, which are gathered and used as substitutes for tea. One of these species is denominated velvet tea and abounds in marshy situations. Its leaves are green on the one side and yellow on the other. There is another species called sanspareil, or unequalled. Another kind is called maiden hair. The inner bark of the maple is likewise used in place of tea. A species of evergreen is denominated winter-green tea."[61]

Meals among the farmers of the thirties and forties varied with the age of the settlement and the prosperity

[59]Jameson, op. cit., Vol. I, p. 97.
[60][W. N. Blane]: An Excursion through the United States and Canada during 1822-23. 1824. p. 395.
[61]John McDonald: Narrative of a Voyage to Quebec, and Journey from thence to New Lanark, Upper Canada. 1823. p. 18.

COBOURG IN 1840

SMITH'S FALLS IN THE EIGHTEEN-THIRTIES
The village was first known as Wardsville

Brockville from Umbrella Island, 1828

of the family. There were many who lived on very plain
fare. In 1833 Surveyor Baird and party called for dinner
at a farmhouse near Rice Lake. A large pot of potatoes was
boiled and emptied on the table, and some salt placed near
by. The charge for the meal, as suggested by the very
discriminating host, was "seven pence ha'penny for the
officers and saxpence for the men".[62]

Joseph Pickering, who travelled through many newly-
settled districts in 1826, found that the typical meal he
could get at a farmhouse was "bread or cake, and butter
and potatoes, or 'mush-and-milk', if for supper". The latter
dish he describes as "ground Indian corn boiled in water
to the consistence of hasty pudding, then eaten with cold
milk. It is the favorite dish, and most people are fond of it
from its wholesomeness and lightness as a supper meal".
These meals he found usual for the first year or two after
settlement, but sometimes Johnny cake and meat were
added.[63] The cornmeal "mush" referred to by Pickering
was sometimes called "supporne" by Americans, and was
the only porridge until the late forties, when oatmeal came
into common use.

In the homes of the more prosperous settlers the food
was better. When Patrick Shirreff visited a friend in
Windsor (Whitby) "the dinner consisted of fried pork,
the standard dish of the country, eggs, new potatoes and
pancakes"; this he considered an excellent repast.[64] Mrs.
Jameson was similarly pleased with the food at a clergyman's home in Erindale: "I found breakfast laid in the
verandah: excellent tea and coffee, rich cream, delicious
hot cakes, new-laid eggs—a banquet for a king."[65]

John Langton, whose letters describe pioneer life in the
early thirties on the shores of Sturgeon Lake, refers to
barrelled beef, and turnips, as luxuries "which I reserve
for chance guests or such great occasions as Christmas or
New Year's days". He used fish, ducks and venison for variety in the summer, but from November to April inclusive,
"salt pork is the standing dish for breakfast, dinner and
tea, and a most expensive one it is, each member of my
establishment consuming at the rate of one and a quarter

[62]Poole, *op. cit.*, p. 29. [63]Pickering, *op. cit.*, September 9, 1826.
[64]Shirreff, *op. cit.*, p. 120. [65]Jameson, *op. cit.*, Vol I, p. 304.

pounds per day at 6d. per pound". To make the pork go farther he used many soups, of which "potato soup is the favourite and is so much relished by my men that it has become the ordinary dish at breakfast". This soup was made by boiling a lump of pork, an onion and a dozen or so potatoes "until it has acquired the desired consistency". The pea soup was not as good, consisting of "hard, black pease floating about in weak greasy broth".

Langton tried to make a plum pudding for Christmas, but "currants and suet were scarce, the eggs entirely wanting, and flour by much the preponderating ingredient", so it was a decided failure, although it was eaten. Sugar and milk were very scarce, so tea was usually drunk clear and strong; after the first months of settlement a goat was bought to supply milk. Bread was usually baked "in a frying pan before the fire". In one letter Langton wrote that his men broke out in boils because of the unbalanced pork diet, and he asks for recipes for preserving some of the wild fruits which grew in such abundance; he stated that he hoped to be able to domesticate some of the swarms of honey bees to be found in the woods.

Among the game which Langton occasionally used for food was the porcupine, which "upon the second trial I pronounce very good eating; there is a peculiar smell and taste about the meat which I judged it prudent to mitigate by parboiling, but after that he made a most excellent stew". A method of salting down fish in winter is described: two dozen potatoes were boiled, peeled and mashed in the bottom of a barrel, adding plenty of salt and pepper; then a maskinonge was boiled, and "at a certain stage if you take him up by the tail and give him a gentle shake over the barrel all the flesh will fall off"; salt and pepper is again added in considerable quantity, and the whole process repeated until the barrel is full, whereupon it is headed up and frozen. "It will keep in a cool place good until the beginning of June, and when any is wanted for use take out a sufficient quantity and fry it in little round cakes".[66]

In connection with Langton's cooking it must be re-

[66]John Langton: *Early Days in Upper Canada, Letters of John Langton*. 1926. References to food are found particularly on pp. 35, 38, 57-60 and 83.

membered that his was a bachelor's establishment of lumbermen, though on a comparatively small scale. Samuel Strickland refers to the food in large lumber camps as "fat barrelled pork, and beef pea-soup, and plenty of good bread, potatoes, and turnips. Tea, sugar, onions, or other luxuries, must be provided at their own expense".[67] In later years lumbermen were supplied with strong tea, though seldom with milk or sugar, for which molasses was substituted. Copious supplies of beans became customary with the pork, while pies and cakes in large quantities were made by the shanty cook.

The examples of foods and meals in the rural districts may seem to represent largely the conditions of the earliest and most difficult times. Usually it was only a few years before scarcity was changed to plenty, and often to abundance. As an example of an average meal in the Huron Tract, after the first years of hardship were over, may be taken the breakfast of "green tea and fried pork, honey-comb and salted salmon, pound cake and pickled cucumbers, stewed chicken and apple tart, ginger bread and *sauerkraut*";[68] and dinner and supper were merely a repetition of breakfast. Besides cabbage in the form of *sauerkraut*, other dainties enjoyed by German and Dutch settlers included *kohl* salad and *schmier kase;* these foods were particularly popular among the German settlers who entered Waterloo County in 1800 and succeeding years, and among those of the same nationality who settled in Lincoln, Welland and Haldimand Counties in the eighteen-thirties.

There was often a similar profusion in other parts of the province. Mrs. Stewart describes the food at a picnic in Peterborough County in 1838 as "cold fowl, ham, bread and butter, then melons, apples, wine and water";[69] while at a raising bee in 1841 was served "a roast pig and a boiled leg of mutton, a dish of fish, a large, cold mutton pie, cold ham and cold roast mutton, mashed potatoes and beans and carrots, a large rice pudding, a large bread-and-butter pudding, and currant and gooseberry tarts"[70]—a banquet which would have called forth praises from that lover of

[67]Strickland, *op. cit.*, Vol. II, p. 286.
[68]R. and K. Lizars: *In the Days of the Canada Company.* 1896. p. 55.
[69]Stewart, *op. cit.*, p. 158.
[70]*Ibid.*, pp. 174-6.

good meals, Samuel Pepys. Upon a similar occasion in the Ottawa Valley "the fatted calf or sheep was killed, or the best beef procurable was well roasted with well-boiled potatoes, the best of bread, buns, cakes, crackers, also puddings and pastries, whilst tea, coffee and whisky flowed in equal streams".[71]

The farther one went into "the bush", the more fish and game he found used as food. When Thomas Need (a bachelor) was visited by four travellers from Peterborough in 1833, he got them all to help in the preparation of the meal,—"one baked, another attended to the roast, while a third prepared the vegetables. In due time, I set before them a repast of the usual forest fare—fish, fowl, and venison—which my guests pronounced sumptuous, and enjoyed not the less on account of its novelty".[72] When Lieutenant-Governor Sir John Colborne honoured the infant settlement with a visit during a tour of inspection of improvements in the backwoods of the Newcastle District, Need rose to the occasion with a much more pretentious dinner-party:

"There was a noble maskalongy, supported by the choice parts of a couple of bucks; then for *entremets,* we had beaver tails (a rare delicacy), partridges, wild fowl and squirrels. My garden supplied the dessert, which consisted of melons, raised from English seed, but far exceeding their parent stock in size and flavour, plums, strawberries and apples; there were grapes too, rich in hue and beautiful in appearance, but unhappily tasteless to the palate as the fabled fruit of the Dead Sea shore. The high-bush cranberry, by far the most delicate and admired of all our native fruits, was not yet ripe, but his Excellency was pleased highly to extol the entertainment".[73]

The little village was then christened Rokeby by the Lieutenant-Governor; but as the rapids were called Bob Cajwin, or the Bob, the place ultimately took the name Bobcaygeon.

At Young's Point, Peterborough County, Mrs. Susanna Moodie was entertained by the Youngs in 1835, just before setting out upon an expedition to Stoney Lake. She describes the feast as consisting of "venison, pork, chickens,

[71]J. L. Gourlay: *History of the Ottawa Valley.* 1896. p. 11.
[72]Need, *op. cit.,* p. 71.
[73]*Ibid.,* p. 99.

ducks and fish of several kinds, cooked in a variety of ways; pumpkin, raspberry, cherry, and currant pies, with fresh butter and green cheese (as the new cream cheese is called), maple molasses, preserves and pickled cucumbers, tea and coffee",[74]—an excellent example of that hospitality for which the inhabitants of the rural districts have always been noted. Wedding suppers or Christmas dinners could not surpass the banquets which were often the meals of the pioneer settlers of but a few years previous.

As a general rule fresh meat was obtainable in the towns, but there were times even in Toronto in the late thirties when it was difficult to procure anything but salt pork; it may be assumed, however, that this condition was caused almost entirely by difficulties of transportation in the spring season, when the roads were breaking up, and navigation had not commenced. Mrs. Jameson refers to a comparative scarcity of this kind in Toronto in April, 1837. She was living in the fashionable western suburbs of the city of that day—in the vicinity of Spadina and Palace (Front) Streets— and the remoteness of the Toronto market necessitated management and forethought to keep the larder full.

"Our table, however, is pretty well supplied. Beef is tolerable, but lean; mutton bad, scarce, and dearer than beef; pork excellent and delicate, being fattened principally on Indian corn. The fish is of many various kinds, and delicious. During the whole winter we had black bass and whitefish, caught in holes in the ice, and brought down by the Indians. Venison, game and wild fowl are always to be had; the quails, which are caught in immense numbers near Toronto, are most delicate eating; I lived on them when I could eat nothing else. What they call partridge here is a small species of pheasant, also very good; and now we are promised snipes and woodcocks in abundance. The wild goose is also excellent eating when well cooked. . . . The higher class of people are supplied with provisions from their own lands and farms, or by certain persons they know and employ . . . Those who have farms near the city, or a country establishment of their own, raise poultry and vegetables for their own table. As yet I have seen no

[74]Moodie, *op. cit.*, p. 327.

vegetables whatever but potatoes; even in the best seasons they are not readily to be procured in the market".[75]

In the towns more luxuries were, of course, available. Those who could afford imported foods were usually able to buy them, though some luxuries—oysters, for example— had often to be purchased in large quantities. In the *Upper Canada Gazette,* published at York, occurs the advertisement of James F. Smith, a merchant at the corner of Church and Palace (Front) Streets, and in his announcement, dated March 25, 1830, he states that he "daily expects Oysters (in shell). Lobsters, Mackerel, North Shore Herring and Salmon pickled and smoked". He also advertises for sale a large variety of imported wines and liquors, "Sugar-Double, Single Refined, and moist; Tea of every description; Sauces, Pickles, East India preserves; Candied Lemons, Citron and Orange Peel; Anchovy Paste and Fresh Curry; Codfish of various kinds; Digby and Lockfine Herrings; English Cheese—Dolphin, King's Arms, Berkley, Pine Apple, Truckle and Double Gloucester; Tobacco, Snuff, Havanna Cigars and Pipes."[76] Thirty years earlier much of the tobacco brought into Upper Canada was smuggled from the United States, often hidden in barrels of salt.

The larger towns were provided with confections which might have been presumed to belong only to a later day. Previous to 1800 York had a bakery which supplied bread and cakes; and some of the other towns or large villages had similar establishments after the War of 1812. Even the "backwoods" village of Perth had two bakeries in 1821, though they were engaged chiefly in supplying incoming immigrants with bread. In the early thirties even ice cream, then usually called ices, was sold in York. Thomas Hamilton states that in passing through the streets he was "rather surprised to observe an *affiche* intimating that ice creams were to be had within. The weather being hot, I entered, and found the master of the establishment to be an Italian. I never ate better ices at Grange's".[77]

Some other luxuries available in York a century ago were sent by a friend to Mrs. Thomas Stewart of Peter-

---

[75]Jameson, *op cit.,* Vol. I, pp. 267-9.
[76]*Upper Canada Gazette,* March 25, 1830.
[77]Thomas Hamilton: *Men and Manners in America.* 1833. Vol. II, p. 335.

borough County, during an illness. The delicacies are described as "sago, tapioca, groats, ginger, and all the niceties
for an invalid".[78] It was many years later, however, before
imported fruits and nuts became common in the towns;
even in the sixties they were curiosities. At a conversazione
of Victoria College, Cobourg, on May 11, 1864, the refreshments included oranges, almonds, raisins, candies and
"cupid's messengers"; and it is stated that a soda fountain
was liberally patronized. The description of these delectable
dainties by the editor of the *Cobourg Sentinel* assures us
that such refreshments were quite unique.[79]

The meals in the towns varied according to the means
of the inhabitants. Most people had food similar to that
of the dwellers in the rural districts; but the wealthier
classes ate meals much like those of the Simcoes and Joseph
Willcocks, thirty or forty years earlier. Luxuries could be
purchased from the merchants, and delicacies prepared and
served in style by expert cooks; but it may be doubted that
any town meals ever surpassed in richness and variety
some of the banquets of the settlers in the backwoods.

Special events brought forth the same effort to provide
a good meal, whether people lived in the urban or rural
districts. Ann Macaulay of Kingston writes to her son in
Toronto that there was to be a grand christening, and "some
turkeys and three roasting pigs" were to be served to the
guests.[80] To roast animals whole was a favourite method
of cooking meat in "the good old days": on Queen Victoria's
wedding day, April 2nd, 1840, an ox was thus roasted in
the streets of Toronto, and everyone invited to come and
slice off a piece for himself![81]

With reference to meals in general it may be said with
certainty that most immigrants fared better in Canada
than they had in the Old Land. This fact was well expressed
by a Scotsman who entered into conversation with Patrick
Shirreff while they were chafing at the delay in the stage-
coach scheduled to carry them from Niagara Falls to the
town. The Scotsman volunteered the information that "the

[78]Stewart, *op. cit.*, p. 79.
[79]*Cobourg Sentinel*, May 14, 1864.
[80]Macaulay Papers. Ann Macaulay to John Macaulay, November 28,
    1837. (Archives of Ontario).
[81]Toronto *Mirror*, April 3, 1840.

beef of Canada was so tough that teeth could not chew it;
. . . . but when in the Old Country he got beef only once a
week, on Sunday, here he had it three times a day".[82]

John Howison found the same comparative profusion of
food in Upper Canada. He advised the intending emigrant
that he "must not expect to live very comfortably at first.
Pork, bread, and what vegetables he may raise, will form
the chief part of his diet for perhaps two years"; but while
travelling through the province and living for several
months among the people, he noticed that most settlers were
soon able to vary their diet with venison, poultry, vegetables, milk and various types of bread and cakes. Howison
was of the opinion that "in Upper Canada the people live
much better than persons of a similar class in Britain;
and to have proof of this, it is only necessary to visit
almost any hut in the backwoods. The interior of it seldom
fails to display many substantial comforts, such as immense
loaves of beautiful bread, entire pigs hanging round the
chimney, dried venison, trenchers of milk, and bags of
Indian corn".[83]

E. A. Talbot, who lived in Canada for five years, came
to the same conclusion, but he expresses it in his own peculiarly snobbish style. He usually disliked everything and
everybody, and he considered it humorous that "Irish moun-
taineers or Scotch Highlanders,—who, in their native country had seldom, except 'on some high festival of once a
year', sat down to a more luxurious meal than 'murphies'
and buttermilk, or to an oaten cake and porridge,—surrounded a table in Canada which groaned beneath the
weight of a profusion of sweetmeats and fine fruits, and
'did the honours' with all the politeness of newly-elected
Aldermen".[84]

After the middle of the century there were many
changes in foods, due largely to improvements in transportation and developments in manufacturing. Almost all can-
ning and preserving of fruits and vegetables was done in
the home in earlier times, but canned goods became in-

[82]Shirreff, *op. cit.*, p. 93.
[83]John Howison: *Sketches of Upper Canada.* 1821. 3rd Edition,
    1825, p. 270.
[84]E. A. Talbot: *Five Years' Residence in the Canadas.* 1824. Vol. II,
    p. 11.

creasingly important in the sixties. The introduction of packaged cereals took place some years later. The general use of maple sugar declined with the increasing importation of cane sugar, which was gradually refined from a dark brown, wet, raw sugar, so tightly packed in huge hogsheads that a boy was hired to climb in and hack it out with a hatchet, perhaps finding an occasional piece of cane as a reward for his labours. Tropical fruits, vegetables and nuts were at first a curiosity even in the towns, and some of them, such as the banana, have been introduced in comparatively recent times. Later still came the grapefruit, at first so bitter that one lady, who had purchased some to be in style, told her grocer that when she wanted more quinine she would order it from her druggist! Apple pie, long the standard dessert in town and country, has given place to many an innovation. Artificial refrigeration has not only changed the status of ice cream to a food, but has enabled the introduction of a large variety of frozen desserts, and made possible the extensive importation of fruits and vegetables, now available out of season in a profusion which would have astonished our pioneers.

CHAPTER III

THE "HUNGRY YEAR"

"The century's last decade came with signs
Foreboding evil to the forest land.
The sun and moon alternate rose and set,
Red, dry, and fiery, in a rainless sky;
And month succeeded month of parching drouth,
That ushered in the gaunt and hungry year,—
The hungry year whose name still haunts the land
With memories of famine and of death!"

WILLIAM KIRBY.[1]

AT the close of the American Revolution the British Government determined to do all in its power to assist Loyalist refugees and disbanded soldiers to establish a home in Canada. For three years they were to be provided with such rations as were allowed daily to the private soldier; and at the expiration of this period it was presumed that they would be able to provide for themselves. The requisite supplies were transported by bateau to each township, and depots were established where provisions were dealt out regularly to each family according to the number of children. They were also provided with spring wheat, peas, corn and potatoes for seed, and government grist-mills were constructed at Kingston, Niagara and Napanee for their use; but at the end of three years there were still many unprepared to support themselves, and, as a season of drought and poor crops coincided with the end of the rationing system, a period of unparalleled hardship was the result.

The year of famine,[2] known to some as "the scarce year", "the hard summer", or "the starved year", was 1788,

[1] William Kirby: *The Hungry Year*. 1878. p. 5.
[2] For an account of this unfortunate event we are almost entirely dependent upon the reminiscences of Loyalists who experienced the famine, for there is but little reference to it in official documents or in contemporary publications. Seventy-five years ago, when Dr. William Canniff was collecting the material for his *History of the Settlement of Upper Canada*, many people could remember the "hungry year", and he obtained valuable reminiscences of the event from men upon whose memory had been made a permanent impression of the extreme suffering occasioned by the scarcity. The chief other sources of material relating to the subject are referred to in the accompanying notes, numbers 1, 4, 5, 6, 7, 10 and 11.

though the distress commenced in some districts the year previous and lasted until 1789. While crops were undoubtedly poor in almost every part of Upper Canada, Dr. William Canniff does not emphasise any general failure, but suggests rather that neglect on the part of some, and inability on the part of others, made it impossible for them to supply themselves adequately with the necessities of life when the government suddenly discontinued the distribution of rations. Some settlers had come but recently to Upper Canada and soon used up the supplies they had brought with them; while others relied on the rumour that the King would continue the distribution of food a year or so longer.

Canniff considered[3] that the Commissary Department of the Army might have alleviated the suffering by bringing up larger quantities of stores from Lower Canada, where the scarcity was less acute. It appears remarkable that the system of rationing was not immediately recommenced when the scarcity became so great; but such reports as are available indicate that there was great difficulty in obtaining food in large quantities, even in the United States, while the slow means of transport of that day greatly delayed the distribution of such food as was to be had. Even officials engaged in the public service did not receive the rations upon which they were entirely dependent.

It would appear that the scarcity, commencing with a poor harvest in 1787, developed very gradually and surprised officials and settlers alike in its intensity; and as the severe winter wore away, the spring of 1788 found the inhabitants almost devoid of food and seed. Towards the end of the famine Lord Dorchester allowed free importation of provisions from the United States *via* Lake Champlain, as his dispatch to Lord Sydney, under date of February 14, 1789, states.[4] Had the duties on such imports been removed a year earlier much of the suffering might have been avoided.

The French settlements along the Detroit River, and such Loyalists as had arrived in Essex County did not escape the severity of the famine year. Their communication with the rest of Upper Canada, and with Lower

[3]See William Canniff: *History of the Settlement of Upper Canada.* 1869. pp. 195-201.
[4]Dorchester to Sydney, February 14, 1789.

Canada, was infrequent, and they were not dependent upon supplies from Montreal and Quebec. The main settled districts most remote from Lower Canada, the base of supplies, were those at Niagara and the Bay of Quinté, and there the distress seems to have been most intense; but there was also a very considerable scarcity of food all along the shores of the St. Lawrence.

The authorities seem to have distributed generously such supplies as were available at the garrison towns. The rations of the soldiers were reduced to a biscuit a day at Kingston to relieve the suffering of settlers; while at Niagara the "King's stores" were distributed among the people who lived close enough to come for them. Food was everywhere in great demand. Settlers are reported to have traded 200 acres of land for a few pounds of flour, a cow for eight bushels of potatoes, and a fine three-year old horse for fifty pounds of flour; and half-starved children on the shores of the St. Lawrence were known to beg sea-biscuits from passing boatmen and traders.[5]

In the Niagara district the drought and heat dried up wells and springs, and water was unobtainable at a distance from lake or river. Crops withered, cattle died, and game and wild birds practically disappeared, while frequent forest fires added to the trials of the inhabitants. Colonel John Clark of Niagara refers in his reminiscences[6] to the use as food of roots and greens from the woods, and states that a kind of tea was made from sassafras and hemlock. Captain James Dittrick of St. Catharines recalled many details: "We noticed what roots the pigs ate, and by that means avoided anything that had any poisonous qualities." He considered that the officers of the army did all in their power to mitigate distress, but the supplies were so limited that "only a small pittance was dealt out to each petitioner". He further states that dogs were killed to allay the pangs of hunger, "the very idea bringing sickness to some, but others devoured the flesh quite ravenously and soon became

[5]See T. W. H. Leavitt: *History of Leeds and Grenville.* 1879. pp. 22-3; and W. S. Herrington: *The History of Lennox and Addington.* 1913. pp. 39-40.
[6]Reminiscences of Colonel John Clark, Coventry Papers, Public Archives of Canada. (Most of the material is printed in Ontario Historical Society, *Papers and Records*, Vol. VII).

habituated to the taste". His family had also to kill a horse which could ill be spared from farm work; but there was nothing else to eat, and the horse "lasted a long time and proved very profitable eating".[7]

In reminiscences written for Egerton Ryerson, Thomas Merritt of St. Catharines states that many families had no food left when the harvest was still three months away; and that leaves, ground nuts, herbs and fish were the common foods; but that "in the middle of June moss became so thick in the river that they could not see to fish". Some settlers who had a cow lived on milk for all meals until the wheat had headed sufficiently, whereupon it was boiled for food.[8]

William Kirby's poem, *The Hungry Year*, emphasises the devastation wrought by drought and forest fire, and gives the Indian explanation of the catastrophe.

"Corn failed, and fruit and herb. The tender grass
Fell into dust. Trees died like sentient things,
And stood wrapped in their shrouds of withered leaves,
That rustled weirdly round them sear and dead.
From springs and brooks no morning mist arose;
The water vanished; and a brazen sky
Glowed hot and sullen through the pall of smoke
That rose from burning forests, far and near.

Slowly the months rolled round on fiery wheels;
The savage year relented not, nor shut
Its glaring eye, till all things perished,—food
For present, seed for future use were gone.
'All swallowed up', the starving Indians said,
'By the great serpent of the Chenonda
That underlies the ground and sucks it dry'."[9]

The reminiscences of settlers in the Bay of Quinté district give some additional details of conditions during the famine. In an address delivered at Picton in 1859 Canniff Haight said:

"Men willingly offered pretty much all they possessed

[7]Reminiscences of Captain James Dittrick, Coventry Papers.
[8]Reminiscences of Thomas Merritt, Coventry Papers.
[9]Kirby, *op. cit.*, p. 5.

for food. I could show you one of the finest farms in Hay
Bay that was offered to my grandfather for a half hundred
of flour and refused. A very respectable old lady . . . .
was wont in those days to wander away early in the spring
to the woods, and gather and eat the buds of the basswood
and then bring an apron or basketful home to the children.
Glad they were to pluck the rye and barley heads for food
as soon as the kernel had formed; and not many miles from
Picton a beef's bone was passed from house to house and
was boiled again and again in order to extract some nutri-
ment."[10]

During the winter, fishing was almost impossible, for the
extreme cold froze up lake and river to a depth of two
feet. Powder and shot were scarce or more game might
have been obtained. Some of the inhabitants were so hungry that they did not wait even to dress the game they
caught by snares, but roasted it as it was; others ate so
many fish in the spring that they became ill. Children were
sent to the woods to discover the storehouses of squirrels
and remove the nuts. Catherine White stated that "bull-
frogs were eaten when provisions were scant, and potatoes
which had been planted were dug up to eat".[11] Some
families had nothing to eat for weeks at a time but baked
bran cakes, while millet seed was frequently a substitute
for wheat flour. References are found to the use as food of
such plants as wild rice, pigweed, lamb's quarter, ground
nut and Indian cabbage; while the bark of trees and the
leaves and buds of the maple, beech and basswood were
found edible in some degree when boiled.

Henry Ruttan, whose parents had settled near Adolphustown among the first Loyalists, stated that the severe winter
caused the deer to fall easy prey to the wolves, "who
fattened on their destruction whilst men were perishing
from want". His uncle had a little money which he had obtained from the sale of his captain's commission, and he
used this to send two men two hundred miles to Albany,
the journey being a hazardous one, for there were no roads
and the route was largely by trail through the forests. In

[10]Quoted in Herrington, *op. cit.*, pp. 39-40.
[11]Reminiscences of Catherine Chrysler White, Coventry Papers.
(Printed in Ontario Historical Society, *Papers and Records*,
Vol. VII).

many districts the snow was so deep that progress was almost impossible, but the men finally returned with four bushels of Indian corn. The Ruttans had also a cow, without which "all would have perished in the year of scarcity". The family of eight lived until the next harvest on this small amount of grain and the milk from the cow. By pounding the corn in a hollowed stump or hominy-block it was made into meal which was baked into bread and cakes. Roots, nuts and wild berries supplied additional food for the family.[12]

The famine affected life in all its aspects. There is a record of a "raising bee" where, instead of the copious supplies of food usually found at such gatherings, a pailful of eggs which had been saved for the occasion provided the food. They were beaten up with milk and rum, and the mixture was served as the only refreshment available.[13]

The commissariat officers at Niagara attempted to collect payment in later years for food distributed to settlers during the scarcity. When Prince Edward visited Niagara in 1791 some of the inhabitants approached him for relief from such treatment, and he ordered the officers to cancel all such debts and withdraw any lawsuits which had been instituted. "My father is not a merchant to deal in bread and ask payment for food granted for the relief of his loyal subjects", said the Duke of Kent in his reply to the petition. We have no record of any attempt to charge settlers in other sections of the province for such aid as they received during the famine.

A number of people died of starvation during the period of scarcity, while others met death as a result of eating poisonous roots, or from diseases induced by malnutrition. Henry Ruttan said that five of the inhabitants in the vicinity of Hay Bay were found dead, "including one poor woman with a live infant at her breast".[14]

Miraculous events are related as accompaniments of the famine. It is said that while one settler went on a journey in search of food, his wife and family were saved from starvation by being supplied with a rabbit every day by

[12]See Henry Ruttan: *Autobiography*. (In *Transactions* of the United Empire Loyalist Association of Ontario, 1899, pp. 77-8).
[13]Canniff, *op. cit.*, p. 201.   [14]Ruttan, *op. cit.*, p. 77.

the family cat, which had never been known to catch a rabbit previously, nor did it ever do so again after the father had returned eight days later with a little food. An old couple were reported to have been saved by wild pigeons who flew to the house and allowed themselves to be killed.[15] Such remarkable accounts may have been largely the product of over-wrought imaginations; but, in the absence of more exact historical material which it is possible to verify, these reminiscences enable us to picture some of the circumstances of a deplorable situation which for a time threatened the extinction of the infant Loyalist settlements.

The following year, 1789, brought relief to most of the inhabitants. A series of excellent crops rewarded those whose industry enabled them to sow a quantity of grain and potatoes, and the "hungry year" passed into memory as the most distressing period in the annals of pioneer life in Canada.

[15]See Leavitt, *op. cit.*, p. 23.

CHAPTER IV

GRINDING GRAIN INTO FLOUR

THE RELIGIOUS MILL

"The religious mill was the Shantz Mill at Port Elgin, operated by a man named Leader. The miller refused to run a minute after twelve o'clock on Saturday night. On one occasion, during a period of special pressure, a helper in the mill proposed to run right through the last night in the week in order to catch up. A man who happened to be present at the time, for a joke on the helper put some wet grain in the hopper as the clock was nearing the midnight hour. Exactly on the stroke of twelve the wet grain struck the stones and the mill stopped dead. 'I told you," said the joker, 'that this was a religious mill and would not, under any circumstances, run on Sunday.' "[1]

WHEN the Loyalist settlers came to Upper Canada, they were for three years supplied with food by a grateful government; but one of the greatest difficulties with which these pioneers were beset was to get the grain which had been given to them ground into flour. Many of those who settled in Glengarry County, and in other districts along the St. Lawrence, were provided with portable mills, consisting of revolving steel plates; these mills were turned by hand like a coffee- or pepper-mill, but do not appear to have been popular, owing to the difficulty of their operation. No such utensils seem to have been distributed in the Bay of Quinté settlement or farther west, and the settlers in these regions had to get their grain crushed as best they could.

Various modes of milling flour at home were adopted, but in all of them the work was done by hand. The Indians were known to have used a hollowed-out stump for the purpose, or to have employed stones to crush grain into meal in finely-woven reed or wooden baskets; similar means were therefore adopted by the early settlers. Sometimes the grain was crushed with an axe upon a flat stone, but a more satisfactory method was the hominy-block or plumping-mill; this was a mortar made in the stump of a tree, or in a section of the trunk. A hardwood stump, often ironwood, was chosen, and it was hollowed out by building

[1] Reminiscences of Patrick Cummings of Bruce County, quoted in W. L. Smith: *Pioneers of Old Ontario*. 1923. p. 259.

a fire in the centre and keeping the outside wet, or by the use of a red-hot cannon-ball or other piece of iron. The hole was then cleaned out with axes and knives.

The size of these mills varied; sometimes the mortar contained only a few quarts, but frequently it held a bushel or more of grain. A pestle or pounder, of the hardest wood, was used to crush the grain; this pestle was six or eight feet long, about eight inches in diameter at the lower end, and at the top sufficiently small to be spanned by the hand. At first hand-power alone was used for grinding, but later a sweep-pole, sometimes attached to the bough of a tree, was added, and this made the work somewhat easier. Canniff describes it as "similar to a well-pole; and, a hard weighty substance being attached to the pole, much less strength was required to crush the grain, and at the same time a larger quantity could be done".[2]

Two men usually worked together at the plumping-mill. It was comparatively easy to make meal out of Indian corn or wild rice by this crude means, but the grinding of wheat was very difficult, and a great deal of labour was necessary to obtain even a coarse, brown flour. Captain James Dittrick of St. Catharines gives a few additional particulars of the hominy-block in his reminiscences of Loyalist days:

"The mills of rude workmanship were thinly scattered about the country, so that we had to content ourselves with a hollow stump to pound our grain in, which was done with a cannon-ball, fastened to a cord or bark of a tree, and affixed to a long pole which served as a lever. The bread or cakes thus made were not particularly white, but were eaten with a good appetite and proved wholesome."[3]

Early settlers occasionally boiled Indian corn in strong lye made from wood ashes, until the grains burst open; whereupon, after being well washed in clear water and allowed to dry thoroughly, it was easily ground in the plumping-mill.

The grinding of grain by these primitive means did not result in a very refined product. The bran was sometimes

[2]William Canniff: *History of the Settlement of Upper Canada*. 1869. p. 194.
[3]Reminiscences of Captain James Dittrick. (Coventry Papers, Public Archives of Canada.)

John Ross Robertson Collection   Mrs. John Graves Simcoe

MILL ON THE APPANEE RIVER, 1795

The location of this early government mill was the left bank of the
river, in Fredericksburg Township

W. H. Bartlett

MILL AND BRIDGE ON THE RIDEAU RIVER, NEAR BYTOWN, 1840

A scene typical of almost any mill-stream in pioneer days

John S. Gordon, A.R.C.A.

OLD KIRBY MILL, BRANTFORD

Homer R. Watson, R.C.A.

THE FLOOD GATE

separated from the flour by a horse-hair sieve, one of which often served a whole community; other settlers used a thin cloth for the same purpose, or winnowed the meal by sifting it in the wind. The entire work of making flour was quite frequently done by women, and the use of the hominy-block continued for many years, particularly in districts where grist-mills were remote. Early settlers describe long trips by canoe or bateau to obtain the precious "stone" flour which only the mills could produce. The white flour thus procured was often reserved for special occasions; though even milled flour was sometimes "black and bad",[4] owing to defective apparatus for cleaning the wheat.

The obtaining of satisfactory flour by any of the domestic methods was so difficult that the government ordered a grist-mill to be built near Kingston for the convenience of settlers along the St. Lawrence, in the Bay of Quinté district, and along the shores of Lake Ontario. This mill was erected in 1782-3 on the Cataraqui River, seven miles north of the fort, a location chosen as a central point to which the Loyalist settlers, who were about to be brought in, might most conveniently come from east and west. Robert Clark, a millwright, was employed by the government to take charge of the construction of the mill, and soldiers of the garrison at Kingston were detailed to do some of the rougher preparatory work in 1782. The mill and mill-house were constructed at a "raising bee" in 1783 by the united efforts of the first Loyalist soldier settlers to arrive in the district.

For four years no other mill was available to the inhabitants of this part of Canada, and grain was hauled to Cataraqui from such remote districts as Cornwall in the east, and Ontario and Durham Counties in the west. Many a settler carried his grain a long distance on his back or by hand-sleigh in winter, or in canoe, bateau or raft in summer. Roger Bates, for example, used to make the trip in the early seventeen-nineties from Darlington Township, Durham County; the journey took five or six weeks to accomplish by bateau, and at night the boat was pulled up on shore and used for shelter. In winter the lack of roads

[4]Frances Stewart: *Our Forest Home.* 1889. 2nd Edition, 1902, pp. 76-7.

forced some to tramp through deep snow many a dismal mile, following an Indian trail or the windings of the lake shore. No charge was made for grinding grain at the Cataraqui Mill, but the congestion was frequently so great that a man had to wait several days before his turn came. The original mill remained standing until 1836.

In 1783 the government constructed a similar mill in the Niagara district, near the mouth of 4-Mile Creek. After a few months as a government mill it was operated by Captain Daniel Servos. Early settlers at the head of Lake Ontario had to make a two-day journey to this grist-mill, which was for two years the only one in the western district. In 1784 it was planned to erect a church and a mill at the Mohawk Village, near Brantford, but though the church was erected in 1785 it was several years before the mill was built.

In 1785 another mill in the Bay of Quinté district was commenced by the government, and it was located on the Apanee, or Napanee, River. The name is said to be Indian for "flour", but the falls was called by that name before the building was constructed. Not until 1787 was the mill ready to commence operations, some of the machinery not being installed until late in 1786. A bill of expenses gives the cost of the materials and work, a considerable part of the expenditure consisting of the purchase of rum for those who aided in the raising.[5]   In 1792 this mill seems to have been rebuilt.

Though there was no charge at the Kingston mill, a small toll was collected at Napanee; but the convenience of getting their grain ground nearer home and without so much delay was of great value to the Bay of Quinté settlers, and the mill was long the best in the province. The third grist-mill in this district was Van Alstine's, erected about 1796 at Lake-on-the-Mountain. In all of Upper Canada's early mills more corn than wheat was ground at first, but, as the clearing of the land increased, wheat-growing became more widespread.

Farther eastward, on the St. Lawrence, the Loyalist settlers established a number of mills before the close of

[5] Account book of Robert Clark, millwright, quoted in Canniff, *op. cit.*, pp. 207-8.

the eighteenth century. At New Johnstown (Cornwall) water-mills were found to be impracticable owing to the shoving of the ice, so two windmills were early constructed there. In 1788 the first grist-mill in Dundas County was erected by Messrs. Coons and Shaver; this was a small structure in Matilda Township, one mile above the village of Iroquois, and it had one run of stone capable of grinding 100 bushels of grain per day. Soon afterwards John Munroe of Matilda built a larger mill with three run of stone. As early as 1791-2 Joel Stone, Loyalist founder of Gananoque, had a small grist-mill in operation at the mouth of the Gananoque River. As an example of average development in the front townships of the St. Lawrence after the War of 1812 may be taken Charlottenburgh Township, in Glengarry; here in 1816 there were "four grist-mills, with two additional pairs of stones, one of which additional pairs is for hulling barley and oats".[6]

On November 7, 1792, a "Statement of the Mills in the District of Nassau, specifying by whom erected, by what authority and what year, etc.", was issued by D. W. Smith, Surveyor-General, and Augustus Jones, government surveyor. The district of Nassau included the entire region from the Trent River to Long Point, but all of the mills were then located in what may be termed the Niagara district—between the head of Lake Ontario and Port Colborne. Of nineteen mills mentioned, four are both saw and grist, five are grist only, seven saw only, all of which had been built; and one grist- and two saw-mills were in process of erection. The report is worth quoting in full, but the saw-mills will be omitted as outside the scope of the present work. The details of location and ownership make possible the location of the exact sites of many of these very early enterprises; while other occasional details show that permission had to be obtained from the government before the mill was commenced, and give other interesting sidelights upon the subject. The list of grist-mills follows:

1. "A saw- and grist-mill near the Falls of Niagara, on the west shore of the River St. Lawrence, in the town-

[6]Robert Gourlay: *A Statistical Account of Upper Canada.* 1822. Vol. I, p. 559.

ship of No. 2, on lot No. 174, by John Burch, Esq., in the year 1785 by permission of Major Campbell, the commandant at Niagara.

2. "A saw- and grist-mill on a creek called the Twelve-Mile Creek, township No. 3, and lot No. 23 in the 10th concession, by Duncan Murray, Esq., in the year 1786; but he dying before they were completed, they were transferred to Robert Hamilton, Esq., who finished them in the year following.

3. "A grist-mill on a creek called the Four-Mile Creek, township No. 1, lot 2, 4th concession, in the year 1787, by Peter Secord, senior, on the verbal promise made him by Lord Dorchester at the house of the late Major Tice in presence of Mr. Burch and others.

4. "A grist-mill on a creek called the Forty-Mile Creek, lot No. 10, 1st concession, in the year 1789, by John Green.

5. "A saw- and grist-mill on Thirty-Mile Creek, township No. 5, Lot No. 22, 4th concession, in 1790, by William Kitchen.

6. "A grist-mill on a branch of Twelve-Mile Creek, in township No. 10, lot No. 5, 4th concession, in the year 1791, by David Secord.

7. "A grist-mill on Four-Mile Creek, near the King's Mills, in the year 1791, by David Servos, on ungranted lands.

8. "A grist-mill on a creek near the Sugar Loaf Hills, Lake Erie, by Christian Savitz—unsurveyed.

9. "A saw- and grist-mill on a creek that empties into the head of Burlington Bay, by Bargely and Wilson, in 1791.

10. "A grist-mill now erecting near Fort Erie, on the west shore of the River St. Lawrence, at the Rapids, (on a lot of John Gardiner's) by Mr. Dunbar."[7]

This report is concerned only with privately-owned mills, the King's Mills at Four-Mile Creek being only incidentally mentioned in number 7, above. The mill "near the Sugar Loaf Hills, Lake Erie", (Number 8, above), was in the vicinity of the present Port Colborne. Green's Mill, (Number 4, above), was located on the Stoney Creek Road, five miles east of the site of Hamilton. At one time this mill ground all the flour for the garrisons of Upper Canada.

[7]Quoted in John Lynch: *Directory of the County of Peel.* 1874. pp. 9-10.

In 1794 there were about 100 settlers at the Forty (Grimsby), where Green's Mill was situated.

The development of milling facilities along the shores of Lake Erie followed the arrival at Long Point of Loyalists who removed thither from the Maritimes. Towards the close of the eighteenth century Captain Samuel Ryerse built the first mill on Long Point, and it was for many years the only one within seventy miles. In 1805 a grist-mill was erected at Turkey Point, and there were soon others at various locations along the Lake Erie shore. The first mill in the Talbot Settlement was erected at Port Talbot in 1807. When it was destroyed by American raiders in 1814 Colonel Talbot did not rebuild it, and for some years the settlers had to make a journey of several weeks in open boats—or with hand-sleighs upon the ice in winter— to the nearest mill at Long Point. Jonathan Doan's Mill at Sparta, South Yarmouth, was the second mill in the Talbot Settlement, and enabled many people to avoid the laborious journey to Long Point.

In 1819 two of the inhabitants of the district invented a type of hand-mill called a "bragh", and before the end of the year there was one in almost every house in the Talbot Settlement. It was made of granite stones fitted into a framework, the smaller stone being on top, and a massive bolt passing through the centre of both to fasten them together. By means of a large eye at the top of the bolt the mill was made portable, for a handspike could be inserted in the eye. One of the inventors of this hand-mill was Peter McKellar, and by his ingenuity he also erected a watermill on the Sixteen-Mile Creek. He himself made all the wheels and gearing for his establishment, the irons were from Colonel Talbot's old mill, and the neighbours helped to construct a raceway. The water was sufficient to provide power from March to June, and for a time McKellar ran the mill all alone, day and night, from 2 am. Monday until 9 p.m. Saturday. Most of the settlers immediately gave up the use of their hand-mills, and men and women might be seen trudging over the roads with bags of grain, and home again from McKellar's with their meal.

To the westward of the Talbot Settlement in the valley of the Thames River, there were grist-mills before the close of the eighteenth century. Smith's *Gazetteer* of 1799 refers to the "good mills" in Delaware Township,[8] and to a mill at Chatham;[9] while still further west the milling facilities antedated by half a century the establishment of the province. The first settlements in Upper Canada were those made during the latter part of the French period along the Detroit River. Between 1734 and 1756 a considerable number of French settlers, many of them former soldiers, were allotted land in this locality under feudal tenure. One of the conditions of settlement was the erection of grist-mills, so windmill forts, combining utility with protection, became common; when there was a good wind one of these mills would grind one hundred bushels of wheat within twenty-four hours. The Montreuil Windmill at Sandwich was a noted landmark of the district until 1875, when it was demolished.

There were other methods of grinding grain in this locality in later days. Patrick Shirreff, an English farmer who visited the district in 1833, noted the grist-mills driven by the wind, and also "several propelled by oxen walking on an inclined plane, and they are very poor machines". In addition to these he saw some driven "by oxen and horses attached to a large wheel, moving horizontally a few inches from the ground". While he was at Sandwich he heard that a steam-power grist-mill was about to be erected there.[10] Besides the windmills in this district there were others at various points in Upper Canada where water power was not convenient or could not be used to advantage. They were early constructed, for example, at Cornwall, Prescott, York, Niagara and Fort Erie, and remained noted landmarks many years after their use was discontinued.

Flour-milling developed eastward from the head of Lake Ontario in much the same manner as it had elsewhere along "the front"; energetic inhabitants, not infrequently Americans, soon established grist-mills at strategic centres of settlement along the Lake Ontario shore. The first grist-mill in York County was erected by William Berczy,

[8]D. W. Smith: *A Short Topographical Description of His Majesty's Province of Upper Canada* . . . . 1799. p. 41.
[9]*Ibid.*, p. 39.
[10]Patrick Shirreff: *A Tour through North America.* 1835. p. 213.

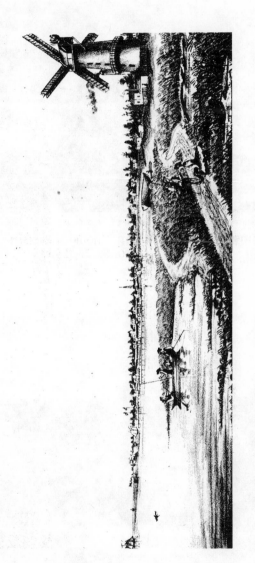

WILLIAM GOODERHAM'S WINDMILL AT YORK (TORONTO), 1833

Armstrong

THE BURNING OF THE GOODERHAM MILL, TORONTO,
OCTOBER 26, 1869

THE "OLD MILL" ON THE HUMBER
A wooden mill was erected on the site in 1833-4, and a stone mill in
1837; the walls of the latter still stand

founder of the first settlement in Markham Township. He brought in his German-American settlers in 1794, and in the same year constructed both saw- and flour-mills on the Rouge River, his establishment being commonly called "the German Mills". The grist-mill was described as having "a pair of French burs and complete machinery bolting superfine flour",[11] and as it was the only mill between the head of the lake and Belleville, settlers brought grain to it from all directions, many of them following the shore of Lake Ontario and continuing up the Rouge.

Soon after were erected the first saw- and grist-mills on the Don River, commenced in the autumn of 1794; these were located on lot 13, East York Township, along the east bank of the stream, just below Todmorden. As they were operated by Timothy Skinner they were known as Skinner's Mills, but they were built through the initiative of Parshall Terry and a few other inhabitants of York. The approach to them by land was over the old Don Mills Road, a continuation of Broadview Avenue. The wife of the first Lieutenant-Governor of the province visited the mills in winter, driving on the ice of the Don "a mile beyond the Castle Frank, which looked beautiful from the river. The ice became bad from the rapidity of the river near the mill".[12]

A saw-mill was operated on the Humber by the government as early as May, 1794, but there was no grist-mill there at that early date. The saw-mill was located near the site of the present "Old Mill' and was not used after the War of 1812. A location for a grist-mill was reserved by the government and leased to John Wilson in 1798, but the lease expired without his having made any progress. A grist-mill was in operation on the Humber after the War, and settlers as far west as Peel County carried their grain to it to be ground.

The history of the site of the present "Old Mill" is of interest. In 1833-4 a wooden grist-mill was built there by Thomas Fisher, and replaced in 1837 by a stone mill erected by William Gamble. An English officer visited the establishment in May, 1840, and describes it as "conducted

[11]Advertisement of sale in the *Upper Canada Gazette*, April 27, 1805.
[12]*Diary of Mrs. John Graves Simcoe*, February 3, 1796.

on a very large scale. About one hundred people derive employment from it. It is supplied with corn for the most part from the United States. It is driven by two large breast wheels".[13] The stone walls of this mill still remain, though the structure was destroyed by fire in 1847, and another built in 1848. For some years longer it remained a centre of trade and business, but the coming of the railways in the fifties diverted the trade, and the establishment was closed in 1858. Previous to this date several other mills were being operated on the upper reaches of the Humber.

The first grist-mill along the Lake Ontario shore between the Rouge River and the Bay of Quinté was that erected in 1794 by Colonel Myers on Myers' Creek (also known as the Moira River), on the present site of Belleville. The earliest settlers at Smith's Creek (Port Hope) made a trip to this mill with their first grain in the winter of 1794-5, "the grain being dragged through the pathless woods on rough sleds".[14]

The Statement of Mills in the District of Nassau, quoted above, notes that a mill-site had been chosen "on a creek called Smith's Creek, north side of Lake Ontario, in the Township of Hope, lot No. 6 in front, at the head of a small pond".[15] Peter Smith had established a trading-post at that point in 1778, near the Indian village Cochingomink (or Pemiscutiank), and in 1790 he was succeeded in the Indian trade by one Herchimere. In 1793 the first settlers arrived, and in the following year the government offered a Loyalist, Elias Smith, a large grant of land on the shores of the creek if he would agree to build saw- and grist-mills. Work was commenced upon them in the spring of 1795, and the flour-mill was completed during that year under the direction of Captain John Burns; but the mill-race was unfinished, and the following spring the frost caused the banks to give way, resulting in a failure of the whole enterprise. Finally, in 1798, the mill was moved down the creek by an American millwright for $1,000, and saw- and grist-mills were in operation on the east bank of the

[13]Quoted in K. M. Lizars: *The Valley of the Humber*. 1913. p. 78.
[14]W. A. Craick: *Port Hope Historical Sketches*. 1901. p. 10.
[15]Lynch, *op. cit.*, p. 10.

creek a few months later. The excellence of the Smith's Creek mills resulted in their being patronised by settlers from far and near. About 1801 White's grist-mill was established seven miles to the east, near Amherst (Cobourg), and gradually others were erected on the main creeks and rivers along the north shore of Lake Ontario.

Some of the proprietors of early mills overcharged the settlers for grinding their grain, and consequently an Act was passed by the first parliament of the province to regulate the tariff. This law, which well exemplifies the practical utility of the acts of Simcoe's *régime*, forbade millers to take more than one-twelfth of the grist as payment for their work. The story is told that one-tenth was being considered, but one miller said this was not enough and suggested one-twelfth, which was thereupon made the legal rate![16]

It is, of course, not possible, nor would it be desirable, to refer to the development of milling facilities in every section of Upper Canada; but, the general course of events along the St. Lawrence and the Lakes having been described, some account of flour-milling in the rear of the earliest settlements will show the characteristic trend.

One of the first settlements back from the Lakes was that of Oxford County. Blenheim Township was surveyed for these settlers, of whom Thomas Horner was the first, by Augustus Jones in 1793, when the closest white inhabitants were near the Mohawk Village eastward and at Chatham in the west. The first mills in the county, both saw and grist, were erected by Horner in the vicinity of Princeton, on the Governor's Road. He had a saw-mill ready for use by 1798. The grist-mill was first operated in 1802, but in 1809 it was burned down and was never rebuilt. The second grist-mill in Oxford County was erected by James Burdick at Centreville in 1806-7. Both of these early enterprises were conducted in buildings only sixteen feet square.

When the first German settlers emigrated from Pennsylvania to Waterloo County in 1800-2 the nearest grist-

---

[16]A variation of this story, (which appears to have been current in early times), is given in Joseph Pickering: *Inquiries of an Emigrant.* 1831. April 2, 1826.

mill was at Dundas. To reach it an almost impassable road through the Beverly Swamp had to be traversed, and the great inconvenience and hardship of such a journey led to the erection of a small mill where the village of Shade's Mills (Galt) later developed. John Miller of Niagara erected the building, and one Maas was the first miller. The structure was of one and one-half storeys and measured twenty-four by twenty-eight feet. In later years many settlers far away in the "Huron Tract" carried their grain to be ground at the Galt mill, the trip being frequently made from North Easthope Township in the days before a mill was erected at Stratford.

As settlement proceeded in the various sections of the country a mill was almost the first consideration. The American settlers in Hull Township, on the Ottawa, were provided between 1802 and 1804 with a grist-mill, a saw-mill, a hemp-mill and a tannery by their leader, Philemon Wright, after whom the main settlement was appropriately named Wright's Mills (Hull). Across the river, in Upper Canada, the first soldier settlers began to arrive in Carleton County after the close of the War of 1812. The earliest arrivals patronised Wright's establishment, but in 1818-19 the government provided the first mills in the county at Richmond. Hamnet Pinhey erected saw- and grist-mills for the settlers of March Township, and other enterprising inhabitants of the county similarly benefitted their community as settlement proceeded.

In the valley of the Rideau the development was similar. When the settlement of the district was commenced in 1816, Perth, the central depot for the distribution of the soldier settlers, was soon provided with a grist-mill; while farther eastward in Lanark, Smith's Falls had mills operated in the early twenties by A. R. Ward, after whom the settlement received its first name, Wardsville.

It might have been presumed that the difficulties of grinding grain experienced by the earliest settlers in Upper Canada were not present in the later pioneer periods; but the hardships of settlement were often just as severe, and the methods just as primitive as in earlier times. This is well illustrated by the experiences of the first inhabitants of Peterborough County. In 1818 a few families moved into

Smith Township, far in "the backwoods". In the first years of settlement they had to carry their grain thirty or forty miles over a blazed trail to the mill at Port Hope, or afterwards to a small establishment on Galloway's Creek, in Cavan Township. In 1821 Adam Scott built small grist- and saw-mills on the Otonabee River, and around them grew the small settlement of Scott's Mills (Peterborough); but this grist-mill often broke down, and was insufficient to meet the needs of even the few settlers then in the district.

Many people in Smith went for weeks without bread, and Jacob Bromwell stated to Sir Peregrine Maitland in 1826 that he had had to resort to the expedient of making a miniature mill of himself, and had actually chewed corn until it became soft enough to bake into bread for his children. The Lieutenant-Governor was impressed with the lack of proper milling facilities, and in 1827 the government provided a good mill to replace Scott's. It was purchased soon after by John Hall and Moore Lee and operated successfully by them for some time. A few years later it was closer for some settlers in the district to travel to Purdy's Mills (the nucleus of Lindsay), where William Purdy, an American, erected a grist-mill in 1830, aided by his sons Jesse and Hasard.

The difficulties were the same in other districts. When the first settlers pushed northward from Uxbridge into Eldon Township in 1829, some of them were forced to grind their first grain "between two grindstones that were made to revolve with a crank turned by hand. The wheat was poured by hand through a hole in the upper stone. Between dark and bed-time enough would be ground to provide for the next day's needs. Later on we thought we were well off when we got a coffee-mill to do the grinding".[17]

Coffee-mills were also in use among many of the settlers in the district colonised by the Canada Company, and in the still larger territories to the north of the Huron Tract known as "the Queen's Bush", comprehending Dufferin, Grey, Bruce and Wellington Counties. An early settler at Belfountain, near Georgian Bay, stated that the work of grinding grain by the hand-mill was so laborious that men

[17]Reminiscences of Colin McFadyen, Eldon Township, quoted in W. L. Smith, *op. cit.*, pp. 140-1.

would rather "chop all day in the bush than grind a half bushel of wheat in the old coffee-mill".[18]   In the forties there was a grist-mill in operation at Belfountain, and early settlers from the vicinity of Meaford and Owen Sound brought their grists in home-made sleighs called jumpers, which were hauled by oxen; in summer the same crude sleds were often hauled over the trails, (which were seldom passable for ox-carts), or the grain was carried by men on their backs.

Where water transport was available it was much easier to carry grain to the mill by canoe or bateau.   Roswell Matthews, the first white settler in the vicinity of Elora, took his first grain to market at Shade's Mills (Galt).   With the help of his sons he had hollowed out a pine log thirty feet long.

"Eagerly launching this dug-out a mile and a half below the Falls, they embarked with sixteen bags of wheat, and paddling down to Galt they found a purchaser in Absalom Shade, who paid them fifty cents a bushel in cash.   The dug-out was sold for two dollars and a half, and they returned home afoot, blithe as any birds of the forest."[19]

On some occasions when it was impossible to get grain ground Matthews was forced to boil wheat when it was in the milk.   A few years after his arrival he attempted to establish a mill near the spot where he had first launched his canoe; but ice-packs destroyed two mill-dams in quick succession, and this, coupled with the fact that an Englishman was commencing a mill two miles below, discouraged further attempts.   There was no mill in the vicinity until after the arrival of Captain William Gilkison, who founded Elora in 1832, moving westward from Prescott, of which also he had been the founder in 1811.

In other sections of Upper Canada the first mills were similarly a boon to the settlers for many miles around.   The old "Red Mill" at Holland Landing served all the farmers in the vicinity of Crown Hill and Barrie; another early mill in this region was that at Newmarket, and it was followed in 1833 by one operated by the government at Coldwater.

In Peel County a number of mills were early established

---

[18]Reminiscences of Robert Brock, quoted in W. L. Smith, *op. cit.*, p. 184.
[19]G. M. Grant (Ed.) : *Picturesque Canada*. 1879. Vol. II, p. 482.

on the Credit River, one of the finest mill-streams in the province. Among the first was Timothy Street's Mill at Streetsville, erected soon after he had surveyed the district in 1819. The Etobicoke was in general a poor milling stream, but John Scott of Brampton erected a small structure for grinding or chopping grain for his distillery. His establishment attracted considerable attention because he had his mill-stones move vertically instead of horizontally, as was the usual practice, and some considered Scott's idea a decided improvement.

In a similar manner might be traced the first mills in each county in Ontario; but while it gradually became true that every settlement where there was sufficient water-power to turn the wheels had at least one mill, yet it was long not unusual for men, and even women, to have to carry grain many miles on their backs, and return home the following day with their flour. One of the Scotch fishermen from the Isle of Lewis who settled about the middle of the century in Huron and Bruce Counties once carried in a barrel on his back 100 pounds of flour for fourteen miles, and when asked how he felt he replied that he was not tired, "but she'll be a little pit sore apoot the back".[20]

Along the shores of Lake Huron the first settlers were served by a few mills erected by enterprising inhabitants. Brewster's Mill, on the lake shore of McGillivray Township, was used in the eighteen-forties by people many miles away in all directions. In the fifties the Harris Mill was the rendezvous of all inhabitants of Kincardine Township and the surrounding district, the farmers putting up at a log tavern near by while their grain was being ground. Those who lived farther inland, in the vicinity of Durham and Orangeville, carried their grists fifty miles or more to the mill at Guelph.

In many districts distilleries were early established in connection with grist-mills. In this manner the poorer grades of grain, such as wheat which had been frosted or rusted, as well as the surplus of the better grades used in the grist-mill, were utilised in the manufacture of whisky. As examples of distilleries operated with flour-

[20]Reminiscences of John S. McDonald, quoted in W. L. Smith, *op. cit.*, p. 258.

mills may be mentioned that of Adam Scott at Scott's Mills
(Peterborough), and the York Windmill, erected in 1831-2
at the mouth of the Don by William Gooderham and James
Worts; this building was first used as a grist-mill, and in
1837 was enlarged to include a distilling plant. In early
days distilleries and breweries were almost as common as
grist- and saw-mills.

The cost of mills varied from £180 to £600 ($2,400),
according to the size of the dam and the way of finishing
the establishment. A "common grist-mill" with one run of
stones usually cost from £200 to £250, while a "good
merchant's mill" was valued at from £800 to £1,000, the
York Windmill costing the latter sum to construct. The
capacity varied similarly, the small mill usually grinding
from 4,000 to 15,000 bushels of grain *per annum*, while
the better ones sometimes ground 40,000 bushels. Almost
all of them could, if the necessity arose, increase their production by one-third by speeding up the process and working in the evenings and on Sundays, as many of them did in
busy seasons.

The mill operated by water-power had one great draw-
back in the forced suspension of milling, often for long
periods, in times of low water; the windmill, too, was
obviously useless when there was no wind. In 1836 there
were about 600 grist-mills in Upper Canada, a number
which remained quite stationary, for in 1854 there were
610. Steam mills began to be fairly common at the middle
of the century, though for many years the water-mills
continued to form a large majority of the total number: in
Oxford County, for example, there were in 1851 seventeen
establishments, only three of which were worked by steam.

Flour-milling enjoyed its palmiest days in the forties,
just previous to the discontinuance of the Canadian preference in the British market as a result of the abolition of
the Corn Laws in 1849. Flour-millers in Montreal led in
the annexation movement of that day, but the agitation
soon died down, and the condition against which it was
a protest was remedied temporarily by Lord Elgin's Reciprocity Treaty with the United States, 1854-1866. During
the existence of this treaty, and particularly in the late
fifties, railway and wagon, schooner and steamboat were

busily employed in the carriage of grain and flour. Men still living in the town of Cobourg, for example, remember double lines of wagons extending half a mile from the harbour, awaiting their turn to unload. The American Civil War still further increased the grain and flour trade in many parts of Upper Canada, though certain localities experienced a depression.

Coincident with developments in transportation and changes in economic conditions was the passing of the small mill, the ruins of many of which are to be seen on river and creek throughout rural Ontario. In the sixties the iron turbine wheel was introduced and proved much more satisfactory than the old type. Most of the wheat is now sent to large mills which supply flour to retail merchants, who, in turn, distribute it to the consumer. With greatly improved machinery and methods much finer grades of flour are produced. The harder wheat grown in the Canadian West supplies the people of Ontario with most of their best flour, a development accelerated after the completion of the Canadian Pacific Railway in 1885 by a gradual change in Ontario from grain-growing to mixed farming, owing to the predominance of the Prairie Provinces as grain producers. The Ontario farmer, who used to haul his grain laboriously to the mill and return home with his flour, now buys it through his own United Farmers' Co-operative Society, or from a chain store, if indeed he needs much flour in a day when his wife buys her bread from the baker.

CHAPTER V

LUMBERING

"Let us recall the brave days of sail, with the great timber rafts dropping down to the coves, and the French-Canadian rivermen singing *En roulant ma boule,* or some such *chanson*: sun-bronzed, red-shirted men, with calks in the soles of their heavy boots, and surprisingly agile in leaping from log to log around the booms; hard brawny fellows, who scanned the Irish timber-stowers for the sight of some opponent in past waterfront fracas to seek or avoid."

F. W. WALLACE.[1]

No phase of pioneer life was more picturesque or more typically Canadian than the lumber industry. Long before the settler pushed his way into the backwoods the lumberman had slashed a bush road through many a remote forest and hauled timber to market. As settlement progressed, every farmer was for some years chiefly a lumberman, though he burned the timber instead of using it. Only enough logs for a primitive home were saved, for it was usually impossible in the early years of settlement to attempt to market lumber. Thousands of beautiful and irreplaceable trees of butternut, walnut, bird's-eye maple and many other varieties common at the time were piled in huge heaps and burned; timber was something to be got rid of as quickly as possible.

Our "second-growth" timber gives us but a poor idea of the extensive forests and huge trees of former times. Fortunately, however, early artists have provided a few representations which recall the days when the trees were towering giants. Pioneers tell of white pine trees sold for masts, over one hundred feet in length and three feet in diameter one-third the way up from the butt-end. Among hardwood trees the oak often attained a remarkable size. Samuel Strickland describes a notable tree which was long a landmark in the territory controlled by the Canada Company. It was located "near Bliss's Tavern, in the Township of Beverly", a short distance from Galt, and was called the Beverly-oak. Concerning its size Colonel Strickland says: "I measured it as accurately as I could about six

[1] F. W. Wallace: *Wooden Ships and Iron Men.* 1924. p. 101.

Lieutenant Philip Bainbrigge

A BUTTONWOOD TREE NEAR CHATHAM

W. H. Bartlett

A TIMBER RAFT IN A SQUALL ON LAKE ST. PETER, 1840

National Development Bureau

MODERN TIMBER RAFTS ARE TOWED BY STEAM TUGS

From the *Illustrated London News*, February 28, 1863   G. H. Andrews

TIMBER COVES AT QUEBEC

feet from the ground, and found the diameter to be as
nearly eleven feet as possible, the trunk rising like a
majestic column, towering upwards for sixty or seventy
feet before branching off its mighty head".[2] Another oak
felled by lightning was found to have a diameter of five
feet three inches twenty-four feet from the ground.[3] Even
black cherry trees, now usually of small size, were to be
found ten or eleven feet in circumference seven feet from
the ground.[4] The magnificient appearance of these primeval
veterans of the forest seldom prevented their destruction,
however, though occasional trees remained to give later
generations some conception of the original grandeur.

In the French period an export trade in ship-building
material, masts and spars had developed with the West
Indies previous to 1700. Some oak planks and pine masts
had also been exported to France, but they were entirely for
government use. In later years shipbuilding, begun in a
small way under Intendant Talon, became an important industry along the St. Lawrence River; ten vessels of from
forty to one hundred tons were built in Canada in 1752.
Saw-mills were to be found in considerable numbers towards
the close of the French period, fifty-two being operated in
Quebec east of the Ottawa River in 1734. The exports of
lumber at the end of the French period do not appear extensive from the modern point of view, amounting in 1759
to a value of only $31,250.

General Murray, the first Governor after the British
conquest of Canada, was instructed in 1763 to set aside
as a reserve for naval purposes a certain section of each
township if suitable timber was to be found there; there
were other suggestions of the kind from time to time, but
no reserves were established other than those for religious
and educational purposes, which hampered settlement to
such an extent that public opinion would probably not have
tolerated any other unused land in the settled districts.

At the commencement of the British period the first important transatlantic trade in lumber developed. The
British bounties and tariff preferences were not large

[2]Samuel Strickland: *Twenty-seven Years in Canada West.* 1853. Vol.
    I, pp. 253-4.
[3]*Ibid.,* Vol. I, pp. 256-7.   [4]*Ibid.,* Vol. I, p. 253.

enough, however, to allow successful competition by the inhabitants of British America with the Baltic timber. At this time, and for about half a century longer, the activities of the world were largely centred on wood, but in later years iron usurped the position of primary importance.

A considerable amount of "Quebec yellow-pine" found its way to the London market before 1800, but the great development in Canadian lumbering occurred when Napoleon's Continental System was operating in full force in 1808. In that year the imports from the Baltic countries fell away to one-eighth of their total in 1806, a reduction due to the success of the French in preventing the trade. To obtain the lumber necessary for the British navy the colonial timber industry was thereupon encouraged in 1809 by a preference, and within a year British North America was supplying Britain with 50,000 shiploads of lumber annually, of which total the Canadian exports were valued at about $400,000.

The trade increased rapidly in succeeding years, the duties reaching their crest in 1813 and being retained until 1842, except for a slight reduction in 1821. Though the Baltic lumber soon became available again, a considerable amount of apprehension remained in Britain, and this, with the desire to trade within the empire, continued the Canadian commerce. By the end of the Napoleonic War the value of the British timber imports from Canada was greater than those from the Baltic, and so remained until the early sixties.

In the French period the Richelieu River system had provided most of the lumber; but as settlement was extended westward and northward after the American Revolution the shores of the St. Lawrence and Ottawa Rivers and their tributaries, and the Bay of Quinté district, were extensive sources of supply. The demand was chiefly for squared timber of pine and oak, although a considerable number of masts were also exported, and there was a good market at Montreal and Quebec for planks, and staves for casks. The squared timber trade necessitated considerable waste in the rough squaring of the logs with the axe, but the process enabled easier packing on ocean ships, and, in addition, was desired for the British market.

Many Loyalist settlers along the St. Lawrence and the
Bay of Quinté found the lumber industry more profitable
than agriculture.   The first timber raft from the Bay of
Quinté was taken to Quebec by Samuel Sherwood in 1790;
it was made up of masts cut three miles east of Trenton,
and as there were then no cattle in that district he used
tackle to haul the logs to the water.

Philemon Wright's American settlers on the Ottawa,
near Hull, were early engaged in lumbering, which was soon
the paramount industry in that district.   In 1806 Wright
examined the rapids along the Ottawa in preparation for
driving down his first timber raft.   This notable event took
place the following spring, and the journey to Quebec from
the banks of the Gatineau took thirty-five days.   "But,"
Wright says, "having from experience learnt the manner
of coming down, we can now (1823) oftentimes come down
them in twenty-four hours."[5]   Wright was also the first to
run a raft through the Long Sault and the Chute au Blon-
deau on the St. Lawrence.

In 1823 over 300 rafts of timber, often loaded with other
produce, made the trip down the Ottawa to Quebec, and by
1835 the lumbermen had penetrated to Lake Timiskaming
—400 miles up the Ottawa.   The characteristics of the
lumber industry in this district are well described by John
MacTaggart:

"The shantymen live in hordes of from thirty to forty
together; throughout the day they cut down the pine trees,
and square them in the 'pineries', or the oaks in the groves,
and afterwards draw the logs to what is termed the bank,
with oxen.   When spring draws on, they form the lumber
into small rafts, called cribs, and drop away down the
rapids to market.   When they come to any extensive sheets
of still-water, the cribs are brought into one grand flotilla;
masts, white flags and sails are sported; while with long
rude oars they contrive to glide slowly along.   Thus they
will come from Lake Allumette, on the Ottawa, to Wolfe's
Cove, Quebec, a distance of nearly 800 miles, in about six
weeks.

[5]Philemon Wright: *An Account of the First Settlement of the Town-
    ship of Hull.* 1823.   (Appendix to Andrew Picken: *The
    Canadas.* 1832. p. xxviii.)

"On these rafts they have a fire for cooking, burning on a sandy hearth; and places to sleep in, formed of broad strips of bark, resembling the half of a cylinder, the arch about four feet high, and in length about eight. To these beds or 'lairs', 'trams' or handles are attached, so that they can be moved about from crib to crib, or from crib to the shore, as circumstances render it necessary. When they are passing a 'breaking-up' rapid they live ashore in these lairs, until the raft is new-withed, and fixed on the still-water below."[6]

In 1828 Philemon Wright's son, Ruggles Wright, erected a timber slide at Hull to avoid the Chaudière Falls. This was the first to be constructed, but soon afterwards these timber chutes, of crib-work construction with sluice gates to admit water, were common at the worst rapids of the rivers where lumbering was extensively carried on. Along the larger streams many of the slides were constructed by the government and a small charge was made for their use; in 1861, for example, the "slide dues" collected in Canada amounted to $55,546. Sometimes these chutes were narrow raceways which would carry only one log at a time; but for rafts they were about twenty-five feet wide, and a crib containing forty tons of timber, with the cookhouse and lumbermen on board, was easily carried over them to the quiet waters often fifty feet below. The Prince of Wales (later Edward VII) made a trip over a timber slide at Ottawa during his visit to Canada in 1860. His experience was, no doubt, similar to G. M. Grant's:

"We embark on board a crib above the slide-gates at the Falls of the Calumet. The raftsmen bid us take firm hold of one of the strong poles which are driven between the lower timbers of the crib. Above the slide the waters of the Ottawa are still and deep; at the left side, through the intervening woods, we can hear the roar of the cataract. The slide-gates are thrown open; the water surges over the smooth inclined channel; our crib, carefully steered through the gateway, slowly moves its forward end over the entrance; it advances, sways for a moment, then, with a sudden plunge and splash of water, rushes faster and faster between the narrow walls. The reflow of the torrent

[6]John MacTaggart: *Three Years in Canada.* 1829. Vol. I, pp. 241-2.

RAFTSMEN IN THE CALUMET RAPIDS, OTTAWA RIVER

W. H. Bartlett

TIMBER SLIDE AT LES CHATS, 1840
The location is Fitzroy Harbour, twenty-five miles above Ottawa

A TIMBER CHUTE

streams over the crib from the front; jets of water spurt up everywhere between the timbers under our feet; then, dipping heavily as it leaves the slide, our crib is in the calm water beneath."[7]

At some timber chutes, notably that at the Cedars on the St. Lawrence, rafts and men were sometimes temporarily submerged during their progress. The turbulent Lachine Rapids were avoided by the use of the Back River, north of Montreal. Oak and pine, the two woods in demand at Quebec, were generally rafted together to help the oak keep afloat. Cash could usually be obtained at Quebec for lumber, almost all of which was exported to England for use in the navy, the ships of which were constructed of thick oak planks, while the masts were usually of pine. As much as $200 was paid at Quebec for a good mast. In a day when long-term credit and barter were the usual means of carrying on business, many a settler "drove" timber to Quebec, pitching camp on his raft, and sometimes taking produce to market both for himself and his neighbours.

After 1800, timber rafts were extensively used by merchants and traders in conveying the produce of Upper Canada to the lower province. Eight hundred barrels of flour, pork, ashes, or other produce were sometimes transported on one raft, which usually carried a large number of square sails to aid the oarsmen in moving it along with the current, a method of transport long a characteristic sight on our main river systems. It was sometimes attempted to move timber rafts on Lakes Erie and Ontario and other large bodies of water, but it was found to be both costly and dangerous owing to sudden storms. An early newspaper describes the loss of a valuable raft in 1826:

"We are sorry to learn that on Monday last, in attempting to tow across Lake Ontario, by the steamboat *Canada*, from the River Humber to the Welland Canal harbour, a large raft, consisting of 15,000 feet of choice timber, belonging to the Lock Company, a strong south-west gale arose, when about twelve miles out, and continued with such violence as to separate in pieces, in spite of every exertion by those concerned to prevent it, which scattered in

[7]G. M. Grant (Ed.): *Picturesque Canada*. 1879. Vol. I, pp. 229-30.

different directions, and floated off entirely at the mercy of the waves. It is probable, when we consider that westerly winds generally prevail at this season of the year, that this timber will drift ashore towards the lower end of the lake, and should this be the case it is earnestly hoped that all those who may observe or fall in with any of this valuable lot of lumber will take measures to secure the same, and immediately give information to Mr. Oliver Phelps, the Company's agent at St. Catharines, U.C., either by mail or otherwise as may be most convenient."[8]

Before the building of railroads the only districts in Upper Canada from which timber could be profitably exported were those near the waterways. By 1820 the western section of Lake Ontario was providing square timber for the trade at Quebec, while by 1830 Lake Erie, and, twenty years later, Lake St. Clair and even lower Lake Huron were sending their quota of the product. In the early forties the "back lakes" almost as far west as Lake Simcoe were being utilized to float square timber by way of the Trent system of lakes and rivers to Lake Ontario, and on down to Quebec. One of the noted timber slides erected in the Kawartha Lakes to prevent damage to the logs was "the Big Chute" at Burleigh Falls, Stoney Lake.

John Langton, an early settler on Sturgeon Lake, drove timber to Quebec over this route, the journey taking several months and costing about £2 15s. per piece of timber; but as the price obtainable at Quebec was £5 or more per piece, according to quality, the business was profitable in good years.[9] The largest mast ever shipped to Quebec is thought to have come from a township in the Lake Simcoe region, for Innisfill once sent one out of a length of 116 feet.

The life of the lumberjack was a hard one, but it attracted many young Canadians who wished a carefree and adventurous existence. Few who had experienced the excitable, if laborious life of the lumberman ever gave it up for the tamer pursuits of farming. Many an early settler hired out as a chopper for a farmer along "the front", or worked at a saw-mill in the summer or a lumber camp in

[8]York *U. E. Loyalist*, October 14, 1826.
[9]See John Langton: *Early Days in Upper Canada, Letters of John Langton*. 1926. pp. 201-9.

the winter in order to add to the meagre earnings produced by farming his own land. A contemporary writer observed that "the lumber trade is of the utmost value to the poorer inhabitants by furnishing their only means of support during the severity of a long winter, particularly after seasons of bad crops, and by enabling young men and new settlers more readily to establish themselves on the waste land".[10] Many settlers along the St. Lawrence neglected their farms to engage in lumbering, which was at times more profitable than agriculture; but in the "bad years", when the Quebec market was glutted, many a lumberman lost all he had ever made in the business.

Lumberjacks are the pioneers of civilisation, the first to open up wild lands and make them available for settlement. To "make timber" the lumberman had first to secure a "limit" from the government, though many dispensed with this formality and merely trespassed on Crown lands. After 1826 the government attempted a better system of regulation, but there was no definite forest policy until the middle of the century. Neither was the system of issuing licenses well-defined: any one could get a "timber berth" by sending to the Crown Timber Office an application accompanied by a surveyor's plan and a year's ground rent of $1 per square mile.

Timber limits varied in size from ten to one hundred square miles or more, and they provided considerable revenue, the rents or dues for lumbering rights on Crown lands amounting in 1861 to $327,503. The first men to enter the limit compose the exploring party of five or six experienced woodsmen, who look over and estimate the timber by climbing some of the tall trees; they also pick out the site for the camps and shanty, and lay out the course of the roads to the most convenient watercourse or "drivable" creek, where the "roll-way" is to be located.

The "head-swamper" and his gang then cleared a bush road from the interior to the roll-way. A line of small evergreens was the method of marking the track to the depot whence supplies for man and beast had to be drawn to the camp. During the winter the men worked in gangs, felling

[10]Quoted in Herbert Heaton: *History of Trade and Commerce*. 1928. p. 227.

the trees, clearing away the branches and cutting the trunks into lengths; cant-hooks were used to roll them into position, the logs were squared if square timber was desired, and they were transported by oxen or horses over the road to the roll-way.

As many as fifteen teams of oxen were used to haul sleigh-loads of huge logs, or one 100-foot mast, to the river bank. To get all the oxen to move at the same time, and to keep them in steady motion, was no easy matter, and the shouting of the half-breed drivers as the great loads were hauled through the woods increased the excitement of the work. On each log was imprinted the "bush-mark" of the company, important for purposes of identification when more than one group of men are driving logs on one river. Some lumbermen not only cut down timber but also cleared the land and cultivated farms to provide provender for stock, and food for the men; and many added to their profits by developing by-products such as potash, wood-oils and medicinal bark.

The lumber-shanty was a large structure with a huge stone fireplace in the centre, and bunks built in tiers on the walls. There was seldom a chimney, but a large opening in the roof let the smoke out and ensured good ventilation. A great fire was necessary to keep the shanty warm under such conditions. The long winter evenings were passed by many in gambling and card-playing, or in singing and dancing to the fiddle; others were employed in drying and mending their clothes or sharpening their axes, while, perhaps, a comrade entertained them with *chansons de bois* depicting the hardship and adventure of the wild and free life in the Indian Territories.

French, Indians, half-breeds and Scotch Highlanders were the predominant nationalities found in pioneer lumber camps. In general the men were, "like sailors, very loose in their habits, and careless of their own souls. . . . It is hard to make any provision to reach their moral and spiritual wants".[11] On rare occasions, however, the visit of a Roman Catholic priest provided an opportunity for many to confess, and mass was said in the woods amid surroundings

[11]W. Fraser: *The Emigrant's Guide, or Sketches of Canada.* 1867. p. 48.

hardly less primitive than those under which, over two centuries earlier, Father Le Caron had sung the first masses in Champlain's bark lodge, surrounded by Huron warriors.

Plenty of food, similar to that of the average settler, was prepared by the lumber camp's cook. Salt pork, pea soup, bread and potatoes were the foundation of all meals, which were served in basins and washed down with copious draughts of strong tea, in early times provided only at individual expense. Whisky was forbidden at lumber camps, a regulation of great advantage in the woods, but which led to excesses when the gangs returned to civilisation. In later years molasses, beans and turnips were added to the menu of the lumberman, and pies and cakes became characteristic of their diet, the severe nature of their work enabling them to eat large quantities of rich and greasy food.

The typical costume of the early lumberman,—gray cloth trousers, flannel shirt, blanket coat fastened round the waist with a red or tri-coloured sash, cow-hide boots with heavy spikes, and a *bonnet rouge* for the head,—formed a picturesque *ensemble,* long familiar on our main river systems in summer, and in the vicinity of most settlements in winter.

When spring arrived the timber was released from its position on the shore; this was usually effected by moving the "key-log", located in such a position that it held all the others in place. Then commenced the long journey to market. In a good current the logs needed little attention except in shallow rapids, where dangerous lumber jams often occurred. Many a man risked his life in breaking up these blockades with the handspike by skilfully extracting the key-piece of the jam; for more serious jams a block-and-tackle was used, or the logs were blown up with gunpowder. Such work necessitates quick thinking and as speedy execution.

To keep the timber in motion it was often imperative to jump from log to log, even amid rapids, and a lumberjack required great nerve and dexterity, and a constitution which was not affected by the necessity of walking for many hours at a time in cold water. Cribs and rafts were formed in the larger bodies of quiet water, over which they were moved by long oars or sweeps, frequently of red pine, seven or eight men working at each sweep. When the wind was favourable large numbers of sails were hoisted, and where the current was strong the great rafts moved along at a good rate.

Withes, or twisted saplings, were often employed to link up the cribs into rafts, but a more convenient method was by the use of planks into which auger holes had been bored; these were placed over upright posts. Ninety or one hundred cribs were frequently joined to form a raft of an area of 30,000 or 40,000 square feet and a value of $15,000 to $25,000.

On the St. Lawrence the transport of timber was based not on the crib but upon the dram; this was a huge raft of many layers and frequently drew six feet of water. It took fifteen men a month to build the average dram, in which withes of birch and hazel fastened the traverses above to the timbers below; no nails or spikes were ever used in timber rafts, and only in the later period did chains and cables become customary as small steam-tugs replaced sweep and sail. Wooden houses took the place of the bark lairs of the early lumbermen, and the men were not infrequently accompanied by their families.

It could hardly be expected that lumberjacks would be among the quietest citizens when they returned to civilisation, though Colonel Samuel Strickland of Peterborough County wrote that he found the bad accounts of the lumbermen greatly exaggerated. He states that, "although large bodies of them have been lumbering close around me for the last four or five years, I have received nothing but civility at their hands; nor has a single application for a summons or warrant against them been made to me in my magisterial capacity".[12]

In other districts the same could not generally be said, however. Richmond and Bytown (Ottawa) were noted for extreme lawlessness in the early days, caused chiefly by fights among lumbermen, Irish labourers and ex-soldier farmers; for Bytown was often the first stopping-place on the way to Quebec:

[12]Strickland, *op. cit.*, Vol. II, p. 285.

"A Bytown c'est une jolie place
Ou il s'ramass' ben d'la crasse;
Où ya des jolies filles
Et aussi des jolis garçons.
Dans les chantiers nous hivernerons."[13]

The lumbermen, as the more transient class of the population, were probably in large measure to blame for the
quarrels which were the usual result of their arrival in any
settled district. All along their route to Quebec they were
a disturbing element, and fights and brawls with the inhabitants on the shores were a common occurrence. When
they had disposed of their timber the lumberjacks often
remained in city or town during the summer, or until their
money had all been spent on "the fiddle, the female or the
fire-water."[14]   Then in the early winter they were off
to the woods to start the wild and adventurous round anew.

During the predominance of the squared timber trade,
which was at its height between 1840 and 1858, Wolfe's
Cove, near Quebec, was the great *entrepôt* of the lumber
industry. At Quebec were established the representatives
of British firms which had moved to British America from
the Baltic, where they had long engaged in the trade. The
Canadian connections of these firms were frequently maintained by the younger sons of families whose names were
a byword in the industry. Charles Poulett Thompson's interest in the Baltic timber trade was the chief reason for
the great objections emanating from Quebec and St. John
against his appointment as Governor-General in 1839.

The trade was early of a most speculative nature—often
a mere gamble in which money was tied up for two years
or more. At first firms obtained timber by contract, but in
later years there was a free market at Quebec. Dry rot and
fungus spoiled much timber, while the variability of freight
rates made it difficult to be sure of a fair price even for the
best. At Wolfe's Cove were located the "cullers", who
graded the timber according to quality, the refuse wood, or
culls, bringing an inferior price. MacTaggart, who wrote
in the late twenties, states that "there is a good deal of cor-

[13]Quoted in Grant, *op. cit.*, Vol. I, p. 179.
[14]Sir Richard Bonnycastle: *Canada and the Canadians*. 1846. Vol. I,
    p. 70.

ruption and bribery going on in this business, and many rafts of timber get a worse character than they deserve".[15] At that time nearly two-thirds of the timber brought to Quebec was white pine, "which generally brings five-pence, currency per cubic foot at Quebec, red pine eight-pence, and oak ten-pence".[16]

Timber-making was from the first an amateur work, and many settlers were ruined financially in the business. There was no concerted policy on the part of producers, and an excessive output, which commonly followed a prosperous year, glutted the market and caused heavy losses and hard times. In 1845, for example, 27,704,304 feet of squared timber was brought to market, but great over-production depressed the trade to a ruinous extent during the next three years.

The heavy work of loading the vessels was the last phase of the trade. As many as 300 boats might be seen shipping square timber at one time. The sailing-ships used to carry the wood to England had bow and stern port-holes for taking in the huge timbers, which were manipulated by tackle and windlass with man-power and horse-power. The intense activity is well described by F. W. Wallace:

"Engaged in this work were expert gangs of timber-stowers, mostly Irish, and rough, powerful men who could work like horses throughout the heat of a Canadian summer, and drink and fight with equal ability. These men were variously classed as timber-swingers, hookers-on, holders, porters, and winchers.

"When the rafts of timber were floated alongside the ship, members of the stowing gangs took their stations on the squared logs in the water and deftly extricated the individual timbers from the mass and pike-poled them into position for loading. On the ship's fo'c'sle-head, other men superintended the manipulation of the tackles for raising the timber up into the open port and swinging it inside the ship. In the hold, other members of the gang sweated with cant-hooks and hand-spikes, stowing the wet and heavy cargo.

"The tackles used to be operated by muscle-power in the

[15]MacTaggart, op. cit., Vol. I, p. 245.
[16]Ibid.

Picturesque Canada. 1879

A LUMBER SHANTY

Picturesque Canada. 1879

MASS IN A LUMBER SHANTY

Picturesque Canada. 1879

THE ROLL-WAY

John Ross Robertson Collection   From a drawing on stone by Josh. Harwood

THE TIMBER-DROGHER COLUMBUS, 1824
A ship constructed of square timber to avoid the British Timber Duty

early days, with men tramping around the ship's capstan or turning a crab-winch, but later the portable donkey-boiler and steam winch were used. The scene around the coves was one of tremendous animation. Ships, as far as the eye could see, were being loaded, towed in or out, or departing, sometimes under sail or with a tug-boat pulling them to a fair wind or open water."[17]

In 1824 an unique type of ship was built at Quebec. The Scotch designer of the *Columbus,* Charles Wood, conceived the idea that he could evade the British timber tax then in force on oak and squared pine if he built the ship of such timber and broke it up on arrival in England. The *Columbus* was specially constructed to make this possible without damage to the timber, and the boat, known as a "timber-drogher", was launched on July 28, 1824, in view of 5000 people, a band being hired to provide suitable accompaniment.

The *Columbus,* 294 feet long and flat-bottomed, was packed solid with timber, and, rigged as a four-masted barque, successfully made the trip to London, but there was eighteen feet of water in her hold on arrival. The owners then decided not to break her up, and sent her back to Canada for another load; but on this voyage she foundered. Another ship of the same type, the *Baron of Renfrew,* a somewhat larger boat of 5294 tons, was launched in 1825 and sailed to England, but grounded near Dover and eventually broke up on the French coast. It was reported that insurance amounting to the huge sum of $5,389,040 was paid to cover the loss of the two boats.[18]

The Canadian preference in the British timber market came to an end during the forties and fifties, when Britain gradually changed from Protection to Free Trade. The administration of Sir Robert Peel greatly reduced the preference in 1842, and by 1846 it had suffered a further reduction along with the duties on grain and West Indian sugar. The trade in square timber received its last impetus in the early fifties with the outbreak of the Crimean War; this was followed by a depression in 1857, after which business revived to a considerable extent. The last vestige of protection vanished in 1860, and a few years thereafter the

[17]Wallace, *op. cit.,* p. 99.   [18]See *ibid.,* appendix, pp. 14-17.

square timber trade declined, a movement accelerated by
the ever-increasing use of iron steamships in place of
wooden sailing-ships.

In 1862 about 25,000 persons were directly engaged in
lumbering in the Canadas, and there was no appreciable
diminution in later years, for coincident with the decline
of the squared timber trade there was fortunately a great
increase in the export of sawn lumber to the United States
and Great Britain. Much of the new trade was in deals—
planks at least three inches thick—and there was some
measure of protection accorded this trade at first. It developed more slowly than had that in square timber, because
machinery and skilled labour were necessary; but it did not
fall away to the same extent when the protection was
removed.

The trade in square timber gradually became less and
less, and almost disappeared during the early years of the
present century. In 1910 there appears to have been none of
it carried on, but there are occasional revivals from time
to time. Only two years ago (1930) the old Booth firm
of lumbermen were cutting square timber in Algonquin
Park for the British market; but such survivals serve only
to recall a famous trade whose greatness lies in the past.

The lack of saw-mills in early Loyalist days led to a
considerable importation of sawn lumber from the New
England states; but after the first few years of settlement
saw-mills began to be erected at about the same rate, and
often on the same sites as grist-mills. The first Canadian
mills were on the shores of the St. Lawrence in Quebec,
and, as settlement proceeded along the upper part of the
river and on the Bay of Quinté, saw-mills to provide lumber
for local purposes became common.

The earliest west of the Bay of Quinté, excepting the
Detroit settlements, were those in the Niagara district. A
report made by Surveyor-General D. W. Smith and Augustus Jones on November 7, 1792, mentions thirteen saw-mills
in the Nassau District, which extended from the mouth of
the Trent River to Long Point, Lake Erie. These were
built between 1785 and 1792 in the following locations,
the mills being given in the order of their erection: (1)
near Niagara; (2) on 12-Mile Creek; (3) on 40-Mile Creek;

(4) on 15-Mile Creek; (5) on 30-Mile Creek; (6) on Black
Creek, seven miles in the rear of Fort Erie; (7 and 8) on
4-Mile Creek; (9) on Small Creek, called the Muddy Run,
near the Whirlpool; (10) on a creek emptying into Burlington Bay; (11) on a branch of 12-Mile Creek; (12) one being
erected on 12-Mile Creek; (13) one being erected on 40-Mile
Creek.[19] These mills were the source of supply of sawn
lumber for all settlers in the district. It will be noticed
that they are all in the Niagara region, which contained at
that time almost all of the settlers in the central part of
Upper Canada.

In later years the saw-mill, like the grist-mill, usually
followed close upon settlement in any district, their number,
size and equipment increasing greatly after the War of
1812. Thomas Need, in the eighteen-thirties the owner of a
saw-mill around which grew the village of Bobcaygeon,
states that "the erection of a saw-mill is always the first
marked event in the formation of a settlement in the Bush.
. . . This induces many to come into the neighbourhood, from
the facility it offers for building. Then, as the settlement
increases, some bold man is persuaded to erect a grist- or
flour-mill, which again serves as an attraction; a growing
population requires the necessaries of life at hand; stores
are opened, a tavern licensed, and in a few years a thriving
village, or, as in the case of Peterborough, an important
town, springs up in the heart of the forest".[20]

Need's establishment, which may be taken as typical of
the smaller mills, sawed 2000 feet of planks a day from
about six logs costing 15s. After paying a sawyer 5s. and
a labourer 2s. per day he found that he had a profit of
£1 2s. 6d. a day, the lumber selling readily at 30s. per 1000
board feet. Concerning the activities of his mill he says
further: "Having little else to do at this season, I took
my turn at the mill regularly, until the yard was cleared
out and all the logs of the neighbours sawn up. The principal demand was for deals, though several oak, elm, and
cedar logs were cut up for furniture and other domestic
purposes."   Need states that a considerable amount of

[19]The report is quoted in John Lynch: *Directory of the County of
    Peel.* 1874. pp. 9-10.
[20]Thomas Need: *Six Years in the Bush.* 1838. pp. 106-7.

timber was brought to him by neighbours, especially in the
early years of the mill's existence; and that, "according
to the practice of the country they leave half their planks
in return for the use of the mill".[21]

Saw-mills operating on a large scale were to be found in
Upper Canada soon after the commencement of the nineteenth century. In 1816 the best in the province was
located in Hawkesbury Township, on the Ottawa River.
Some eighty men were employed at this establishment,
which was first owned by one Mears of Hawkesbury, and
later by an Irishman named Hamilton. From the first work
of providing a few neighbouring settlers with boards for
doors and sashes for windows, the saw-mills had developed
into manufactories of large quantities of all kinds of sawn
lumber, which could be purchased in the eighteen-twenties
for $5 per thousand board feet. At that time the wood
supply in the eastern United States was becoming exhausted, and sawn lumber exports from Canada were soon
of great importance.

As time passed the trade became increasingly extensive,
and in 1854 there were 1,618 saw-mills in Upper Canada,
with a production of nearly 400,000,000 board feet of lumber; of these mills 1,449 were water-wheels. In 1861 the
Canadian lumber exports were valued at $8,693,638. The
sawn lumber trade with the United States reached the
peak during the course of the Reciprocity Treaty, 1854 to
1866, which, with the American Civil War in the early
sixties, created a period of great prosperity for Canadian
lumbermen.

With the decline of the squared timber trade and the
rise of that in sawn lumber the process of lumbering under-
went some changes. The squaring of the logs, which often
wasted nearly one-quarter of the wood, and always left
the forests in a dangerous condition because of the debris,
was no longer necessary, and the timber was merely run
down to the nearest saw-mill; this was not infrequently,
however, a distance of 200 miles. In difficult and dangerous
rivers no driving was attempted, but the logs were merely
thrown in from the roll-way, and such as reached the mill
without being dashed to pieces were sawn up into lumber.

[21]*Ibid.*, p. 103.

On lakes and less turbulent rivers, or where locks had been built making possible the avoidance of the worst rapids, the lumbermen often carried a shanty along with them on a crib. The drives of logs, kept together by large boom-logs chained to one another, moved slowly along lake and river with the aid of the current, horse-power or steam tugs. At rapids the booms were released and the logs were guided by the pike-poles of the men among the rocks or through the chutes, to be collected again in the quiet water below.

The type of lumber varied with the locality. The Credit River district was early noted for oak, and staves were floated down to its mouth during the days of the squared timber trade, and afterwards to the mills along its banks. Many a log of fine walnut was sent down the Thames River from Dorchester and vicinity, and brought 75c. each at Detroit. A typical mill at the middle of the century was that at Nassau, near Peterborough, early the centre of a large lumber trade from the back lakes. This establishment, one of the best in the province for some years, was erected in 1854 by Charles Perry, and was situated three miles north of the town. It is described as having "two 'Yankee Gangs', a 'Slabber', 'Stock Gang', and an 'English Gate', containing in all 130 saws, besides circulars for butting, cutting laths, etc. It has also a very ingenious machine for grinding slabs. This mill has cut 90,000 feet in twelve hours".[22] In 1866 the mills of Peterborough County sawed 50,650,000 feet of lumber for export, most of it being shipped over the Midland Railway to Port Hope, and thence to the United States by schooner.

In the seventies the export of forest products from Canada amounted to over $20,000,000 annually. The Canadian lumber exports to Great Britain were first exceeded by those to the United States during the years of the Civil War; and thereafter the American trade gradually superseded the British, in spite of the fact that the United States Government placed a tariff on milled lumber, though admitting saw-logs free of duty. During the last twenty-five years the Canadian lumber exports have remained practically stationary, averaging about two billion board feet valued at over $60,000,000 *per annum;* of the total the

22*Peterborough Directory.* 1858. p. 65.

United States receives nearly 85 *per cent.* and Great Britain less than ten *per cent.* In recent years the possibility of developing an extensive export of lumber to the Orient *viâ* the Panama Canal has become prominent. Lumber is not, however, the all-important feature of our export trade that it was in the pioneer period: in 1830 nearly eighty *per cent.* of the total exports were of wood, while in 1904 only about sixteen *per cent.* could be placed in that category. Saw-mills, too, have decreased in number, as there are at present only about 1,000 in the province.

From early days the lumber industry in Ontario has moved through a series of zones from the St. Lawrence and its tributaries to the Ottawa and the lower lakes, and thence to Georgian Bay, and beyond to Lake Superior and the Hudson's Bay slope. Soon after 1860 the lumbermen ascending the tributaries of the Ottawa were meeting those working inward along the rivers flowing into Lake Huron.

Since the eighteen-sixties the outstanding development in lumbering has been the pulp and paper industry, which has become increasingly important with the passing of the years. Soft woods, such as hemlock, spruce, balsam, jack pine and poplar, of comparatively small value as sawn lumber, are now extensively used in the manufacture of paper, particularly newsprint. Another important change has made the timber supply of the future more secure, for the various provinces of the Dominion have all established policies of forest conservation and reforestation, the principles of which were almost unknown in pioneer days.

The industry has followed the capitalistic trend of the times in that larger and larger companies, many of them directed by forestry experts, control most of the trade. With the exception, however, of the use of small railways in place of ox-teams for transport, and the introduction of improved machinery in mills, the lumberman's life has not materially changed since the old days when the turbulent rivermen floated their mighty timber rafts down the Ottawa, singing

"Oh, when we get down to Quebec town, the girls they dance
    for joy.
Says one unto another one, 'Here comes a shanty-boy!'

G. H. Andrews

From the *Illustrated London News*, January 3, 1863

BREAKING A TIMBER JAM

LUMBER ARCH, UNION SQUARE, OTTAWA, 1860

150,000 board feet without a nail; erected to welcome H.R.H. the
Prince of Wales

From the *Illustrated London News*, October 20, 1860

THE PRINCE OF WALES DESCENDING A TIMBER SLIDE AT
OTTAWA, 1860

One will treat us to a bottle, and another to a dram,
While the toast goes round the table for the jolly shanty-
man.

I had not been in Quebec for weeks 'twas scarcely three,
When the landlord's lovely daughter fell in love with me.
She told me that she loved me and she took me by the hand,
And shyly told her mamma that she loved a shanty-man.

'O daughter, dearest daughter, you grieve my heart full
sore,
To fall in love with a shanty-man you never saw before.'
'Well, mother, I don't care for that, so do the best you can,
For I'm bound to go to Ottawa with my roving shanty-
man.' "[23]

[23]*Ye Maidens of Ontario.* The words and music may be found in
Franz Rickaby: *Ballads and Songs of the Shantyboy.* 1926.
pp. 79-81.

CHAPTER VI

Maple Sugar Making

"Whan that Aprille with his shoures sote
The droghte of Marche hath perced to the rote,
And bathed every veyne in swich licour
Of which vertu engendred is the flour;
Whan Zephirus eek with his swete breeth
Inspired hath in every holt and heeth
The tendre croppes, and the yonge sonne
Hath in the Ram his halfe cours y-ronne,
And smale fowels maken melodye
That slepen al the night with open yë, ..."

GEOFFREY CHAUCER: Prologue to *The Canterbury Tales.* (1386).

AMONG the domestic manufactures of pioneer days few processes were more interesting or more important than the making of maple sugar. A comparatively small amount of coarse cane sugar was imported into Canada at the time, but it was obtainable only in the larger settlements and at high prices. While some settlers procured maple sugar from the Indians in trade, yet the scarcity of money prevented the purchase of things which could be made at home; so almost every farmer who had a sugar-bush spent a few weeks in the spring at sugar-making .

The art of making maple sugar, and the birch canoe, are among the few contributions of the American Indian to our civilisation. When the Jesuit missionaries began their work among the Indians shortly after 1600 they found them making sugar each spring in their primitive manner. In the Jesuit *Relations* there is reference to "a certain liquor that runs from the trees toward the end of Winter, and which is known as 'Maple Water' ".[1] Father Paul LeJeune writes in 1634: "When they (the Indians) are pressed by famine they eat the shavings or bark of a certain tree, which they call *Micktan,* which they split in the Spring to get from it a juice, sweet as honey or as sugar. I have been told this by several, but they do not enjoy much of it, so scanty is the flow."[2] The only reference in the *Relations*

[1]R. G. Thwaites: *The Jesuit Relations and Allied Documents.* 1896-1901. Vol. LVI, p. 101.
[2]*Ibid.*, Vol. VI, p. 273.

to the process of manufacture is the following short account:

"There is no lack of sugar in these forests. In the Spring the maple trees contain a fluid somewhat resembling that which the canes of the islands contain. The women busy themselves in receiving it into vessels of bark when it trickles from these trees; they boil it, and obtain from it a fairly good sugar. The first which is obtained is always the best."[3]

The process of sugar-making among the early Indians was comparatively crude. They gashed the tree in a slanting direction with a tomahawk, and inserted a wooden chip or spout to carry the fluid drop by drop into birch bark receptacles resting on the ground. The Mohawk Indians commonly used a hollowed-out basswood log for a sap trough, the log being burned out as much as possible and then cleaned out with a stone adze.

Two methods of boiling the sap were in use. Earthenware pots were made by all but the Pacific coast Indians, and in these the sap was usually boiled; but when it was more convenient, red-hot stones were dropped into the sap trough, and, by removing these when cold and adding more hot stones, the sap was eventually boiled down, and the desired result achieved at the expense of a great deal of labour. Such primitive methods enabled the Indians to make only a comparatively small quantity of poor sugar, but it was highly prized as the only sugar available, and among some tribes it formed a considerable part of the food.

With the coming of the fur trader and settler, the Indians obtained iron kettles, and made sugar in a manner similar to, though somewhat cruder than that used by the early settlers. Thomas Need observed the Chippewas engaged in the work near Pigeon Lake in 1835, and wrote concerning the process:

"As soon as the sap begins to rise, which is early in April, the squaws betake themselves in families, or select parties, to the Maple Groves, or Sugar Bushes, as they are called; there they erect a camp, and prepare troughs and firewood, and collect all the kettles they can borrow or hire in the neighbourhood; this done, they begin to tap the trees

[3]*Ibid.*, Vol. LXVII, p. 95.

with a tomahawk, inserting a tube in each incision to receive the sap and conduct it into troughs underneath: each
family or firm has its own bush, consisting generally of
three or four hundred trees; these are visited in turn by two
or more of the younger ladies, whose office it is to collect the
sap and bring it to the fire.

"The most experienced among them is there placed to
regulate the heat, which ought to be tolerably equal, and
round her the rest of the party are busied in watching
the process of boiling, and arranging the contents of the
kettles; and finally, when by steady boiling the consistency
of sugar is obtained, in delivering it over to others whose
business it is to keep stirring the boiling mass as it gradually cools and settles. . . . There were several women and
girls busily employed, while their lords· and masters, as
usual, were idling about or carelessly looking on. It is,
however, but fair to state, that, as they do not assist in the
labour, so neither do they share in the profits, which are
sometimes considerable, and may always be looked upon
as pretty pin-money for the ladies of the bush. . . .

"After the season was over, the party brought me a
present of ten or twelve pounds of excellent sugar in return
for the loan of my kettles." The sugar was weighed, and
packed into neatly-sewn birch baskets by the Indians, and
was then ready for the market. Need states that a camp
produced between three and four hundred pounds in a
favourable season.[4] Mrs. Simcoe notes in her diary that she
purchased several baskets of maple sugar from the Indians,
paying $3 for thirty pounds.[5]

Henry Schoolcraft, a noted authority on the Indians, describes the manufacture of maple sugar as "a sort of
Indian carnival. The article is profusely eaten by all of
every age, and a quantity is put up for sale in a species of
boxes made from the white birch bark, which are called
mococks or *mokuks*. . . . The boxes designed for sale are of
all sizes; from twenty to seventy pounds weight. They are
sold to merchants at six cents per pound, payable in
merchandise. The number made in a single season by an
industrious and strong-handed family is known to be from

---

[4]Thomas Need: *Six Years in the Bush*. 1838. pp. 104-6.
[5]*Diary of Mrs. John Graves Simcoe*, April 3, 1796.

thirty to forty, in addition to all the sugar that has been consumed".[6]

An early settler in Bruce County stated that a considerable amount of the maple sugar made in Canada by the Indians was sent to Montreal refineries, and eventually emerged as ordinary commercial brown sugar. He remembered seeing the northern Indians bringing their sugar to market: "A picturesque scene occurred in the spring of the year when the Indians came down from Manitoulin to sell their maple sugar. The journey was made in mackinaws,—open boats with a schooner rig; and the sugar was carried in mococks,—containers made of birch bark, each holding from twenty to thirty pounds."[7]

Early fur traders and *voyageurs* sometimes manufactured their own sugar, and during the process usually ate nothing but the product. Alexander Henry, one of the first British traders to enter the north-west after the British conquest, writes that "each man consumed a pound a day, desired no other food, and was visibly nourished by it".[8]

The method of sugar-making used by our pioneer settlers was capable of but little variation, and it is only in the last fifty years that there have been any appreciable changes in the process. The commencement of sugar-making depends upon the season: in some years the trees are tapped as early as February, in others as late as April; but as a general rule the work commences about the twentieth of March. The following description of the process is based largely upon the experiences of Colonel Samuel Strickland, a writer whose accounts of pioneer life are among the most authoritative.[9]

Before commencing actual operations it was necessary

[6]Henry Schoolcraft: *The Indian Tribes.* 1851-6. Vol. II, pp. 55-6.

[7]Reminiscences of John McNab, quoted in W. L. Smith: *Pioneers of Old Ontario.* 1923. p. 264.

[8]Alexander Henry: *Travels and Adventures in Canada and the Indian Territories, 1760-1776.* 1807. p. 218.

[9]See Samuel Strickland: *Twenty-seven Years in Canada West.* 1853. Vol. II, pp. 298-311. A detailed account of the maple industry from selecting the trees to making taffy may be found in W. M. Brown: *The Queen's Bush.* 1932, Chapter XXII. This is of special interest in that it describes a number of local variations in process as they applied to the Lake Huron and Georgian Bay counties, which were settled in the latter half of the nineteenth century.

to clear the sugar-bush of all underbrush, rotten logs and fallen trees. The area was then usually fenced in so as to prevent cattle from entering, for sometimes when this was not done they would upset the troughs or drink so much sap that they died from the effects. As near as possible to the centre of the bush was located the boiling-place, and from it roads radiated in all directions. These enabled an ox-sled holding a barrel to be used in collecting the sap from the buckets or troughs at the trees. A large store trough, often a hollowed-out half-log, served to hold the sap at the boiling-centre. This trough had frequently a capacity of over one hundred pails.

A round, wooden spout, hollow in the centre, and variously known as a tap, spile or spigot, was inserted from a half inch to an inch into the tree, the hole being best made with an auger. A gash made by an axe was found to produce a better flow, but was hard on the tree, and the method was therefore not generally used except when the trees were soon to be cut down. The troughs, made of pine, black ash, cherry, or butternut, were capable of holding three or four gallons each, and were set exactly level immediately under the drip of the sap. In later days these troughs were replaced by every variety of pail available on the farm. The sap was found to run better on warm days after frosty nights, and experience taught also that the tap should be placed on the south side of the tree in the early part of the season, but on the north side if it needed renewing towards the close of the run.

Iron or copper kettles were used in boiling the sap, and care had to be taken to keep the fires burning day and night. When the sap had been boiled down to a thin molasses or syrup it was poured into a deep wooden vessel, where it was allowed to settle; then the liquor was poured into a copper boiler and clarified of earth and other impurities. Various clarifiers were used in pioneer days, among them milk and eggs. Six eggs beaten up with about a quart of syrup and poured into the sugar-boiler would clarify fifty pounds of sugar. After the mixture was well stirred the boiler was hung upon a crane over a slow fire, and when the liquid began to simmer, the beaten eggs and the impurities would rise to the surface. The moment the boiling-point was reached the crane was swung off the fire, and the surface carefully skimmed; if this was properly done the molasses was bright and clear. It had still to be boiled down to sugar, and great care was necessary to prevent its boiling over. Various tests were applied to find when the syrup was sufficiently boiled down, one of the more common being to drop a little of the syrup into the snow, and if it hardened it was ready to remove from the fire. The syrup was then poured into pans and moulds, often of fancy shapes, and the cakes of maple sugar worth from 4d. to 7d. a pound were the result.

The first run was found to be best for sugar, so the more acid sap obtained towards the close of the season was often made into vinegar. The process was to boil down three pails of sap to one, adding a little yeast while the liquid was still warm. The barrel was then set in a sunny place to ferment. Some of the settlers discovered that maple sap would also make good beer, especially if essence of spruce or ginger was added to it. The juice from the yellow birch was similarly used by some settlers to make vinegar and beer. Occasionally, too, the sap of the black walnut was made into sugar, for Mrs. Simcoe in describing the refreshments served at Adam Green's house, near the head of Lake Ontario, states that "the sugar was made from black walnut trees, which looks darker than that from the maple, but I think it is sweeter".[10]

Samuel Strickland estimated that in a good season from eight to twelve hundred pounds of sugar and syrup might be made from a sugar-bush containing five hundred trees.[11] Bouchette's estimate of five and a quarter pounds per tree[12] may have applied occasionally in Quebec, but appears to be too high for an average yield in Upper Canada. In the pioneer period comparatively little syrup was made, almost all of the sap being boiled down into sugar. Robert Gourlay, writing a few years after the close of the War of 1812, found the sugar maple common in every settled district. He states that the sap was particularly useful "to the inhabitants in the early stages of their settlement; and

[10]Simcoe, *op. cit.*, June 12, 1796.
[11]Strickland, *op. cit.*, Vol. II, p. 300.
[12]J. Bouchette: *The British Dominions in North America,* 1831. Vol. I, p. 372.

might be rendered of more extensive and permanent use by proper attention to the preservation of the trees, the manner of tapping them, and some practical improvements in the process of reducing the sap to sugar".[13]

It was estimated that the amount of maple sugar made annually in the thirties and forties reached an average of 100 pounds per family;[14] but many settlers are known to have made from 1,000 to 3,000 pounds in a good season. As an example of maple sugar production at the middle of the century may be taken that of Oxford County, which in 1850 produced 477,320 pounds. In 1851 the production in Upper Canada totalled 3,669,874 pounds, and ten years later it was nearly double that amount.

After the middle of the century, however, the average farmer did not make maple sugar to the same extent as he had done earlier, the increase in total production being explained rather by the advance in population, and by the gradual development of maple sugaries where the manufacture of sugar was the main business of the farm. A contemporary writer states that the farmer soon found, after his land was mostly cleared, that his time could be spent more profitably on the cleared land than in the sugarbush; and "the moment he thinks he can earn on his cleared land in ten days as much as will purchase a larger quantity of sugar than he can make in ten days in the bush, he abandons sugar-making".[15] The increasing cheapness of imported cane sugar had, of course, an important influence on the Canadian maple sugar industry in that it obviated the necessity of domestic manufacture.

Sugar-making is referred to by a pioneer who engaged in it as "one of the most laborious processes which the early settler had to undertake".[16] It was one, too, in which accidents frequently occurred, resulting in considerable loss. Another writer, who was an observer rather than a participant, considered that the work was not usually laborious, but that "the sugar season is rather deemed one of festivity than toil".[17] There is no doubt, however, that sugar-

[13]Robert Gourlay: *A Statistical Account of Upper Canada*, 1822. Vol. I, pp. 151-2.
[14]Strickland, *op. cit.*, Vol. II, p. 298.
[15]Thomas Shenston: *The Oxford Gazetteer*. 1852. p. 64.
[16]Strickland, *op. cit.*, Vol. II, p. 304.
[17]Bouchette, *op. cit.*, Vol.I, p. 371.

From Henry Schoolcraft's *The Indian Tribes*

AN INDIAN SUGAR CAMP

From Carlile and Martindale's *Recollections of Canada.* 1873

A MAPLE SUGARY

Public Archives of Canada   Lieutenant Philip Bainbrigge

A BUSH ROAD IN UPPER CANADA, 1842

PAPER MONEY ISSUED BY THE VILLAGE OF COBOURG, 1848

making was usually a merry time among the young people, for the approaching spring lent romance to the occasion.

"Soon the blue-birds and the bees
   O'er the stubble will be winging;
So 'tis time to tap the trees
   And to set the axe a-ringing;

Time to set the hut to rights,
   Where the girls and boys together
Tend the furnace fire o'nights
   In the rough and rainy weather;

Time to hew and shape the trough,
   And to punch the spile so hollow,
For the snow is thawing off
   And the sugar-thaw must follow.

Oh, the gladdest time of year
   Is the merry sugar-making,
When the swallows first appear
   And the sleepy buds are waking!"[18]

It is said that children seldom appeared in the sugar-bush during the early stages of the process, but came in large numbers, well-armed with spoons and ladles, when the sugar or syrup was being made. The boiling-centre was a favourite location for "sugar-eating bees" and other picnic parties, but the depredations of the younger set were usually regarded good-naturedly, for, after all, was not this season one of the compensations for the many hardships of pioneer life? Thomas Conant recommended the "sugaring-off" as one of the greatest of life's pleasures:

"Reader, if you have not already tried it, don't fail to make an effort to get to a sugaring-off, and my word for it you will never regret it. . . . The wax is so sweet, so pure and pleasant, and it's all so jolly, that such experiences are always red-letter days in one's life calendar."[19]

During the past half century there has been an advance

[18]Quoted in William Canniff: *History of the Settlement of Upper Canada.* 1869. p. 203.
[19]Thomas Conant: *Life in Canada.* 1903. p. 128.

in maple sugar manufacture similar to that in other branches of agriculture. It is now a highly-organized commercial industry in which co-operative methods and labour-saving devices have been introduced; while at the same time much of the waste resulting from pioneer methods has been eliminated, and markets have been expanded. In early days the syrup made was often dark in colour and strong in taste, while now the best producers are exceedingly careful to maintain a reputation for fine quality, for the 50,000 Canadian manufacturers of maple products are in the business not to supply their own needs, as in pioneer days, but to sell in a competitive market in which only the highest grade commands adequate remuneration.

Some 8,000,000 trees are tapped annually in Eastern Canada, and produce on the average about two and a half pounds of sugar per tree. It is estimated by the Department of the Interior that there are approximately 60,000,000 sugar maples in Eastern Canada, so that the industry has by no means reached its maximum development. While in pioneer days comparatively little syrup was made, two-thirds of the total production is now in that form. The maple sugar output varies in direct ratio with the market price of cane sugar, the greatest production of maple sugar being in 1921 when cane sugar was very scarce. The industry is confined to the four eastern provinces, with Quebec the banner province, producing nine-tenths of the sugar and three-fourths of the syrup. Ontario comes second in production, Nova Scotia third and New Brunswick fourth.

A report on maple sugar production during 1931 is contained in a recent issue of the official monthly Dominion Government bulletin on agricultural statistics.[20] According to this report the production of maple sugar in Canada during the spring of that year was 5,484,100 pounds valued at $930,000, while that of maple syrup is placed at 1,314,700 gallons with a value of $2,606,900. The value of sugar and syrup was the lowest for some time, the highest point reached in the last six years being in 1929 when the total value of the output was $6,118,656.

Of the total production of sugar in 1931 Quebec supplied 4,726,000 pounds, Ontario 636,000 pounds, Nova

[20]Dominion Government *Bulletin on Agricultural Statistics*, June, 1931, pp. 184-5.

Scotia 63,000 pounds, and New Brunswick 58,500 pounds. Quebec's primacy is not so marked in the maple syrup branch, for that province produced 737,000 gallons, Ontario 572,400 gallons, and Nova Scotia and New Brunswick approximately three and two thousand gallons, respectively. The best remaining opportunities for the extension of the industry are to be found within the extensive Crown forest reserves in Eastern Canada, and in addition to legislation, and encouragement by its agencies, the government issues permits for the operation of sugaries on Crown lands.

The chief export market for Canadian maple products is the United States. In the calendar year 1930, out of 116,705 gallons of syrup exported, 114,202 gallons went to the United States, while of exports of maple sugar totalling 5,997,436 pounds, all but about 40,000 pounds went to the same market; most of these exports are used in the curing and manufacture of tobacco.

Discoveries of great practical value have recently been made by L. Skazin of the National Research Laboratories at Ottawa, and it is expected that they will enable the greater use of maple products as food, and in ice cream and confectionery manufacture. It will now be possible to prevent cakes of maple sugar from deteriorating into a hard and mottled condition; and, by a process of intensification, syrup can be made fifteen to twenty times stronger in maple flavour than heretofore.

It is quite apparent that, while the pioneer made the product almost entirely for his own consumption, the industry now relies to a large extent on the United States' market. But there are still many farmers who manufacture maple sugar in much the same manner as their forefathers did, and for them the season retains much of the *joie de vivre* of the "merry sugar-making" of pioneer days, so well described by Mrs. Susanna Moodie:

> "When the snows of winter are melting fast,
>   And the sap begins to rise,
> And the biting breath of the frozen blast
>   Yields to the Spring's soft sighs,
>   Then away to the wood,
>   For the maple, good,

Shall unlock its honied store;
And boys and girls,
With their sunny curls,
Bring their vessels brimming o'er
With the luscious flood
Of the brave tree's blood,
Into cauldrons deep to pour.

The blaze from the sugar-bush gleams red;
Far down in the forest dark,
A ruddy glow on the tree is shed,
That lights up the rugged bark;
And with merry shout,
The busy rout
Watch the sap as it bubbles high;
And they talk of the cheer
Of the coming year,
And the jest and the song pass by;
And brave tales of old
Round the fire are told,
That kindle youth's beaming eye."[21]

[21]Susanna Moodie: *The Maple Tree: A Canadian Song.* See 1923 Edition of *Roughing It in the Bush*, pp. 504-6.

CHAPTER VII

FISHING

"No life, my honest Scholar, no life so happy and so pleasant, as the life of a well-governed Angler; for when the Lawyer is swallowed up with business, and the Statesman is preventing or contriving plots, then we sit on Cowslip-banks, hear the birds sing, and possess ourselves in as much quietness as these silent silver streams, which we now see glide so quietly by us. Indeed, my good Scholar, we may say of Angling, as Dr. Boteler said of Strawberries. 'Doubtless God could have made a better berry, but doubtless God never did'; and so, if I might be Judge, 'God never did make a more calm, quiet, innocent recreation than Angling.'"

IZAAK WALTON: *The Compleat Angler.* (1653.)

EVEN before John Cabot returned from America in 1497 with the news that the shoals of fish off the Grand Banks were so great that they "stayed his ship", Basque fishermen are thought to have visited the fishing-grounds off Newfoundland. The first explorers of the interior of Canada found the fish in the same profusion. When Champlain passed through Lake Simcoe in 1615 he observed that the Indians carried on fishing "by means of a large number of stakes which almost close the strait, only some little opening being left where they place nets in which the fish are caught".[1] Because of the hurdles or stakes used in the construction of these fish-traps in the shallow water, the lake was sometimes known to the French as Lac aux Claies. The fishing industry was of similar importance along the St. Lawrence River in the latter part of the French period, and for a time fish were used in some localities as a type of money, in which the value of other commodities was measured.

When Alexander Henry, the famous fur trader, visited Cadot (Sault Ste. Marie) in 1762 he saw the Indians catching whitefish in the rapids with a long-handled net. He states that a skilful fisheman could sometimes catch as many as five hundred in two hours, some of them weighing from ten to fifteen pounds.[2] Another type of net, made from

[1]Samuel de Champlain: *Voyages.* (The Prince Society, Vol. III, p. 124.)

[2]Alexander Henry: *Travels and Adventures in Canada and the Indian Territories, 1760-76.* 1807. p. 59.

the bark of trees, was frequently used in the Straits of Mackinaw. In the days before the coming of the white man, and to a lesser extent afterwards, the Indians are known to have shot fish with arrows; but the spearing or netting of fish in summer, and in winter through holes in the ice, became common in the latter part of the French period, and only natives who had no contact with the white trader continued to use the more primitive bow and arrow.

It was customary for the Indians to come to the St. Lawrence and the Great Lakes on fishing expeditions twice a year; their wigwams were raised on the banks, and their encampments, with both men and women busily engaged in fishing or in curing, were an interesting sight to early travellers. In 1789, when Anne Powell was journeying from Montreal to Detroit, she observed the Indians fishing on the St. Lawrence:

"I walked out to enjoy a very fine evening. The bank of the River was very high and woody, the Moon shone bright through the trees; some Indians were on the river taking Fish with Harpoons, a mode of fishing I had never seen before. They make large fires in their Canoes which attract the fish to the surface of the water, when they can see by the light of the fire to strike them. The number of fires moving on the water had a pretty and singular effect."[3]

Methods which Indian and early trader used on the Humber River are typical of fishing during the last half of the eighteenth century. A traveller noted in 1760 "the extraordinary method of catching fish; one person holds a lighted torch, while the second strikes the fish with a spear. September is the season in which the salmon spawn in these parts, contrary to what they do in any other place I ever knew them before."[4]

Salmon-spearing was an occupation of intense enjoyment to the Indian, and one in which he would exert himself in body and mind for many hours at a stretch. There were two types of spears used,—the javelin, and the three-pronged fork, with an ash handle often twelve feet long. Night fishing was carried on by the Indians in canoes, by the use of a torch of birch bark at the end of a long pole; some-

[3]See W. R. Riddell: *Old Province Tales, Upper Canada.* 1920. p. 73.
[4]Quoted in K. M. Lizars: *The Valley of the Humber.* 1913. p. 113.

Royal Ontario Museum   Paul Kane

SPEARING SALMON BY TORCHLIGHT

From *Picturesque Canada.* 1879   H. Hamilton

A TROUT POOL

FISHING SCENE AT WELLINGTON, LAKE ONTARIO, 1840

THE FISH MARKET, TORONTO, 1840

The site of the St. Lawrence Market. At the rear right is Weller's Stage Office, at the junction of Front, Wellington and Church Streets

times, however, they attracted the fish by lighting a fire on the bank of the river. Early traders and settlers improved upon the Indian method by using a jack-light in the bow of canoe or bateau. The socket in which the light was placed was a circular iron grate on pivots that kept the fire upright, and pieces of pitch-pine, about eight inches long and one and a half thick, would make a flare three feet high.

An adaptation of the Indian fire on the shore was a stage erected in the river and supplied with a torch-light; from this platform, or from a boat close by, men speared the fish as they went up stream. If shoals of fish appeared, two men sometimes killed enough during one night to fill eight or ten barrels holding 200 pounds each.

During the day fish could frequently be speared from a boat if the sun was bright. A more common method of fishing by day, however, was to fell a tree at the water's edge, and spear them from it; quiet and careful fishermen could catch forty or fifty in a few hours in this manner. A spearman had to learn to strike nearer than the fish appeared, or he almost invariably missed his object. Eels were sometimes speared, but were more often caught on night-lines.

In the eighteen-forties Paul Kane, the artist, saw the Indians of the Middle West engaged in the spearing of fish, and the sight recalled his boyhood days at York:

"We saw some Indians spearing salmon; by night this has a very picturesque appearance, the strong red glare of the blazing pine knots and roots in the iron frame, or light-jack, at the bow of the canoe, throwing the naked figures of the Indians into wild relief upon the dark water and sombre woods. . . . As the light is intense, and being above the head of the spearsman, it enables him to see the fish distinctly at a great depth, and at the same time it apparently either dazzles or attracts the fish. In my boyish days I have seen as many as 100 light-jacks gliding about the Bay of Toronto, and have joined in the sport."[5]

A method of fishing through the ice is described by Samuel Hearne, the noted explorer of the Canadian north-land:

"Angling for fish under the ice in winter requires no

[5] Paul Kane: *Wanderings of an Artist among the Indians of North America*. 1859. pp. 30-2 .

other process than cutting round holes in the ice from one to two feet in diameter, and letting down a baited hook, which is always kept in motion, not only to prevent the water from freezing so soon as it would do if suffered to remain quite still, but because it is found at the same time to be a great means of alluring the fish to the hole."[6]

Mrs. Simcoe fished in a similar manner for red trout through the ice of the Don and Humber Rivers: "At the mouth of the Don I fished from my carriole, but the fish are not to be caught, as they were last winter, several dozen in an hour. It is said that the noise occasioned by our driving constantly over this ice frightens away the fish, which seems probable, for they are still in abundance in the Humber, where we do not drive. Fifteen dozen were caught there a few days ago."[7]

Thomas Need noticed that the Chippawa Indians exercised great patience in the spearing of fish in Pigeon Lake a century ago:

"We observed some forty or fifty or them in picturesque gipsy-like tents, watching for fish. They will stand many hours together over a hole in the ice, darkened by blankets, with a fish-spear in one hand, and a wooden decoy fish, attached to a line, in the other, waiting for a maskelongy or pike, which they strike with almost unerring certainty the moment the bait is seized. In this way a skilful fisherman will sometimes catch 150 or 200 lbs. weight of fish in a day; though, of course, very frequently they are a long time unsuccessful."[8]

One calm night in April, Need took his birch canoe, "fetched a spear and torch, and sallied forth amongst the floating ice, with so much success that in two hours I had captured nearly a hundred weight of fish. . . . As I was slowly moving along, a huge fish made a stroke at the gaily-painted paddle: he took me so entirely by surprise that I lost my equilibrium, and nearly upset the boat; and instead of spearing him, which I might easily have done, I was only thankful when he discovered his error and released his hold".[9]

[6]Samuel Hearne: A Journey from Hudson's Bay to the Northern Ocean in the Years 1769-1772. 1795. Journal, March 9, 1770.
[7]Diary of Mrs. John Graves Simcoe, February 3, 1796.
[8]Thomas Need: Six Years in the Bush. 1838. pp. 44-5.
[9]Ibid., p. 104.

Until about a century ago sea salmon used to run up the
St. Lawrence River into Lake Ontario, where they were
caught in large quantities in the streams which flow into the
lake. Isaac Weld, who travelled in Canada in 1796, wrote:
"Lake Ontario, and all the rivers which fall into it, abound
with excellent salmon and many different kinds of sea fish
which come up the St. Lawrence."[10] For some unexplained
reason they stopped running up, and have never been seen
since. As their disappearance coincided rather closely with
the extensive use of steamboats, it has been suggested that
this was the cause of it; but there were other reasons of
more importance. The lack of salmon-leaps in streams
caused serious injuries to many fish, while thousands were
slaughtered or taken in gill nets at the foot of falls or mill-
dams which they could not surmount. Travellers noted
that huge numbers of fish were caught below Niagara Falls,
which blocked their further passage up the river. A very
early visitor, who estimated the height of Niagara at from
700 to 800 feet, stated that "the Beasts and Fish that are
thus killed by the prodigious Fall serve for food to fifty
Iroquese, who are settled about two Leagues off, and take
'em out of the water with their Canows".[11]

In addition to these hazards, and the reckless slaughter
of the salmon, the sawdust from mills was injurious to all
types of fish and helped to deplete the fisheries. As early
as 1806 an effort was made to conserve salmon, when an
Act was passed forbidding the netting of these fish in the
creeks of the Home and Newcastle Districts; in general,
however, effective measures were not taken until it was too
late to save the fisheries.

Reports from a variety of sources testify to the abundance of fish in Upper Canada during the pioneer period.[12]
The garrisons at the forts varied their food, and at the same
time amused themselves, by netting large numbers of whitefish and sturgeon, some of the latter caught at Niagara
being six feet long; while along the Detroit River the

[10]Isaac Weld: *Travels through the States of North America*. 1799.
p. 295.
[11]Louis Lahontan: *Nouveaux Voyages dans L'Amérique Septentrion-
ale*. 1703. Thwaites Edition, Vol. I, p. 137.
[12]See Vol. I, Chapter XV, of Robert Gourlay: *A Statistical Account
of Upper Canada*, 1822, for a full description of the fish found
in Upper Canada in the early pioneer period.

soldiers sometimes speared large sturgeon with their swords. The reminiscences of early inhabitants contain many allusions to the numbers and size of fish in the lakes and rivers of Upper Canada, and the ease with which they could be caught. Referring to the early years of the nineteenth century, one settler states that "a crotched pole would procure salmon in any of the creeks which flow into Lake Ontario";[13] another recalls that an old man speared seventy salmon in one afternoon.[14] Fishing was often left to the boys, because men were too busy in pioneer days to spare the time for such an occupation; and it is said that "the fish were so plentiful that the boys often waded in and threw them out with their bare hands. Few people had time for angling in those days so a pitchfork was used to catch all the fish you needed. By the use of a jack-light of fat pine it was no trouble for a few boys to throw out a wagon-load of fish in an evening".[15]

For many years pike were very plentiful in early spring in the creeks flowing into the Great Lakes; while whitefish and herring were caught in large numbers in the lakes in summer, and in November with seines in the creeks. Thomas Conant writes that schools of fish used to be so numerous along the shore near Oshawa that at times they prevented canoes from making any progress.[16] A century ago the harbour of Goderich "appeared to swarm with fish. When the sun shone brightly you could see hundreds lying near the surface. There was no difficulty in catching them, for the moment you threw in your bait you had a fish on your hook".[17]

The following description, which has reference to Wilmot's Creek, a stream flowing through Clarke Township into Lake Ontario, is quoted from a report prepared in 1869 by Messrs. Whitcher and Venning of the Federal Department of Fisheries, and may be taken as typical of the remarkable fishing to be found everywhere:

"In early times it was famous for salmon, great num-

[13]Reminiscences of Roger Bates, Coventry Papers. (Public Archives of Canada.)
[14]Reminiscences of Catharine Chrysler White, Coventry Papers.
[15]Letter of Dr. William Herriman to the *Cobourg World*, November 26, 1920.
[16]Thomas Conant: *Life in Canada*. 1903. p. 30.
[17]Samuel Strickland: *Twenty-seven Years in Canada West*. 1853. Vol. I, p. 270.

bers of which frequented it every autumn for the purpose of spawning. They were so plentiful forty years ago that men killed them with clubs and pitchforks, women seined them with flannel petticoats, and settlers bought and paid for farms and built houses from the sale of salmon. Later they were taken by nets and spears, over a thousand often being caught in the course of one night."[18]

Those who had no time to engage in the sport had no need to go without, for fish were traded to settlers by the Indians at a very low price. Mrs. Traill obtained a twenty-pound maskinonge from a Mississaga Indian for a loaf of bread; on the Humber River a salmon of ten to twenty pounds brought "one shilling, a gill of whisky, a cake of bread, or the like trifle";[19] while Samuel Strickland writes that "the Indians on Lake Huron traded fresh salmon trout for whisky and apples. One of our passengers purchased the largest I ever saw for a quart of whisky: it weighed no less than seventy-two pounds".[20]

Though stories are common of the great number of huge fish to be caught in pioneer days, the imagination of the people does not appear to have run to accounts of sea-serpents. Yet they were not without their fish stories. Among the notable tales related as truth was the statement that seals were to be found in both Lake Ontario and Rice Lake, (perhaps this is the origin of the present "Rice Lake Hudson seal" coats!) ; while the appearance of a Lake Superior mermaid, seen in 1782, was described and sworn to before the Court of King's Bench in Montreal. In Mrs. Simcoe's diary there is an interesting fish story which sh describes as follows, under date of February 18, 1796: "I heard an anecdote of black bass, which, if true, renders it probable they remain in a torpid state during the winter. An old hollow tree, which lay on the margin of the lake (Simcoe), half under water, being stopped and taken out, thirty black bass were taken out of it."[21]

In the "back" lakes and rivers trout were to be found in large quantities, as well as bass, maskinonge, whitefish, and

---

[18]The report is quoted in E. T. D. Chambers: *The Fisheries of Ontario.* (In *Canada and its Provinces*, Vol. XVIII, p. 604.)
[19]Lizars, *op. cit.*, p. 115.
[20]Strickland, *op. cit.*, Vol. II, pp. 132-3.
[21]Simcoe, *op. cit.*, February 18, 1796.

many other varieties, and they formed no small part of the
menu of settlers. As the intensive work of settlement in
the woods gradually decreased, men found time occasionally for sport, and great sport it must have been. John
Langton, who settled on Sturgeon Lake in 1833, writes:
"The bass is our staple commodity, and a most excellent one
it is; if you are on the lake, tie a line, baited with a piece of
red cloth, round your wrist, and proceed on your journey,
and it is ten to one that before you have proceeded a quarter
of a mile you will feel your prize." Langton states that
maskinonge and eel were generally speared; and he considered whitefish, salted in barrels, almost as good food as
herrings.[22]

Samuel Strickland, early settled near Peterborough,
refers to the excellent fishing in Stoney Lake, at the foot
of Burleigh Falls. In October, 1849, he camped there, and
"one morning between breakfast and dinner my two eldest
sons and myself caught with our trolling-lines thirty-five
salmon trout, eight maskinonge, and several large lake bass,
the total weight of which amounted to 473 pounds."[23]
Twenty years earlier Colonel Strickland had been an employee of the Canada Company, which was organized to
establish settlers in Upper Canada, particularly on the
"Huron Tract". While in that district he often engaged
in trout fishing on the Speed River, which he found "without exception the best for that species of fish I ever saw.
I have frequently caught a pailful of these delicious trout in
the space of two or three hours".[24]

It was not necessary in early times for Great Lakes
fishermen to go far from shore to lay their nets. The
Cobourg Star of June 28, 1831, describes "a very animat-
ing scene witnessed by us with much delight on Friday
last, on the beach immediately in front of our town". A
large net had been placed between the two piers then being
constructed to form a harbour. Shortly afterwards the net
was pulled in amid intense excitement, for most of the
inhabitants of the village had come down to see the result.
A haul of over twelve hundred fish was made, and the net

[22]John Langton: *Early Days in Upper Canada, Letters of John
    Langton.* 1926. pp. 34-5.
[23]Strickland, *op. cit.*, Vol. II, p. 238.
[24]*Ibid.*, Vol. I, p. 218.

set out again with almost equal success. "So", the *Star* says, "a sufficient supply being obtained, the whole were distributed with impartial and praiseworthy liberality among all present, every man, woman and child being loaded with large portions of this wholesome and nutritious food."[25]

Almost every settlement along the main lakes and rivers had its quota of fishermen. York's earliest fish market is described in an interesting manner by Dr. Scadding:

"In the interval between the points where now Princess Street and Caroline Street descend to the water's edge was a favourite landing-place for the small craft of the bay—a wide and clean gravelly beach, with a convenient ascent to the cliff above. Here, on fine mornings at the proper season, skiffs and canoes, log and birch bark, were to be seen putting in, weighed heavily down with fish, speared or otherwise taken during the preceding night in the lake, bay or neighbouring river. Occasionally a huge sturgeon would be landed, one struggle of which might suffice to upset a small boat. Here were to be purchased in quantities, salmon, pickerel, masquelonge, whitefish and herrings; with the smaller fry of perch, bass and sunfish. Here, too, would be displayed unsightly catfish, suckers, lampreys, and other eels; and sometimes lizards, young alligators for size. Specimens, also, of the curious steel-clad, inflexible, vicious-looking pipe-fish were not uncommon."[26]

The preserving of fish by salting them in barrels was early practised by the settlers in Upper Canada. A supply of food for future use was thereby obtained, and in addition there soon developed a trade, both local and with the United States, in barrelled fish. Salted salmon was worth from 30s. to 35s. a barrel of 200 pounds, while Lake Erie white-fish, caught in seines, sold at from 27s. to 32s. per barrel.

Fishing gradually assumed a position of prime importance. In the period just previous to the War of 1812 hauls of whitefish of one thousand or more were commonly taken at Niagara, and at almost any village on the shores of the Great Lakes. In later years, when fishing developed on a large scale, the hauls were much greater. A resident of Barrie recalled that he "once helped haul in a net near

[25]*Cobourg Star*, June 28, 1831.
[26]Henry Scadding: *Toronto of Old*, 1873. p. 31.

Willard's Beach, in Prince Edward County, that contained 14,000 fish".[27] In some parts of Lakes Erie and Ontario single hauls of 90,000 whitefish were not unusual. In the Detroit River fish used to be driven into pens where they were captured and dried by hundreds of thousands, to be used later as fertilizer; similarly, Lake Ontario whitefish were sold to farmers in the eighteen-sixties and used for manuring the land.

In addition to the eventual depletion of the fisheries, another result of the wasteful methods of netting fish was a demoralised market. People still living remember when fisherwomen carried large baskets through the streets and sold choice fish for five cents each. The slaughter continued, however, in spite of low prices, and it was not long before the waters were comparatively barren. Only in recent times has commercial fishing recovered through restocking from government hatcheries; and there are now several thousand men engaged in the industry in Ontario.

Commercial fishing first became important in the thirties and forties, and groups of hardy fishermen carried on the industry at almost every port, where their nets, drying in the sun, were long a characteristic sight. Towards the middle of the century the coastal fisheries had become depleted, and nets were of necessity laid at a considerable distance from shore. To row or sail small boats far out into the lake was dangerous, for sudden storms often arose. On April 1, 1875, a harrowing lake tragedy occurred off Cobourg. Four boats had gone out several miles from shore to inspect their nets, but an unexpected storm alarmed them and they attempted to return to the harbour. Two of the boats finally reached Cobourg with their crews in a state of complete exhaustion; but the other two never returned. Six men and three young boys lost their lives on this occasion, long remembered as one of the greatest tragedies among Great Lakes fishermen.

[27]Reminiscences of Henry Smith, in W. L. Smith: *Pioneers of Old Ontario*. 1923. p. 88.

CHAPTER VIII

PIONEER CO-OPERATION—"BEES"

"Many and sundry are the means which Philosophers and Physicians have prescribed to exhilarate a sorrowful heart, to divert those fixed and intent cares and meditations; but, in my judgment, none so present, none so powerful, none so apposite, as a cup of strong drink, mirth, musick and merry company".

ROBERT BURTON: *The Anatomy of Melancholy.* (1652.)

"After the specific duties of the bee were ended, the young men indulged in trials of strength, while their elders discussed the crops, prices, local politics and the prospects of the ensuing year. The elderly women extended the circulation of the personal gossip of the neighbourhood, while the younger ones, after disposing of the rude accompaniments of the feast, were ready for the dance, the round of country games and the repartee of flirtation."

ADAM SHORTT.[1]

ONE of the most notable characteristics of pioneer life in Canada was the spirit of co-operation. Remarkable generosity both in time and money is exemplified by the rebuilding of settlers' homes when destroyed by fire, the loss usually being entirely made up by the voluntary work and subscription of neighbours. One example out of many that might be quoted is noted in the *Cobourg Star* of January 25, 1831, where a fire is described which destroyed the cedar log home of one of the citizens. The account continues: "The loss of Mr. Hart, including upwards of $60 in cash, must at least amount to £150. We cannot express in too strong language the praiseworthy liberality that has been evinced by the inhabitants of our village upon this occasion. A subscription already amounting to upwards of £70 has been raised, and we have no doubt the entire loss of Mr. Hart will be made up to him."[2]

Such generosity is the more commendable when it is remembered that money was exceedingly scarce a century ago, and most people found it difficult to pay their taxes in cash, barter or long-term credit being usual in other business transactions. An example of praiseworthy co-operation is

[1]Adam Shortt: *The Life of a Settler in Western Canada before the War of 1812.* (Queen's University *Bulletins of History*, Vol. XII, p. 10.)
[2]*Cobourg Star*, January 25, 1831.

afforded by the action of the early settlers in a township where religious feeling ran high. The "Cavan Blazers", ardent Orangemen of the northern part of Durham County, had many a "run-in" with the Irish Roman Catholics of Peterborough County; but when the only Roman Catholic settler in Cavan took sick at harvest-time, the Blazers came secretly and prevented loss by harvesting his crop.

In many another way was pioneer life made bearable through co-operation. Roads were built by the subscription and labour of those who lived in the district through which they were to pass; settlers took turns in getting mail and supplies for their neighbours; but the most notable means of aiding one another was the "bee", or gathering of neighbours to help with farm work, a form of co-operation prevalent throughout the pioneer period and which still survives in barn-raisings and harvesting bees.

All bees provided entertainment and social intercourse as well as hard work. On that account they were usually called "frolics" in New Brunswick and the United States. Besides large quantities of food and drink, it was customary to provide a dance or "hoe-down" as the main amusement, while those who chose not to dance engaged in sports, games, and conversation. In pioneer days almost every activity was the occasion of a bee. Mrs. Moodie observed that "people in the woods have a craze for giving and going to bees, and run to them with as much eagerness as a peasant runs to a race-course or a fair; plenty of strong drink and excitement making the chief attraction of the bee".[3]

When new settlers arrived in a district it was quite usual for those already located to help construct the first shanties for the newcomers. The next work was the clearing of a piece of land, an almost endless task if one worked alone. A good workman might clear an acre of land in a week, but he could not burn it all. A half dozen men working together sometimes chopped and burned an acre in a day, but as a general rule a settler was fortunate if he could clear ten acres per year. There were various methods of clearing the land for cultivation: "slashing" was the

[3]Susanna Moodie: *Roughing It in the Bush.* 1852. Edition of 1923, p. 305.

felling of the trees with the intention of leaving them where they fell, and burning them later when they were dry; "windrow felling" was the same procedure except that the trees were so cut that they fell in rows; while "girdling" or "ringing" consisted of the clearing away of underbrush, and then cutting a ring in the bark of the larger trees and allowing them to stand until dead, a method which saved time but was not advantageous in producing good crops.

The devastation which resulted from this means of killing trees is well described by Mrs. Anna Jameson, who saw, on the main road between Hamilton and Brantford, "a space of about three miles, bordered entirely on each side by dead trees, which had been artificially blasted by fire, or by girdling. It was a ghastly forest of tall white spectres, strangely contrasting with the glowing luxurious foliage all around. . . . Without exactly believing the assertion of the old philosopher, that a tree feels the first stroke of the axe, I know I never witness nor hear that first stroke without a shudder; and as yet I cannot look on with indifference, far less share the Canadian's exultation, when these huge oaks, these umbrageous elms and stately pines, are lying prostrate, lopped of all their honours, and piled in heaps with the brushwood, to be fired,—or burned down to a charred and blackened fragment,—or standing leafless, sapless, seared, ghastly, having been 'girdled' and left to perish".[4]

Settlers of means frequently hired "American choppers", Irish immigrants, half-breeds, or other inhabitants anxious to earn extra money, to clear their land at a price varying from $10 to $20 an acre; but whatever means was chosen it was usual for chopping and burning to continue all the first summer, and thereafter during the winter. When oxen were not available the laborious "hand-log" method had to be used to remove the timber. In some low-lying districts, such as Lambton County and the front of Glengarry, logging was complicated by the superabundance of water. When the land was but little above the level of lake or river the soil was often of such gluey nature that oxen and logs sank in sloughs of mud.

[4] Anna Jameson: *Winter Studies and Summer Rambles in Canada.* 1838. Vol. II, pp. 102-3.

In general, however, logging was not beset with such difficulties. At the middle of the nineteenth century much of Huron County was in process of settlement, and one settler in McGillivray Township describes how he chopped eight acres the first winter, "and next spring my wife and I logged most of it by hand. I cut the logs in short lengths so that they would be easier to handle, and cut the trees off close to the ground so that the stumps would not be in the way of cultivation. It was certainly no light winter's work to cut up the trees, many two and three feet through, growing on eight acres".[5] John McDonald, who settled in 1855 in Kincardine Township, Bruce County, did what thousands of pioneers had done from Loyalist times down through the years: "For four successive years I spent the winters in chopping, the springs in burning and seeding, and the summers in working for other farmers at 'the front' ".[6]

It was so difficult to do this work alone that the logging bee was early the most typical example of pioneer co-operation. All the settlers living within a radius of fifteen or twenty miles were invited to the bee, and always brought oxen and implements with them. Sometimes a "butler" or "boss" was placed in charge to give the necessary directions, and after underbrushing the piece of land the workers proceeded with logging.

The trees were usually chopped down in such a manner that they would fall in heaps as far as possible. Several large piles were formed on each acre of land and all the logs were dragged thither by oxen, while men with handspikes built up the heaps until they were about eight feet high. When the region had been entirely cleared, the piles were fired with the help of underbrush and branches.

There was no thought of saving any of the timber: it had to be got rid of as quickly as possible. As the wood was green it often required several burnings to dispose of the piles of logs. The collecting and burning of the half-burnt wood was sometimes called "the branding". Charred logs and rotten wood were gathered by three or four men and a yoke of oxen dragging a single chain between them; a

[5] Reminiscenses of Linwood Craven, quoted in W. L. Smith: *Pioneers of Old Ontario*. 1923. p. 239.
[6] Reminiscences of John McDonald, quoted in Smith, *op. cit.*, p. 256.

James Weston

A Logging Bee in Muskoka

From F. G. Weir's *Scugog and its Environs*

OLD SQUARE LOG SCHOOLHOUSE ON SCUGOG ISLAND

Robert Harris, C.M.G., R.C.A.
Reproduced by Permission of the National Gallery of Canada

A MEETING OF SCHOOL TRUSTEES

"yoke and bow" was used when the larger logs were dragged away, while men picked up the smaller pieces. Walter Riddell, an early settler near Cobourg, describes a day in the branding-field as one long to be remembered: "With a blazing sun overhead and ashes heated like unto a fiery furnace underneath, the men looked like a lot of chimney-sweeps after a day at branding."[7] Women still living recall the noisy shouting at the oxen as the men laboured all day at this work, and the preparation of meals "for thirty blackened men" at the close of the bee.[8] In new settlements during July the whole countryside was illuminated by the burning of log heaps. To see a hundred of these fires blazing at once on a dark night was a spectacle not soon forgotten.

To save the work of chopping the trees into lengths which could be readily handled, small fires, in some districts called "niggers", were occasionally used. These were placed on top of the logs at intervals of twenty or thirty feet, and kept burning until the logs were burned through. A settler in Zorra Township, Oxford County, sent back word to his friends in Scotland that he had one hundred niggers working for him; whereupon "the whole parish was agog with excitement over the Zorra man's wonderful wealth in controlling the services of no less than one hundred negroes".[9]

In later years when the farmer had more leisure the best ashes were usually collected, and either made into potash or sold to a potashery in the nearest village. There was a ready market for pot and pearl ashes in the early days, the product being usually shipped to Montreal in large barrels. The ashes from ten acres of forest would make about five barrels (2500 pounds) of potash, for which a price of from 9s. to 25s. or more per cwt. was obtained, the price depending upon the condition of the market and the grade of the product. Samuel Strickland considered that a settler should receive at least 25s. per cwt. to recompense him for his work.[10]

The ashes were usually stored and kept dry in small log

[7]Reminiscences of Walter Riddell, Hamilton Township, in the *Farmer's Sun*, August 4, 1898.
[8]Reminiscences of Mrs. (Dr.) Richard Jones, Cobourg. (Unpublished.)
[9]W. A. Mackay: *Pioneer Life in Zorra*. 1899. pp. 167-8.
[10]Samuel Strickland: *Twenty-seven Years in Canada West*. 1853. Vol. I, p. 169 fn.

houses built for the purpose, and those settlers who wished to avoid the difficult process of potash-making, sold the ashes for about 4d. a bushel, or took a little whisky or other goods in exchange. One writer advised intending immigrants that "when potash brings a good price, and the land to be cleared has those sorts of timber growing on it the most proper for the purpose, the ashes will often pay for clearing the land. If not preserved at all, land can be hired to be chopped, logged, burned, and fenced at from 45s. to 52s. per acre".[11] Advances in chemistry had seriously affected the ash trade by the late thirties, and eventually put an end to it altogether; but many farmers long continued to make lye from ashes, and, by the addition of grease, to manufacture their own soft soap.

Lime-burning was a process often connected with the logging bee. Large quantities of lime were necessary for filling cracks in the walls, and building chimneys for the log house. It could be purchased at from 6d. to 1s. 3d. per bushel, but many settlers burned their own. The timber from at least half an acre of land was formed into an immense pile, on the top of which was constructed a frame in which to place the limestone. Some twenty ox-cart loads of the stone were then drawn and thrown on top of the heap, after being broken into small pieces by a sledge hammer. The pile was then fired and would be consumed over night, though the red coals remained hot for a week, when the white lime could be collected and covered. Colonel Strickland held such a lime-burning in 1826 at his farm in Douro Township, Peterborough County, and wrote that about one hundred bushels of lime were obtained, sufficient for all purposes for a house thirty-six feet by twenty-four feet.[12]

Enterprising settlers sometimes obtained charcoal from their timber, though charcoal-burning was never practised in Canada on so extensive a scale as was long characteristic of England. John Thomson, who was located near Lake Simcoe, noted in his diary on several occasions that his men were engaged in the work; in October, 1834, for example, he writes that "five hands commenced cutting basswood

[11]Joseph Pickering: *Inquiries of an Emigrant*. 1831. 4th Edition, 1832, p. 107 fn.
[12]Strickland, *op. cit.*, Vol. I, pp. 97-8.

logs and splitting them to make a charcoal heap."[13]   A
settler's first logging, however, almost always resulted in
the burning of all the timber. In later years it was customary to save some of the best pieces for building purposes, and to split logs for rail fences, but it long remained
usual to burn up the greater part of the wood cleared from
the land, and often none whatever was saved.

The free use of liquor at logging bees was characteristic.
In some districts it was customary to provide whisky for
the men in the proportion of one gallon to each yoke of
oxen; while in others a copious supply, without limit, was
available. What was not consumed during the bee lasted
through the night. Sometimes the workers at a logging
were divided into gangs, and each had a certain proportion
of the fallow to clear. Whisky played no small part in keeping up the excitement of the contest, and in urging all to
work at the highest pitch, but it also led to occasional cheat-
ing and considerable fighting. J. W. Dunbar Moodie's short
parody well describes the usual events at a logging:

> "There was a man in our town,
>   In our town, in our town—
> There was a man in our town,
>   He made a logging bee;
>   And he bought lots of whisky,
>   To make the loggers frisky—
>   To make the loggers frisky,
>   At his logging bee.
>
> The Devil sat on a log heap,
>   A log heap, a log heap—
> A red-hot burning log heap—
>   A-grinning at the bee;
>   And there was lots of swearing,
>   Of boasting and of daring,
>   Of fighting and of tearing,
>   At that logging bee."[14]

It is no wonder that the better-class settlers, and especially women bred in homes of refinement, evinced a pronounced aversion to bees of all kinds, and particularly to

[13]Diary of John Thomson, October 14, 1834. (Archives of Ontario.)
[14]Quoted in Moodie, *op. cit.*, p. 304.

those at which excesses were the rule. Mrs. Moodie presents the case very strongly, and shows that the amount of work accomplished at a bee was often less than expected:

"A logging bee followed the burning of the fallow as a matter of course. In the bush, where hands are few and labour commands an enormous rate of wages, these gatherings are considered indispensable, and much has been written in their praise; but to me they present the most disgusting picture of a bush life. They are noisy, riotous, drunken meetings, often terminating in violent quarrels, sometimes even in bloodshed. Accidents of the most serious nature often occur, and very little work is done when we consider the number of hands employed, and the great consumption of food and liquor. I am certain, in our case, had we hired with the money expended in providing for the bee, two or three industrious, hard-working men, we should have got through twice as much work, and have had it done well, and have been the gainers in the end. . . . We had to endure a second and a third repetition of this odious scene before sixteen acres of land were rendered fit for the reception of our fall crop of wheat."

The logging bee from which Mrs. Moodie drew her conclusions was held on a hot July day in 1834, and consisted of thirty-two men. Mistress and maid were busy for two days previous preparing vast quantities of food. The men, a typical aggregation, included half-pay officers and various types and nationalities of settlers of lower rank: "the four gay, reckless, idle sons of ——, famous at any spree, but incapable of the least mental or physical exertion; . . . the two R—s, who came to work and to make others work; my good brother-in-law, who had volunteered to be the Grog Boss; . . . the Youngs, the hunters, with their round, black, curly heads and rich Irish brogue; . . . the ruffian squatter P—, from Clear Lake,—the dread of all honest men; the brutal M—, who treated oxen as if they had been logs, by beating them with handspikes; and there was 'Old Wittals' . . ., the largest eater I ever chanced to know; . . . . there was John—, from Smith-town the most notorious swearer in the district; . . . there was a whole group of Dummer Pines . . . , all good men and true."

At dinner time all sat down to "the best fare that could

be procured in the bush: pea soup, legs of pork, venison, eel, and raspberry pies, garnished with plenty of potatoes, and whisky to wash them down, besides a large iron kettle of tea. . . . My brother and his friends, who were all temper-ance men, and consequently the best workers in the field, kept me and the maid actively employed in replenishing their cups". While some of the men "were pretty far gone" by that time, there was nothing particularly objectionable until supper, when "those who remained sober ate the meal in peace, and quietly returned to their homes, while the vicious and the drunken stayed to brawl and fight. . . . Unfortunately we could hear all the wickedness and pro-fanity going on in the next room. . . . The house rang with the sound of unhallowed revelry, profane songs, and blas-phemous swearing. It would have been no hard task to have imagined these miserable, degraded beings, fiends in-stead of men. How glad I was when they at last broke up and we were once more left in peace to collect the broken glasses and cups, and the scattered fragments of that hate-ful feast".[15]

Similar conclusions as to the inefficacy of bees were reached by the Rev. William Proudfoot, who lived in the London District. Some ninety men, though not all at one time, were busy for three days in raising his log house. Owing to his profession, and to the fact that most of his helpers were members of his own congregation, the Rev. Proudfoot was not required to follow the almost invariable custom of providing food and drink; these requisites were supplied by the workers themselves, and the clergyman considered that he was most fortunate in that respect, for he wrote in his diary: "Had I to give them their victuals and drink the raising would have cost an outlay more than a frame house. Many of the people came for the sole purpose of drinking, and never once assisted in lifting a log."[16].

One of the heaviest and most difficult pieces of work was "stumping", or removing the stumps from land which had

[15]Moodie, *op. cit.*, pp. 305-314. The "Pines" were the Paynes, whose descendants are still prominent inhabitants of Peterborough County. The identity of most of the other participants in this bee is best, for obvious reasons, left undisclosed.

[16]*Diary of William Proudfoot,* June 12, 1833.

been logged. The first crops were usually sown among the stumps, which occupied about one-eighth of the field. Apart from the waste of that much of the land, their presence was not a very great disadvantage in a day of primitive agricultural methods. Stumps of many softwood trees rotted away in a year or two, but those of hardwood lasted eight or ten years, and resinous stumps, like the pine, much longer. In early York stumps were prominent in the streets, from which they were removed by the operation of the Stump Act. Any person found intoxicated might be sentenced to the task of eradicating a certain number of stumps, and, after his "community service", the culprit was usually very sober and very tired, and did not repeat his offence. This law was so beneficial to York that other localities imitated it, as may be seen from an item in the Niagara *Canada Constellation* under the heading "Stump Loyalty".

"The Stump Law, although framed for the particular benefit of York, meets with such universal approbation that it is expected considerable exertion will be made to extend it through the province. Its beneficial influence has been proven at Chippawa, even during the late extremely frosty days, where it has been enforced on several without mercy, and in every instance on those whose law knowledge was too circumscribed, or who found it in vain to plead the jurisdiction or limitations of the act, and, submitting to the hard sentence, dug through the frozen earth singing

'Come all you joyful topers
Come follow, follow me' ".[17]

A more general method of accomplishing this necessary work was a stumping bee. Various methods were used in the work: some of the stumps were chopped out, others were dragged out by oxen after chains had been fastened around the chief roots; many, especially pine stumps too solid to move, were burned out, or removed by blasting. In some districts a stumping-machine, composed of a screw fastened to a framework, was used; this operation consisted in elevating the machine and the root by using oxen or horses to provide power. The stump fences which are still

[17]Niagara *Canada Constellation*, January 4, 1800.

a characteristic feature of the rural landscape recall many an old-time stumping bee.

Philemon Wright, the founder of Hull, describes stumping activities at his settlement fifteen years after its commencement:

"In 1815 I employed some men in taking out the small stumps and roots, and levelling of the roughest places, as the roots began to decay according to the size of the stumps. Beech and rock maple stumps are much more easily taken out after the seventh year; pine, elm, basswood, and hemlock are less liable to rot, and therefore require about fifteen years before they can be taken out, especially those of the largest size. Every season I set apart a certain number of days, and take from two to six pair of oxen, harnessed with strong chains, which are fastened round the stumps and drawn up, collected together into piles, and burnt upon the ground."[18]

The raising bee is one which has survived to the present. There was but little variation in types of buildings in the pioneer period: house, church, store, barn and mill were usually much alike except in size, and a raising bee was the ordinary means of their erection. The first grist-mills in Upper Canada, near Kingston, Niagara and Napanee, were the result of bees, and a considerable part of their cost appears, from the accounts, to have been expended in rum for the entertainment of the Loyalist soldier-settlers who raised the structures.

In 1834 the saw-mill of Thomas Need, founder of Bobcaygeon, Victoria County, was similarly raised by the united efforts of the inhabitants of the district. Need wrote in his journal on July 3rd:

"They assembled in great force and all worked together in great harmony and good will, notwithstanding their different stations in life. When the last rafter was fixed, a bottle of whisky was broken on the top, and, sundry others having been distributed among the humbler members of the hive, the party separated, well satisfied with their day's work. The completion of the saw-mill was an event of vast interest to all the inhabitants of the settlement, who looked

---

[18]Philemon Wright: *An Account of the First Settlement of the Township of Hull*. 1823. (In Andrew Picken: *The Canadas*. 1832. Appendix, pp. XXXII and XXXIII.)

to exchange their rude shanties in a little time for neat frame houses."[19]

"An emigrant farmer of twenty years' experience" describes a raising bee as "a general rising throughout the settlement . . . One small party was in the woods cutting down the timber, followed by a couple of hands to line it out; then came the scorers and hewers, and at their heels again the teamsters, with oxen and horses to haul it to the place, where five men put it up as fast as it was brought to them, and after a day spent apparently more in fun and frolic than in hard labour, the out-shell of a capital log house, with the exception of a roof, was put up."

On the following day some of the neighbours returned to complete the house, (the work was being done in this instance for a shoemaker whose home had been destroyed by fire) ; the rafters were put up, the house boarded, spaces for doors and windows cut out, and everything completed. Some of the neighbours "furnished boards, others shingles, a carpenter the door and sashes, and the storekeeper the glass, putty, nails, etc., all of which the man paid for in work at his trade in the course of the following six months."[20]

One hundred men often gathered to raise the framework of a large barn, teams of oxen being used to haul the largest logs. The process varied with the type of building, but the framework was usually constructed on the ground and then raised into position by the men, who used long pike-poles for the purpose. Sometimes a race was held by the two teams of men at work on the opposite sides of a barn, a competition which enlivened the proceedings but resulted in their taking dangerous risks which occasionally ended in fatal accidents. Mrs. Moodie refers to the raisings in the Peterborough district as "generally conducted in a more orderly manner than those for logging. Fewer hands are required, and they are generally under the control of the carpenter who puts up the frame, and if they get drunk during the raising they are liable to meet with very serious accidents."[21]

Another early settler in the same county, in describing

[19]Thomas Need: *Six Years in the Bush*. 1838. p. 96.
[20][J. Abbott]: *The Emigrant to North America*. 1844. pp. 44-5.
[21]Moodie, *op. cit.*, p. 305.

the raising of her new home in 1841, writes of the huge
preparations which had to be made, for he who "called the
bee" was expected to provide a "spree", as well as to return
the work day for day when similarly called. The young
ladies came to help with the baking of the huge quantities
of pies and cakes which were served for dinner, in addition
to "a roast pig and a boiled leg of mutton, a dish of fish, a
large cold mutton pie, cold ham and cold roast mutton,
mashed potatoes and beans and carrots, a large rice pudding, a large bread-and-butter pudding and currant and
gooseberry tarts". This meal was eaten at noon, and
afterwards the raising continued.

Later on it began to pour rain, so the men went into the
old house and drank punch and smoked cigars, while "the
young people chatted or flirted as they fancied". A substantial tea was served soon after, whereupon dancing
commenced to the fiddling of one of the men, and this continued until eleven. A supper almost as substantial as the
dinner was then brought forth, after which dancing was
resumed and continued until one. As no one could venture
out because of the rain, the whole eighteen were somehow
accommodated for the night. "And I hear", says Mrs.
Stewart, "that they laughed almost all night instead of
sleeping". In the morning all were busy before breakfast,
and by noon the structure was raised, and the hostess considered that they should be glad that nothing but the rain
had interrupted the work, "for often dreadful accidents happen at these raising bees".[22]

The food served at bees was not always of such quality
and in such abundance. During the "hungry year" of
Loyalist days many a gathering received but scant refreshment; at one raising during that period of famine the only
food served was a mixture of eggs beaten up with milk
and rum. In later years, too, workers were not always
luxuriously treated, the exigencies of the times often per-
mitting to be served only such coarse foods as bran cakes,
boiled Indian corn, salt pork, pea soup, and the usual whisky.
In fact such was the generosity and good nature of one's
neighbours, (so we are told in one Emigrants' Guide), that,

[22]Frances Stewart: *Our Forest Home*. 1889. 2nd Edition, 1902, pp.
174-6.

if they knew that a settler's circumstances made it impossible for him to provide meals for the crowd, "some whisky and the evening frolic are sufficient inducements for the attendance of your neighbours".[23]

One of the most interesting accounts of a raising bee is that given by John Thomson, a retired naval officer who located in 1832 in Medonte Township, Simcoe County. Owing to unfavourable weather this raising lasted three days, the third of which was largely spent in an inquest over an Indian who was killed in what is termed "a half-playful wrestling scuffle". There is so much of interest in Thomson's account that it is worth giving in full just as he recorded the events in his diary.

"*Saturday, April 19, 1834*:—Sent off two hands to raise the country to come on Tuesday to get up the frame of the barn . . . .

"*Monday, 21st*:—Very rainy. Poor prospects for tomorrow's work; two hands at the village bringing over a supply of whisky, etc., the other two making the pike poles for raising the frame, cleaning and preparing the shanty for the accommodation of the people coming from a distance. . . .

"*Tuesday, 22nd*:—A bad rainy morning; however, as people came forward we commenced towards 9 o'clock to put the bents of the building together. . . . It was with difficulty we got them persuaded to stay and persevere tomorrow; however, I sent for a fiddler and cajoled and flattered them as well as I could, with the assistance of Mr. Kinsopp, Majors Darlings and Rowes, these being gentlemen and messed in the dining room, while the others, landed proprietors but no gentlemen, lived in the kitchen; (this) caused some envious feeling among certain Yankiefied personages of the latter class, and consequently we mixed among them and did all we could to do away with any bad impression, and pleased them wonderfully well.

"*Wednesday, 23rd*:—Began to put up the frame with thirty men or thereabouts; found the bents so heavy that at first we feared a failure, but, after everyone got themselves fairly put to their mettle, it went up and so did all the others before night. . . . In the afternoon several men

[23]William Hickey: *Hints on Emigration to Upper Canada*. 1834. p. 46.

who had come from Oro, perhaps ten or twelve miles off,
went away, and made our party still weaker. We also
got the wall plates up to the beams ready for putting into
their places in the morning. While the men were at supper
this evening a half-playful wrestling scuffle occurred. . . .
Joseph St. German was thrown down in the kitchen, and,
melancholy to tell, he received some mortal injury, and in
the course of seven or eight minutes expired, to the horror
and regret of everyone. . . .

"*Thursday, 24th*:—Sent a warrant to the constable to
call a jury by daylight; they assembled about half-past 11
o'clock and proceeded to investigate the unhappy occurrence
of last night, and found a verdict of manslaughter against
Ronald McDonald. . . Very cold day: the people could hardly
stand upon the top of the barn to get the plates on; indeed,
had it not been for the detention as witnesses on the inquest,
I believe they would all have decamped by daylight; no
great wonder if they had, as I am sure they must all be
sick enough of the job. The inquest was over by half-past
three, and all hands got away by five o'clock. They have
used a barrel of pork and one of flour with fifteen gallons
of whisky, besides tea and sugar, etc. One of the hands
made a coffin for St. German, and he was removed immediately after the inquest by his friends".[24].

This is by no means the only death resulting from
fights at bees. Magistrates who did not relish being
continually engaged in settling disputes avoided trouble
by making themselves hard to find. "When I became a
magistrate", said Squire George Munro, "I used to go away
to the woods when I heard there was a fight at a bee, and
keep away till the blood cooled down, and that generally
ended the matter".[25]

Colonel Strickland, a magistrate for many years, considered that bees in general were "a continual round of dissipation—if not of something worse. I have known several
cases of manslaughter arising out of quarrels produced by
intoxication at these every-day gatherings".[26]

There were often local variations in the conduct of
raising bees. In some communities it was customary to

[24]Diary of John Thomson, April 19-24, 1834. (Archives of Ontario.)
[25]Quoted in C. O. Ermatinger: *The Talbot Regime*. 1904. p. 102.
[26]Strickland, *op. cit.*, Vol. I, p. 37.

"christen" buildings with whisky, like ships at launching. Benjamin Waldbrook, who lived near Oakville, remembered barn-raisings where this ceremony was performed.

"Once, at a raising near Ancaster, I saw a man, bottle in hand, run up the peak where two rafters joined. There, balancing on one foot, he sang out:

> 'It is a good framing
> And shall get a good naming.
> What shall the naming be?'

When the prearranged name was shouted back the man on the rafters so declared it as he cast the bottle to the ground. Was the bottle broken? No, indeed! As it contained the best liquor supplied at the raising, care was taken to see that it fell on soft ground, and the moment it fell it was surrounded by a crowd of men, still thirsty despite the liberal libations already supplied."[27]

David Dobie, who lived in Ekfrid Township, on the banks of the Thames, recalled a case of human life destroyed by wild beasts. This unfortunate incident, perhaps unique in pioneer annals, happened as a result of drunkenness at a raising:

"One night after a raising, a party of helpers were on their way home, and one, who had imbibed more freely than the others, refused to go further. He was accordingly left in a fence-corner to sleep off the effects of the liquor. Next morning, on his failure to return home, some men started out to look for him. They found the place where he had slept, but there was scarcely a shred of body or even of clothing left. Wolves had found him helpless, torn him limb from limb, and feasted on the mangled carcass."[28]

The amount of whisky distributed at bees by the "whisky-boys", "grogmen" or "grog-bosses" was so great that there are records of as much as eighty gallons consumed at one bee.[29] "One man had charge of the bottle, and

---

[27]Reminiscences of Benjamin D. Waldbrook, near Oakville, quoted in Smith, *op. cit.*, p. 176. Spirited accounts of a logging bee and a raising, with local variations as they applied to the later-settled counties between Lake Huron and Georgian Bay, may be found in W. M. Brown: *The Queen's Bush*. 1932. Chapters XVIII and XIX.

[28]Reminiscences of David Dobie, quoted in Smith, *op. cit.*, pp. 223-4.

[29]Patrick Shirreff: *A Tour through North America*. 1835. p. 125.

AN OLD TIME BARN-RAISING NEAR BRANTFORD

A MODERN BARN-RAISING AT WOODBRIDGE, ONTARIO

Harold McCrae, O.S.A.
Reproduced by Courtesy of the Artist and the T. Eaton Co., Ltd.

THE QUILTING BEE

From Heriot's *Travels through the Canadas.* 1807   George Heriot

MINUETS OF THE CANADIANS
A dance was the inevitable end of every bee

if he was judicious the people went home sober";[30] if he was not, fighting and other disorders were the inevitable consequence. The whisky habit was so deep-rooted that, until Temperance Societies began to gather headway in the forties and fifties, it was difficult to get men to come to a bee under any other conditions. We find that in 1832 a citizen of Wentworth County accomplished the remarkable feat of getting his saw-mill erected without whisky; but it was evidently a most unpopular move on his part, for when he tried to arrange a barn-raising under the same conditions he had to send to the Methodist Indian mission on the Credit before he could obtain men.[31]

Another instance of the same kind occurred in Cobourg in the forties. A builder named Bradbeer, who had "signed the pledge", found that his usual helpers refused to come to raise a barn when they heard that no liquor was to be served. The cause of temperance was vindicated, however, for with the aid of the town clerk a large number of "temperance people" were obtained to help with the raising, and they enjoyed tea and coffee as refreshment.[32]

Here and there other men with strength of character fought against the abuses of the whisky habit and strengthened the temperance movement. Among the first to abolish liquor at bees were Quakers and Methodists. John Gunn, early settled near Beaverton, put an end to liquor at loggings on his farm after a fight had occurred; similarly Abner Chase of Yarmouth Township succeeded in getting a barn raised without the aid of whisky. The example of these and other men exerted a good influence which spread far beyond the confines of the communities in which they lived.

After the rise of Temperance and Total Abstinence societies an ever-increasing number of men were found on the side of common sense and law and order at bees, and whisky-drinking gradually declined. Among other "temperance settlements" was that of Flos Township, near Georgian Bay. The first settlers in this district were mainly the sons of Oro Township pioneers. One of them states that "no whisky was even seen at raising or bee in this section. . . .

[30] J. L. Gourlay: *History of the Ottawa Valley*. 1896. p. 11.
[31] Cited in Emily Weaver: *The Story of the Counties of Ontario*. 1913. p. 165.
[32] Letter of James H. Bradbeer in the *Cobourg Sentinel-Star*, June 3, 1920.

To that fact is largely due the prosperity of the settlement".[33] Many of the inhabitants of rural Ontario were
pioneers in the temperance movement just as they were
pioneers in settlement, and they formed the nucleus of the
campaign for temperance legislation, which reached its
culmination in Canada during the Great War.

Bees were very democratic institutions, even in a day
when social distinctions were rigidly drawn. In the Adelaide military settlement in the London District occurred a
logging bee in which a man later Chief Justice of Upper
Canada, another a county judge, a third afterwards a
rector, and an old colonel, participated. There were times,
however, when some of the more aristocratic "gentlemen"
did not at first appreciate the full force of democratic sentiment, and had to be compelled to eat with the mob instead
of separately, as they intended. This attitude on the part
of refined people is not to be wondered at when we consider the low level of manners and the excesses which were
characteristic of the gatherings.

There were numerous other occasions when settlers
assembled from far and near to help with farm work—and
at the same time to "let off steam", for bees provided a
social outlet for the emotions. There were hauling bees,
ploughing bees, bees at hay-cutting and harvest-time, bees
to build stone or rail fences. A British magazine quotes a
traveller to Upper Canada in 1819 as of the opinion that the
English "are more offended with the fences than anything
else they see in this new country". But the ease with which
they could be made at a bee, one log often providing eighty
rails, soon reconciled them to rail or stump fences, particularly since stone walls could be erected only at great expense of labour and money, and the hedges of England were
unsuitable and inconvenient in a new country "on account
of harbouring vermin".[34]

Samuel Strickland attended a mowing and cradling bee
in Darlington Township in 1825, and found thirty-five men
cutting hay and rye, and ten cradlers. So well did they
work that by evening the whole of these crops had been
harvested, and there was time for gymnastics, trials of

[33]Reminiscences of Noah Cotton, quoted in Smith, *op. cit.*, p. 301.
[34]James Strachan quoted in the *Farmer's Magazine*, August, 1820,
    p. 331.

strength, running and jumping, and other popular pastimes such as throwing the hammer and putting the stone. During the day the "grog-boss" dealt out plenty of refreshment from a pail, while a couple of meals were served, consisting of "roast lamb and green peas, roast sucking-pig, shoulder of mutton, apple-sauce, and pies, puddings and preserves in abundance, with plenty of beer and Canadian whisky".[35]

Butchering day, or "the killing" was a busy time, when six or eight pigs, and perhaps some cattle as well, were slaughtered and dressed, the whole work—even to making sausages—being of necessity done in one day. Among the women there were paring bees, preserving bees, quilting bees,—where each woman worked on one section of a patchwork quilt,—fulling, and linen-spinning bees. Colonel John Clark, a Loyalist settler near Niagara, remembered linen bees where the young people spun from flax as much as sixty yards of fine linen, the only payment being a supper and a dance.[36] Logging and quilting were sometimes combined into a "double bee", and in the same manner the quilting in the afternoon often preceded the husking in the evening, in which the men participated. As W. S. Herrington neatly puts it: "The afternoon tea now serves its purpose very well, but modern society has yet to discover the equal of the quilting bee as a clearing-house for gossip."[37]

Perhaps the husking bee provided most pleasure to the participants. Piles of corn were arranged in the barn, which was illuminated by candles placed in tin lanterns. Walter Riddell gives an excellent description of the course of events: "At these bees lads and lassies occupied alternate seats, and when one of the former found a big red ear of corn he had the privilege of kissing the girl next him. And it is surprising what a lot of big red ears were found." The husking was followed "by a dance, and refreshments in the form of cake, home-made cheese and punch".[38]

[35]Strickland, op. cit., Vol. I, pp. 35-37.

[36]Reminiscences of Colonel John Clark, Niagara. (Coventry Papers, Public Archives of Canada.)

[37]W. S. Herrington: Pioneer Life on the Bay of Quinté. (In Lennox and Addington Historical Society, Papers and Records, Vol. VI, p. 17.)

[38]Reminiscences of Walter Riddell, Hamilton Township, in the Farmer's Sun, August 4, 1898.

Pumpkins were early an important food, used in a variety of ways. A settler near Kirby, Clarke Township, recalled that "the pumpkin bee was a social function, and lads and lassies gathered from miles around to peel and string pumpkins for drying, just as those of a later generation had their apple-paring bees. And what delicious pies those dried pumpkins did make."[39]

The later paring bees were interesting events, at least in Dundas County, where "each of the boys, accompanied by his peculiar home-made paring machine, would bring his best girl. . . . The boys tossed the peeled apples from the machines, which were caught by the girls, who quickly completed the work".[40] A common type of paring machine reresembled a two-pronged fork, upon which the apple was placed; there was generally an attachment which enabled the coring of the apple. It was usual to slice the apples and place them to dry on racks above the fireplace or kitchen stove. Perhaps the following account is typical of the proceedings at the average apple-paring bee:

"The young folks make a grand night of it when the bee comes off. The laughing and frolic is unbounded; some are busy with their sweethearts; some, of a grosser mind, are no less busy with the apples, devouring a large proportion of what they pare; and the whole proceedings, in many cases, wind up with a dance on the barn floor."[41]

In addition to the bees which had as their main purpose the accomplishment of work, there were "house-warmings", spelling bees, maple sugar-eating bees, and other frolics where no work was done. Perhaps the best description of this type of gathering is that written by a young Scotch traveller who played a most important part in what might be called, in the vernacular of the day, a "sparking bee", or —in more modern terms—a "petting party". When he arrived at the home to which he had been invited, David Wilkie found "a goodly cluster of misses with smooth, smiling faces, beaming beneath a load of clear and glistening tresses, that seemed to have cost them a deal of extra trouble for the occasion. . . . I was introduced to the good old squire himself, with whom I was soon knee-deep in a

[39]Reminiscences of H. L. Powers, quoted in Smith, *op. cit.*, p. 312.
[40]J. S. Carter: *The Story of Dundas County.* 1905. p. 49.
[41]C. Geikie: *Life in the Woods.* 1873. p. 326.

sea of humdrum prosification of and concerning the state
of the foreign markets, sour cider, and the price of pork.
We were regaled with refreshments, small cakes, currant
tarts, and similar puffery. . . . As the room became more
obscure, the masters and misses drew closer together. . . .
The moon, (for luckily there was one), smiled beautifully in
upon them".

Soon the squire slipped away and the visitor was invited
to join "this round-robin of honest men and bonnie lassies.
Being naturally endowed with Scotch caution, I intended,
whatever might chance, to keep a sharp look-out after my
heart!" Wilkie soon found, indeed, that this was no place
for him! A large bone button was passed from hand to
hand, and he was asked to guess where it was, in which he
was not correct; he was, therefore, sentenced to place himself "between the two young squiresses on the window-seat.
They were quite in the shade, for the moonbeams merely
glanced along the outlines of their flowing curls and snowy
necks. . . .

"The fair one on my right hand . . . complied with the
sentence which followed by placing herself on one of my
knees, to which I kindly assisted her, to render the penance
as light as possible. The lady on my left . . . . was consigned
to the precious support of my vacant limb. . . . The lock-up
house was my knee, and the chains that bound them were
my arms. Not content with the extent of the penal duties I
was already made to perform, the master of ceremonies,
with more refined wickedness, brought me once more
beneath the lash of the law, and awarded the additional
penance that I do forthwith salute the two culprits in the
condemned cell. Time had got so far ahead that we had
now to think of home; and I was obliged, however re-
luctantly, to resign my romantic post and dive into the
woods, leaving all the alluring fascinations of the magical
button behind, which, I doubt not, has often before the occurrence of this busy bee caused many a heart to ache, and
many a head toss over a sleepless pillow".[42]

Except among families where dancing was considered
sinful, and the fiddle an instrument of the devil, the invariable end of every bee was a dance in the house, the barn,

[42]David Wilkie: *Sketches of a Summer Trip to New York and the
Canadas*. 1837. pp. 182-6.

or the "ballroom" of a tavern. Quadrilles, reels and jigs, waxing fast and furious as the fiddler struck his stride, and the aching muscles of even the old men were limbered up, alternated with rustic plays and "kissing games" until the small hours of the morning, when every laddie saw his lassie home, perhaps with the help of a flambeau of dry cedar bark.

Such were the bees of the pioneer period. In a day of severe and unremitting toil, of privation and hardship, they provided social intercourse and diversion as important to the life of the people as the work accomplished.

CHAPTER IX

AMUSEMENT AND SOCIAL LIFE IN THE RURAL DISTRICTS

"After dinner we fell to dancing, and continued, only with intermission for a good supper, till two in the morning, the musick being Greeting and another most excellent violin, the best in town. And so with mighty mirth and pleased with their dancing of jigs afterwards several of them, and among others Betty Turner, who did it mighty prettily, and then to a country dance again, and so broke up with extraordinary pleasure as being one of the days and nights of my life spent with the greatest content, and that which I can but hope to repeat again a few times in my whole life."

The Diary of Samuel Pepys, March 2, 1669.

THE life of the pioneer settlers in Canada was one of hardship, but the difficulties under which they lived were to some extent relieved by co-operation, not only in work but in play. The "bees" which were so characteristic of early life in Upper Canada supplied that social intercourse which is essential to a well-balanced life. Judged by modern standards some pioneer amusements were crude, leading occasionally to regrettable excesses; but there was a wholesomeness among the vast majority of the people which pervaded their social life, and frowned upon any variation from the spirit of honest fun.

In considering the pleasures of the pioneers it must first be understood that "it takes all kinds of people to make a world"; what is one person's pleasure is another's aversion. There were many who considered all worldly amusement sinful, and to be avoided at any cost. Prominent among these were the Friends or Quakers, who often took disciplinary action against members of their societies guilty of backsliding; we find, for example, that the disfavour of their co-religionists fell upon some who "had attended a noisy, unruly and unlawful assembly called a chivaree"; and likewise upon three Quakers on Yonge Street who were "guilty of assisting in tarring and carrying a woman on a rail".[1] In addition to the more serious breaches of conduct—swearing, drinking, fighting, gambl-

[1]A. G. Dorland: *A History of the Society of Friends in Canada.* 1927. p. 10.

ing, immorality and horse-racing—other less harmful diversions, such as card-playing, music and dancing in one's home, were deprecated, and persons persisting in such practices were expelled from the society.

Though social life in a Quaker community was greatly restricted, yet most Quakers had the same sense of humour to be found among other sections of the population, even though it was usually hidden by a solemn face and quaint garb. In later days they sometimes had debating societies, while at all times "their Yearly, Quarterly and Monthly meetings filled a social as well as religious need in a pioneer state of society which was very simple and had few outlets for demands of this kind. Members would travel great distances to attend these gatherings which were the occasion of lavish hospitality. Indeed these were notable social events which had a large place in the life of the early Quaker community".[2]

The early Methodists were similarly opposed to amusements of a worldly nature; in the days of the first class-meetings the violin was forbidden as a sinful musical instrument (if such a thing is possible!), chiefly because it was commonly used to supply the music for dancing. This prohibition of the one common source of music left them without any, for the accordeon and concertina were not invented until 1829, while melodeons and "pianofortes" were not common in Canada until many years later.

The scarcity of musical instruments led to greater stress being laid upon singing in the home and the church. Singing-schools were organised each winter in many neighbourhoods and provided a means of social intercourse, though the unfortunate singing-master often found it difficult to keep order among those who did not come to sing. The Methodists were particularly noted for singing in unison at their religious services, the congregational singing at the York Conference of 1831 being described as "most delightful and heavenly".[3] The Jesuit missionaries had a small organ in Quebec as early as 1661, but organs were uncommon a century ago in the churches of Upper Canada. One method of obtaining the key in which the congregation

[2]*Ibid.*
[3]Anson Green: *Life and Times.* 1877. p. 153.

Public Archives of Canada From an Old Print

THE RED MEETING-HOUSE, STAMFORD, 1800-40

From the *Illustrated London News*, April 18, 1863

CELEBRATION OF THE ROYAL WEDDING DAY, BURLINGTON
BAY, 1863

From Conant's *Upper Canada Sketches* E. S. Shrapnel

A METHODIST CAMP-MEETING

Reproduced by Courtesy of the Maple Leat Gardens, Inc.

18,000 PEOPLE AT DENTON MASSEY'S YORK BIBLE CLASS, MAPLE LEAF GARDENS, DECEMBER 13, 1931

Probably the largest indoor assembly in the history of Canada

sang consisted in the striking of a tuning-fork by the leader.

While not pleasures in the usual sense of the word, the class-meeting and the camp-meeting of the Methodists often provided a "love-feast" which, despite occasional emotional excesses, may be considered as a form of higher spiritual pleasure. The services of the other denominations, while more orthodox and impersonal, were equally important in the social life of the community. Church services were early held in courthouses or other government buildings, ii. taverns, stores or private homes, until it was possible to erect a church building by the subscription and labour of the members.

In most denominations the service was most informal, though a sense of decorum was apparent in the custom of men and women sitting in separate sections of the room. Sometimes the men removed their coats in warm weather, and people frequently walked in and out during the course of the service; while often the week's mail was distributed at the church door at the close. There were Sunday schools for the children in connection with most churches, and in some cases they had a few books to be distributed among those whose education was sufficient to enable them to read. In fact the social life of the pioneer community centred in the church and the school, the clergyman and the teacher being not infrequently the same person. Social intercourse was extended, and education as well as amusement supplied by tea-meetings and socials, singing-schools and spelling-matches, literary and debating societies, though such organised activities were seldom found during the first years of settlement.

Many of the inhabitants of Upper Canada were not as scrupulous with regard to their pleasures as were the Quakers and early Methodists. There were many, too, who were forced by the manners and customs of the times to join upon some occasions in questionable activities which they would ordinarily have avoided. One of the worst of these customs, and the most far-reaching in its effects, was the excessive drinking of spirituous liquors, a habit which, though by no means universal, pervaded social life in all parts of the country, and was as prominent in the backwoods as in the towns. Whisky was early considered an antidote to the hardships and misfortunes of pioneer life, and a means temporarily to forget care and trouble.

At almost every gathering liquor was served in abundance, and it was considered in the thirties that he was "a moderate man who does not exceed four glasses in the day".[4] Many people attended bees, weddings, auction sales, and other social assemblies merely for the purpose of drinking; liquor was frequently taken to revival camp-meetings and consumed by those who came to scoff but did not remain to pray. Even funeral wakes were not exempt from strong drink, and on at least one occasion "so hilarious did the participants become that the corpse was offered a share of the beverage".[5] The poor quality of the drink often made its effects much worse: one writer compares the usual liquor to fire and brimstone, "made of frosty potatoes, hemlock, pumpkins and black mouldy rye".[6]

The number of inns and taverns that existed in Upper Canada in former times would surprise the present generation. Every crossroad had one or more, and the main highways supported many dozens of them. The small city of Toronto had in 1850 a total of 152 taverns and 206 beer shops to supply a population of about 30,000 and such farmers as brought their produce thither to market. Distilleries were among the first establishments in most settlements, and provided large quantities of cheap liquor, usually obtainable at 25c. a gallon, or even less; and almost all taverns were maintained largely by the sale of strong drink. A traveller refers to "taverns and low drinking-houses" as the chief places of public amusement in Upper Canada;[7] while another writer[8] found "every inn, tavern and beer shop filled at all hours with drunken, brawling fellows; and the quantity of ardent spirits consumed by

[4]Letter of William Hutton in the *British Farmer's Magazine*, April, 1835, p. 114.
[5]M. A. Garland and J. J. Talman: *Pioneer Drinking Habits, and the Rise of the Temperance Agitation in Upper Canada.* (Ontario Historical Society, *Papers and Records*, Vol. XXVII, p. 345).
[6]John MacTaggart: *Three Years in Canada.* 1829. Vol. I, p. 199.
[7]Anna Jameson: *Winter Studies and Summer Rambles in Canada.* 1838. Vol. I, p. 293.
[8]"An Ex-Settler": *Canada in the Years 1832, 1833 and 1834.* 1835. p. 25,

them will truly astonish you". Men went from tavern to tavern treating one another all round, and the amount of liquor consumed often led to fatal accidents. Of the sudden deaths investigated by coroner's juries, excessive whisky-drinking was found to be by far the most frequent cause.

The temperance movement originated in the United States, and spread into Canada at the commencement of the second quarter of the nineteenth century. Montreal was long the temperance centre of Canada, and there the first Temperance Society was formed in 1828. A few months later a number of township societies had been formed in Upper Canada, and by 1832 there were 10,000 members of such organisations in the province. The early societies usually restricted their warfare against intoxicants to whisky, rum and brandy, and emphasised temperance rather than prohibition; but in later years beer and wine were added to the proscribed list, and in 1835 the first of a large number of Total Abstinence societies was organised in St. Catharines. The reaction against the drinking habits of the times gathered headway down through the years, though the societies were opposed by many as a "Yankee" institution, which reason, and his own personal appetite, led Colonel Talbot to dub them "damned cold water drinking societies".[9]

Apart from the excessive use of intoxicants there were among the pioneers no very harmful habits which are not present to at least as great an extent now. The use of snuff was comparatively harmless, and both men and women were more or less fond of it in the earlier periods of settlement. The tobacco habit, while by no means universal, was quite general among all classes of the male population. Women were not usually addicted either to tobacco or intoxicants; some of the old ladies did enjoy smoking an old, blackened clay pipe, but cigarettes had not been invented, and smoking by young women in general is a very recent innovation.

Some of the girls of a century ago were not, however,

[9]Speech at St. Thomas, April 23, 1832. See the *Talbot Papers*, Section II, pp. 124-6. (*Transactions* of the Royal Society of Canada, 1909).

averse to appearing sophisticated and *risqué* upon occasion. Joseph Pickering notes in his journal in 1826 that while he was stopping at Loder's Tavern on Talbot Street "some smart lasses came in during the evening, who live just by, most of whom took a smoke with the landlord and the landlady, passing the short black pipe from one to another! Disgusting as this practice is, it is not so much so as one in common use in the eastern part of Maryland, of girls taking a "rubber" of snuff—that is, taking as much snuff as will lie on the end of the forefinger out of a box, and rubbing it round the inside of the mouth"![10]

There were many evils traceable in a large measure to the excessive drinking habits. Drunkenness, "the vice and curse of the country",[11] was generally accompanied by profanity, immorality, lawlessness and crime. Boisterous activities and cruel habits were considered amusing by people of low or degenerate mentality. Murder and robbery were common, and while some men stole sheep, horses and cattle, others repaid a grudge or satisfied a depraved desire by maiming them. Burning barns, breaking windows, smashing store signs, and other types of horseplay and vandalism, were of frequent occurrence, and even in modern times such activities are occasionally carried on where the vigilance of the police and magistrates is insufficient to prevent them. In the first years of villages and towns there was frequently a similar disregard for the rights of property, and early newspapers contain notices of the following type:

"Two Dollars Reward.—Whereas on Friday night last some evil-disposed person fired a gun at the house of the subscriber, ... whereby upwards of twenty squares of glass were broken, and the premises otherwise injured, the above reward will be paid on the conviction of the offenders."[12]

Similarly in York twenty dollars reward was offered for the apprehension of the man "who is so depraved and lost to every sense of social duty as to cut with an axe or knife the withes which bound some of the fence round the

---

[10]Joseph Pickering: *Inquiries of an Emigrant.* 1831. November 2, 1826.

[11]Jameson, *op. cit.,* Vol. I, p. 76.

[12]*Cobourg Star,* January 18, 1831.

late Chief Justice's farm on Yonge Street, and to throw down the said fence".[13]

On many occasions the public conscience was aroused by flagrant disregard for the principles of law and order. Mob justice was not infrequent in some parts of Upper Canada, particularly where the regular course of law enforcement was tardy, and in instances where a moral but not a legal crime had been committed. Prominent in this connection was the "Old Sorrel", a species of summary justice dealt out to those who had offended the sense of morality of the neighbourhood. This punishment consisted in tarring and feathering the culprit, with the addition, at times, of "riding the fence rail"; anyone treated in this manner was expected to leave the district immediately. Altercations arising from such types of mob rule were usually ignored as far as possible by the authorities, even where deaths resulted, though as civilisation advanced such occurrences could not be tolerated and have fortunately become infrequent.

A few men of low, if not perverted tastes took a savage delight in the sufferings of animals, and were to be found— as they occasionally are at the present day—carrying on such sports (?) as bull- or bear-baiting, dog-fighting and cock-fighting. Two centuries earlier these crude activities had been quite common in England, especially during the period of reaction which followed the Puritan repression of Commonwealth days; but even at that time John Evelyn considered them "butcherly sports, or, rather, barbarous cruelties, ... a rude and dirty pastime";[14] while Samuel Pepys, whose interests were universal, and who was by no means fussy in his amusements, found cock-fighting "no great sport", and soon "had enough of it" and its accompaniments—"swearing, cursing and betting".[15] In Canada these so-called old English sports so offended the public sense of fair play and decency that they have been prohibited by law in modern times.

Wrestling and fighting were long popular public amusements. Gourlay stated that "the vulgar practice of pugil-

[13]*Upper Canada Gazette*, July 23, 1803.
[14]John Evelyn: *Diary*, June 16, 1670.
[15]Samuel Pepys: *Diary*, December 21, 1663, and April 6, 1668.

ism, a relic of the savage state", was declining in 1817,[16] but it by no means died out. It was commonly considered that the best man was he who could knock his opponent senseless, and seldom did the rules of the Marquis of Queensbury apply to any such pugilistic encounters. Feats of strength and skill were deservedly popular at bees and other public gatherings; in fact the supremacy of a township frequently rested upon the ability of its representatives to dispose of all comers in some athletic competition. Races were less popular than wrestling or fighting for public spectacles of this kind. On one occasion the "Fifth-towners", as the inhabitants of the Township of Marysburgh were called, considered that the "Fourth-towners", across the Bay of Quinté in Adolphustown, were "too smart and stuck-up"; so they challenged them to pick out three of their best wrestlers to settle the relative "smartness" of the townships. Needless to say they were not to be "stumped", and sent Samuel Dorland, Samuel Casey and Paul Trumpour to uphold the reputation of Adolphustown against the chosen men of Marysburgh, whose names have not come down to us, perhaps because they were worsted in the encounter.

"The hour was fixed, and a nearby field was selected where hundreds were on hand 'to see fair play' and help decide which township had the best men. These were all noted athletes, and they were then young and in their prime. Samuel Dorland, afterwards a colonel in the militia and a leading official in the Methodist Church, was an expert wrestler, and used to boast, even in his old days, that he seldom if ever met a man who could lay him on his back. He soon had his man down. Samuel Casey, who afterwards became a leading military officer and a prominent justice of the peace, was one of the strongest men in the township, but not an expert wrestler. He was so powerful in the legs that his opponent, with all his skill, could not trip him up, and at last got thrown down himself. Paul Trumpour, who was the head of what is now the largest family in the township, was not so skilled in athletics; but he was a man of immense strength. He got his arms well fixed

[16]Robert Gourlay: *A Statistical Account of Upper Canada.* 1822. Vol. I, pp. 252-4.

around his man and gave him such terrible 'bear-hugs'
that the poor fellow soon cried out 'enough', to save his
ribs from getting crushed in, and that settled it. The
Fourth-town championship was not again disputed."[17]

There were among the pioneers many who delighted
in the opportunities which Canada afforded for the field
sports whch they had enjoyed in the Old Land. Dr. Dunlop fills up twenty-one pages in describing—for the benefit
of immigrants!—the rare hunting, gaming, hawking and
fishing available in Canada.[18] But while some had leisure
in which they could enjoy such pastimes, most of the
early settlers were too busy to enter into them unless
necessity compelled them to obtain food in that manner.
Field sports cannot be described in detail here, but it is
sufficient to say that fish, birds and animals now almost
extinct were obtainable a century ago in a profusion which
would astonish the sportsman of today.

Among the activities of this type which were sometimes
a necessity was raccoon-hunting. Many a boy and his dog
amused themselves in the green-corn season driving the
raccoons from the fields to the woods, from which, if
no other artifice availed, they were forced by felling the
trees. The hunting of deer many be taken as a typical
Canadian field sport. A man who frequently engaged in
such amusements during the pioneer period considered
that deer-hunting was "a very exciting sport; but I prefer
still-hunting, (or deer-stalking, as it is called in the High-
lands of Scotland), to driving them into the lakes and rivers
with hounds. The deer are not now (1853) nearly so
numerous as they formerly were. . . . To give my
readers some idea how plentiful these wild denizens of the
forest were some years since, I need only mention that a
trapper with whom I was acquainted, and four of his companions, passed my house on a small raft on which lay the
carcasses of thirty-two deer—the trophies of a fortnight's
chase near Stoney Lake. The greater number of these
were fine bucks.

"I once had seventeen deer hanging up in my barn at

[17]Thomas W. Casey: *Old Time Records*. Quoted in W. S. Herrington:
    The History of Lennox and Addington. 1913. p. 137.
[18]William Dunlop: *Statistical Sketches of Upper Canada*. 1832.
    pp. 32-52

one time—the produce of three days' sport, out of which I had the good fortune to kill seven. Parties are now made yearly every October to Stoney Lake, Deer Bay, or the River Trent. I do not know anything more pleasant than these excursions, especially if you have agreeable companions, a warm camp, and plenty to eat and drink. . . . This is one of the great charms of Canadian life, particularly to young sportsmen from the Mother Country, who require here neither license nor qualification to enable them to follow their game; but may rove in chase of deer or other game at will".[19]

Bird life was found in similar profusion a century ago. Joseph Pickering notes in his diary on April 8, 1826: "Pigeons, in great flocks, going out daily northward; some people with nets and decoy pigeons will catch several hundred in a day, when they sometimes take only their breasts and salt them down, and make beds of their feathers".[20] In the late summer of the same year he observed that "pigeons again made their appearance in large flocks, as also wild turkeys; partridges, larger than the English breed, and quails, less than those of Europe, are also numerous".[21] The wild turkeys sometimes weighed fifteen pounds when dressed.

Fishing, which Izaak Walton so appropriately called "the contemplative man's recreation",[22] has been a noted amusement in Canada from the earliest times. Even the Indian was inclined to look upon it as an exciting pleasure rather than a means to obtain food. Many a pioneer participated in the enjoyments of fishing in a day when even a poor fisherman could well-nigh fill his canoe in a few hours. In general the sport has changed, as the years have passed, from spearing to angling; but even if no fish are caught, the unsuccessful angler's consolation is the same as it was three centuries ago when Robert Burton wrote:

"Fishing is still and quiet: and if so be the Angler catch no Fish, yet he hath a wholesome walk to the Brook-

[19]Samuel Strickland: *Twenty-seven Years in Canada West*. 1853. Vol. I, pp. 78-9.
[20]Pickering, *op. cit.*, April 8, 1826.
[21]*Ibid.*, August 26, 1826.
[22]See the title-page of the First Edition, 1653, of Izaak Walton: *The Compleat Angler*.

Edward Caddy, D.L.S.

STONEY LAKE IN THE FIFTIES

PROWSE'S HOTEL, BEAUMARIS, MUSKOKA LAKES, IN THE
EIGHTIES

Note the emphasis placed upon the Billiard Room

CATARAQUI (KINGSTON) IN AUGUST, 1783

FALL OF MONTMORENCIE IN WINTER
The joys of carrioling are here apparent

side, pleasant shade by the sweet silver streams; he hath
good air, and sweet smells of fine fresh meadow flowers;
he hears the melodious harmony of Birds."[23]

A sporting event early characteristic of the Canadian
summer was the regatta. Canoe races in which Indian and
voyageur vied with settler aroused the greatest interest
among those who lived near the waterways. John Mac-
Taggart, writing in the eighteen-twenties, considered that
there were "few finer scenes than a Canadian Regatta:
fifty canoes on the smooth broad lake, *voyageurs* fancifully
adorned, the song up in full chorus, blades of the paddles
flashing in the sun as they rapidly lift and·dip, while the
watery foam-bells hurry into the hollow of the wakes".[24]
The first regattas were on the St. Lawrence or the Ottawa,
but as early as 1838 there were similar aquatic competitions
at Fenelon Falls, and at other settlements in the "back
lakes" region of the old Newcastle District, which was to
become in later years so popular a summer resort.

Just as characteristic of Canada were the sports of
winter. Snow-shoe and dog-sled had long been necessary
for winter travel over Indian trail and along frozen lake
and river, and they were supplemented in the days of
settlement by sledge and carriole. Travel by carriole was
just as pleasurable in winter as the canoe was in summer,
and it was a time when travelling was but seldom pleasant.
The settler's sleigh was usually home-made and its body
ran very close to the ice; while that of the "gentlemen"
in the towns had runners, and was often a very elaborate
affair. The carriole had no covering, so travellers were well
bundled up in furs. Sleighing-parties have remained a
characteristic Canadian winter pleasure though the motor-
car is gradually replacing horse-drawn vehicles.

Tobogganing, or, as sometimes spelled, "traboggining",
was another winter sport early enjoyed by the young people.
Skating, which originated in Holland, was also a favourite
amusement, though it was frequently considered improper
for girls to participtate in such a form of pleasurable exercise. Curling commenced in Canada towards the close of

[23]Robert Burton: *The Anatomy of Melancholy.* 1652. Dell Edition,
       1927, p. 478.
[24]MacTaggart, *op. cit.,* Vol. I, p. 308.

the eighteenth century, when some of the officers of the garrison at Quebec became interested in the game as a means of relieving a monotonous life. In Upper Canada the game was first played at Kingston about 1820, and on the Don River at York nine years later; soon afterwards it was popular in many another settlement, particularly where the Scotch predominated. In this sport, as in many another activity, the rural settler frequently walked many miles to join his brethren in the nearest village, and all gathered at a favourite stretch of ice on river or lake.

Visiting has always been a popular diversion among all classes of people. Formal calls were made by the social set in the towns, and very informal visits in the rural districts. Births, marriages and deaths provided an excellent opportunity for the exchange of civilities, and it was usual to provide guests with food, and frequently with lodging as well; it is said that farmers thought it "nothing extraordinary to make an excursion of six or seven hundred miles in the winter in their sleighs to see their friends".[25] Sunday was the great day for local visiting, and it was generally considered that no time was so appropriate for "sparking" (courting) as Sunday evening. The improvement of roads and the invention of the motor-car have greatly facilitated travel, and might be presumed to have increased visiting; that this is not the case is the fault of the great amusement of "listening-in", not only to the radio, but also of an older variety,—that major sport of many communities— listening in over the party telephone line!

Surprise parties, where ten or twelve families suddenly descended upon the home—and sometimes the larder—of mutual friends, were a popular form of visiting in the rural districts, and have survived to the present. The women obtained a considerable proportion of their pleasure in visits, for their activities were more restricted than those of the men. Many pioneer women seldom went anywhere beyond a neighbour's, the market, or the general store; their lives were often monotonous, for it was usually considered improper for females to enter into the men's ac-

[25]D'Arcy Boulton: *Sketch of His Majesty's Province of Upper Canada.* 1805. p. 11.

tivities, and there were in the country few libraries and fewer readable books. The men, on the other hand, frequently had occasion to visit the town, and their contact with the official, the merchant and the tradesman was not only diverting, but affected, even if unconsciously, their attitude towards life, and lessened the monotony of their existence. They also engaged from time to time in hunting and fishing, visited taverns, attended bees, fairs, horse-races, militia training, circuses, and elections; some also entered into curling, bandyball, lacrosse, football, quoits and other sports.

Social intercourse among farmers was increased through the activities of Agricultural Societies and kindred organisations. There were a few societies in existence in Upper Canada before 1825, the first being at Niagara in 1793; but they did not become important throughout the province until the thirties and forties. With them came the local fairs and, later, the Provincial Exhibition, which were of value not only in developing agriculture but also in that they provided some contact with the outside world; horse-racing, ploughing-matches, and, in later years, amusements more or less commercialised, were prominent at all fairs, and soon became an attraction of outstanding importance to the average citizen.

Associations among farmers' wives were not formed as early as the Agricultural Societies among the men, but in later years the Women's Institutes became increasingly important in developing social life. The Temperance Societies which became so common in rural Ontario in the forties and fifties provided many people with opportunities for advancement and pleasure similar to those afforded by the agricultural organisations, for in both cases papers were read and debates held upon subjects of popular interest.

The early settlers were too busy to indulge in amusement very often, so it was customary to crowd a great deal into one "spree", as a social gathering was often called. A bee, a wedding, or an auction sale was not always over in one day, for the participants frequently extended the jollification several days longer. This was particularly true of a wedding, which was a notable community event in the early days. A wedding procession of lumber-wagons was often a feature, and "each gallant was supposed to support his partner upon his knee, and thus economise room".[26]

While fighting was common enough at bees and other gatherings, nothing of the kind was allowed at a wedding celebration, where it was considered that everyone should be good-natured. A dance was the inevitable concomitant of a wedding; in fact to dance until daylight during several succeeding nights was not uncommon. The older people seldom attended the wedding celebration, probably feeling that their absence would be appreciated; but they usually joined in the dances.

A species of amusement once very common, and still to be found in some parts of Ontario, was the charivari or chivaree; this was, in early times, particularly connected with second marriages, or when the parties were unequal in age, or unpopular. The custom was to be found in parts of England, and in Canada it originated among the French in Quebec. Gourlay wrote early in the pioneer period concerning the usual reasons which led to the chivaree:

"I have observed no essential peculiarity in the funerals or weddings of this country; but there is a singular custom of 'chereverreeing', as it is called, a newly-married couple, where the match is thought to be unequal or unseasonable; as between an old man and a young girl, or within a short period after the death of a former husband or wife. Sometimes it is in consequence of the offence so frequently caused by a neglect of invitation to the wedding."[27]

The chivaree party would steal up to the home of the newly-wedded, usually after midnight, and suddenly music (?) from tin horns, horse-bells, "bull-roarers", "horse-fiddles", tin pans, and copper kettles would burst upon the ears of those within the house. If the bridegroom did not come forth and meet the demands for refreshments, or money (to be spent at the tavern), the discordant uproar would continue the rest of the night, and often on succeeding nights. Where the marriage was considered particularly objectionable the charivari was much more serious

[26]"An old lady in Ameliasburgh" quoted in William Canniff: *History of the Settlement of Upper Canada.* 1869. p. 239.
[27]Gourlay, *op. cit.*, Vol. I, p. 254.

than a serenade. The roysterers have been known to climb
to the roof of the house and close up the opening of the
chimney with the intention of smoking the wedding party
out; fighting, and occasionally death, resulted from such
proceedings. Gourlay noted that the chivaree was sometimes a subject of prosecution, but that it was generally
considered best to regard it "with good humour, as a joke
unworthy of serious notice".[28]

Bees were, perhaps, the most noted occasions of amusement in the rural districts in pioneer days. An early
settler in the Bay of Quinté district refers to them as
"great institutions in those days. Every settler was
licensed to make two or three each year, provided he furnished a good 'pot pie', and plenty of grog, and never made
any objections to his guests fighting".[29] Races, gymnastics,
wrestling matches, feats of strength such as putting the
stone and hurling the hammer, axemanship, and skill in
handling recalcitrant oxen or horses provided amusement
for many of the younger people at bees. They spent the
evening in dancing, while the older men and women who did
not care to dance concluded the day's work by conversation
about their common interests—the crops, prices, local politics, and such news as had come from the Old Land.

Paring, quilting and the other domestic bees supplied
the women with an opportunity to become acquainted; here
were discussed family affairs, house furnishings, recipes,
new arrivals in the neighbourhood, and the usual run of
petty scandal. It has been said that these bees have never
been equalled as "a clearing-house for gossip";[30] but the
men learned just as much news at the tavern, the blacksmith shop, the general store and, in later days, at the
barber shop, though the last-named sanctuary disappeared
when bobbed hair became the fashion!

The dances or "hops" which almost invariably closed
every bee were frequently held in the barn. Games and
"forfeits" alternated with dancing, and were frequently
accompanied by much flirtation. Such "kissing bees", like

[28]*Ibid.*
[29]"An old settler in Ameliasburgh" quoted in Canniff, *op. cit.*, p. 628.
[30]W. S. Herrington: *Pioneer Life on the Bay of Quinté.* (Lennox and
    Addington Historical Society, *Papers and Records*, Vol. VI,
    p. 17).

all other evils, are stated by some writers to have originated in the United States; though it may be said that in general these amusements were then considered quite innocent, whatever opinion might be held by later generations.

Of all the amusements of early times dancing was the most universal and appears to have given the greatest pleasure to the greatest number. The rhythmic beats of the war dance of the savage have been varied through the centuries into other types of sound, until many consider the jazz of today a reversion to type. The music supplied at dances was not, however, the all-important matter in pioneer days: where a fiddler or a bag-piper was not obtainable the young people whistled, sang, or made music with a comb. In much of the dancing in the rural districts more exercise than grace was apparent. Waltzing was not generally popular, the square dance being most in vogue. In the towns, dancing-schools taught various fancy minuets and quadrilles, but the backwoods settlers were quite satisfied with the usual country dances. Scotch and Irish reels, four-hand and eight-hand reels, jigs and hornpipes varied in popularity with the nationality of the participants.

Above the noise of the dancing could be heard the scraping sound of the fiddle, and the voice of the caller-off as he shouted "Salute your Partners", "Promenade All", or "Grand Chain". Some rustic dances called for equally rustic directions from the caller-off, whose shouts "Balance to the next and all swing out", "Gents hook up, ladies bounce back", "Down the centre and chaw hay", usually exhibited more ingenuity than gentility. Among the popular dance music of pioneer days were prominent *The Soldiers' Joy, Money Musk, Old Dan Tucker* and *Pop Goes the Weasel*. The enthusiasm of the dancers usually increased as the night passed:

"The dancers hop and reel round, toes up and heels down, and turn to the right and left with one foot, and clap their hands and snap their fingers, and whoop, with ever-increasing heartiness. The fiddler gets inspired, plays faster and faster, his foot keeping time on the big chest, making a loud hollow sound. The boys get around him, and every time he rises from the chair they move it a little nearer the edge of the chest. At last the excitement is at its height; up goes a whoop, and down comes the chair, fiddler and all, landing on Farmer M's head, and the heads of two or three others, bringing them to the floor in a heap. Soon order is restored, the fiddle starts again, and the fun goes fast and furious."[31]

While the barn was good enough for most rural dances, it became customary in some localities to hold dances in the dining-room,—or in the "ball-room" over the driving-shed,— of the country tavern. Guests at inns had frequently to vacate their rooms when a large dance was being held. The young men usually took up a collection among themselves to pay the expenses, while the girls brought the refreshments. An old soldier, a negro, or someone else in the neighbourhood who had a reputation as a fiddler, usually provided the music.

A man who frequently officiated as fiddler at dances states that almost anyone was allowed to join in the fun, even if he was a stranger in the community. Once while he and his brother were travelling westward from Port Hope along the Kingston Road, they came to an inn where a dance was in progress, and, upon the invitation of the landlord, joined the party. Scarcely had they entered the room "when two girls came up and invited us to be their partners. (We did not wait for introductions in those days). The dance was the 'opera reel', with girls on one side and boys on the other in parallel lines. It was while holding opposite lines that the fancy steps were put in. My brother was one of the best fancy dancers I have ever seen, and after the girls saw how he could 'step it off' we had no lack of partners for the rest of the evening. I sometimes served as fiddler at local dances, and even yet I can see the bright-eyed girls, clad in homespun, as they swing in the arms of the swains of long ago."[32]

In the "Huron Tract" there were in the thirties, when it was in process of settlement, dances in taverns which were by no means cheap: while the ladies paid nothing, a gentleman's subscription was about $5, for which sum, however, he was entitled to bring with him a partner and a

---

[31]W. A. Mackay: *Pioneer Life in Zorra.* 1899. pp. 180-1.
[32]Reminiscences of H. L. Powers, Clarke Township, in W. L. Smith: *Pioneers of Old Ontario.* 1923. pp. 312-13.

servant, and "to be supplied with wine and other liquors, with tea and supper for himself and them". On producing a ticket anyone was admitted, whether strangers or not, and without any introduction. Before the dance commenced, "a solemn silence reigns, the gentlemen sitting on one side, the ladies on the other"; but once the dancing was under way all formalities were at an end, and the party seldom broke up before daylight.[33]

Rural balls were frequently the most attractive of amusements available to pioneer settlers. People would travel many miles through the bush to participate in the fun. It is said that a certain log schoolhouse in Guelph Township was erected "more for the purpose of holding a yearly dance than for educational purposes". The Paisley Block Ball was inaugurated in 1832 and soon became famous, "waxing beyond the concessions; and ultimately died after a long and brilliant career, through its sheer popularity".[34] Youth, beauty and music—a sugar-kettle outside for the preparation of whisky toddy—a huge currant loaf carried by several men—home-made cheese and home-made biscuits—a song composed for the occasion and sung to the air of *The Wearin' of the Green*—these combined to render the allurements of the Paisley Block Ball high in the public estimation. And even if many of the participants found it difficult to carry on farm work when the rising sun put an end to the festivities, all looked forward with keen anticipation to the next October and a renewal of the event.

In many ways, though often indirectly, were the rural inhabitants influenced by the more highly-developed social life of the towns. In spite of the difficulties of transportation and communication there was not usually that separation between urban and rural dweller which might have been expected. During the early years of all settlements hamlet and village were part of the township, and even the rather dry work of governing the municipality supplied diversion and interest to many a farmer. Until 1842 the township meeting provided the usual means of carrying

[33]R. and K. Lizars: *In the Days of the Canada Company*. 1896. p. 57.
[34]Thomas Laidlaw quoted in Fred Williams: *Do You Know?*, in the Toronto *Mail and Empire*, October 7, 1932.

on such local affairs as were within the powers of municipal-
ities. The District Councils Act of 1841 instituted county
councils, which enabled men to establish a greater contact
with, and interest in their fellow-settlers in other parts of
the county. Town and village councils frequently drew
some of their most public-spirited members from the rural
inhabitants dwelling near by, for anyone living within two
miles of a settlement might be elected to its municipal
council. People took their politics very seriously in pioneer
days, and debate and argument frequently gave way to
personalities and fisticuffs, all of which added to the spice
of life even if it created hostility and enmity between
families.

Among the first commercialised amusements to become
available to all except the most remote settlers was the
circus. Such organisations were almost exclusively of
American origin and their advertisements were always
greatly exaggerated. Appearing first in the towns, they
were soon visiting every settled part of the province,
stopping usually at well-known taverns and putting on
their performance under canvas. It was unusual for them
to attempt any programme, the show consisting of a menagerie, some of the animals of which could perform. From
press advertisements a historian has been able to follow
the itineraries of several of these circuses, and to show
how generally accessible they were, though, of course, remote or "backwoods" settlers had sometimes to walk thirty
miles or more to see them:

"In 1828 one organisation, with a typical itinerary,
stopped at Ancaster on June 16th and 17th, Jones' Inn,
Dundas, the 18th, Summers' Inn, Nelson, the 19th, and
Smith's Inn, Trafalgar, on the 20th. . . . Another circus,
in 1836, after travelling through the Bathurst District,
stopped at Kingston, Bath and Belleville. On reaching
Toronto it remained three days, then went to Markham,
Crew's Tavern at Thornhill, Newmarket, and French's
Tavern on Yonge Street. It next proceeded west to Munro's
Inn and the Nelson Hotel. Thus in the Home District alone
there were nine performances within forty miles. These
examples are ample evidence that the public well patronised

these entertainments, and problems of communication did not make them inaccessible, except to the most isolated settlers."[35]

Many of these travelling shows were American in sentiment to an extent that is so frequently apparent in modern times in the motion pictures of Hollywood; but perhaps it was stretching the point a little to exhibit at a tavern near Ancaster a show including "the glorious victory over the British at New Orleans". No wonder a traveller considered it "a public insult".[36]

Theatrical entertainments, exhibitions and concerts of either local or itinerant talent, and somewhat more ambitious than those attempted at rural taverns, became increasingly common in the towns as the years passed, and they were patronised not only by the townspeople but by many inhabitants of the neighbouring districts. The lodges and other social organisations of the urban centres had also an influence on rural life. The National Societies of St. George, St. Patrick and St. Andrew, though organised in the towns, usually drew many members from the surrounding country; while Agricultural and Horticultural Societies often contained more rural than urban members, though the meetings were commonly held in a tavern at or near the town. The Public Exhibitions of schools and colleges, resembling in some respects the modern "commencement", attracted proud parents from all parts of the country, but they must have been rather monotonous affairs to the vast majority of the audience.

The rural inhabitants also took a prominent part in the militia parades, usually held on the King's birthday, and in such other holiday festivities as took place in the towns. Parade-day, which was held at convenient points in the rural districts as well as in the towns, consisted in a small amount of rather ludicrous drill followed by horse-races and other sporting activities, and frequently ending in fighting engendered by excessive drinking. Mrs. Jameson's description of parade-day in 1837 at Springfield (Erindale),

[35]J. J. Talman: *Social Life in Upper Canada, 1815-1840.* p. 134. (Unpublished). The paging is of the typewritten MS.
[36]Pickering, *op. cit.*, November 5, 1826.

GRAND MENAGERIE
By Permission of the Police.

Zebra.

Camel.

THIS Grand Collection of BEASTS, late of N.
Y. City Zoological Institute, will be exhibited
at COBOURG, on Friday, the 3d day of September
FOR ONE DAY ONLY, from 1 to 5 in the Day.

This collection comprises the largest and most general variety perhaps now travelling. The splendid
preservation of the Giraffe or Camel-Leopard, is
beautiful beyond description. Shortly after shipping
it died, the proprietor sustaining a loss of some $20,
000, but the animal being so extraordinarily fine and
full grown, it was thought proper it should be preserved in the most natural and perfect way, which renders this grand display of Natural Curiosities still
more attractive and complete.

The Keeper Mr. Shaffer, will enter the den of the
Lions, Tigers, &c. and fondle and handle them with
seeming ease; the perfectly cool and collected manner in which he enters and maintains throughout is
perhaps unequalled in the known world, not excepting the celebrated Van Amburg, who has astonished
all Europe in this most daring and unaccountable
manner.

The Proprietors would say to the Public that this
Exhibition is under the strictest discipline in all its
departments, and so entirely foreign in its nature
from all Circus or Mountebark Shows, that it meets
with most cordial and general approbation even in
the most refined and religious communities—from
the fact that it serves rather to instruct than traduce
the nobler qualities of the mind.

ADMITTANCE 1s. 3d. Children Half Price.
Cobourg, Sept. 18th, 1840.   2w48

From the *Cobourg Star*, August 20, 1840

MENAGERIE ADVERTISEMENT, 1840

The typical travelling circus of a century
ago is here described in characteristic
language

　　　　　　　　　Lady Alexander

GRAND MILITARY STEEPLECHASE, AT LONDON, C.W.,
MAY 9, 1843

A "TURN-OUT" OF THE 43RD LIGHT INFANTRY AT THE FALLS
OF NIAGARA, 1839
The various officers may be identified from the original print

in the County of Peel, may be considered typical of the 4th
of June celebration in the rural districts:

"On a rising ground above the river which ran gurgling
and sparkling through the green ravine beneath, the motley
troops, about three or four hundred men, were marshalled
—no, not marshalled, but scattered in a far more picturesque fashion hither and thither: a few log houses and
a saw-mill on the river bank, and a little wooden church
crowning the opposite height, formed the chief features of
the scene. The boundless forest spread all around us.

"A few men, well mounted and dressed as lancers, in
uniforms which were, however, anything but uniform,
flourished backwards on the green sward, to the manifest
peril of the spectators; themselves and their horses,
equally wild, disorderly, spirited, undisciplined: but this
was perfection compared with the infantry. Here there was
no uniformity attempted of dress, of appearance, of movement; a few had coats, others jackets; a greater number
had neither coats nor jackets, but appeared in their shirt-
sleeves, white or checked, or clean or dirty, in edifying
variety. Some wore hats, others caps, others their own
shaggy heads of hair. Some had firelocks; some had old
swords, suspended in belts, or stuck in their waistbands;
but the greater number shouldered sticks or umbrellas. Mrs.
M. told us that on a former parade-day she had heard
the word of command given thus—'Gentlemen with the
umbrellas, take ground to the right! Gentlemen with the
walking-sticks take ground to the left!'

"Now they ran after each other, elbowed and kicked each
other, straddled, stooped, chattered; and if the commanding
officer turned his back for a moment, very coolly sat down on
the bank to rest. Not to laugh was impossible, and defied
all power of face. Charles M. made himself hoarse with
shouting out orders which no one obeyed, except, perhaps,
two or three men in the front; and James, with his horsemen, flourished their lances, and galloped and capered and
curveted to admiration. . . .

"The parade-day ended in a drunken bout and a riot,
in which, as I was afterwards informed, the colonel had
been knocked down, and one or two serious and even fatal
accidents had occurred; but it was all taken so very lightly,

so very much as a thing of course in this half-civilised community that I soon ceased to think about the matter."[37]

Contemporary accounts of holiday celebrations show that excesses were expected, and that the authorities were surprised and quite obviously pleased when the day passed off without "bloody battles", fatal accidents, or other untoward incidents. In the rear concessions, particularly where the lumbering industry was prominent, serious trouble was frequently the result of holidays, fairs, or other occasions where rival elements in the population came together. Bytown and Richmond on the Ottawa were the scene of several such riots, and on many occasions clashes were very narrowly averted.

Elections, held both in the towns and at rural taverns or other convenient locations, usually lasted a week, and were often productive of riotous conditions, for men's political feelings and animosities were easily aroused at a time when life was hard, and kept inflamed by the incitements of the electoral practices of the times—open voting, intimidation and bribery, and, what was even worse, the intoxicants freely distributed at the expense of the candidates. An excellent description of a typical election week is given by Walter S. Herrington:

"Parliamentary elections today are very tame affairs compared with those of a century ago. The open vote afforded opportunities for exciting scenes that the rising generations know not of. The closing of the bars on election day has robbed the occasion of a good deal of romance. The actual voting contest is now limited to eight hours, from nine to five, and one might rest peacefully in a room adjoining a polling booth and not be aware that an election was in progress. It was all very different even fifty years ago. Whisky and the open vote were two very potent factors in keeping up the excitement. Instead of having several booths scattered throughout each township there was only one in the electoral district.

"The principal village in the district was generally selected, but sometimes the only booth was set up in a country tavern, especially if it was in a central location and the proprietor could pull enough political strings. A platform would be constructed out of rough boards and protected from the weather by a slanting roof. On Monday morning of election week the candidates and their henchmen would assemble in the vicinity of the platform, which was known as the husting. The electors would come pouring in from all parts of the electoral district. Each party would have its headquarters at a tavern or tent, or both, where the workers would lay their plans. The forenoon would be spent in listening to the orators of the day, and at one o'clock the polling would begin.

"It is easy to imagine what would happen to the doubtful voter when he arrived at the village. As the poll was kept open every day until Saturday night it is not quite so easy to picture the scene during the last day or two of a hot contest. Couriers with foaming horses were going and coming. Heated discussions frequently terminated in a rough-and-tumble fight in which a score or more participated. Drunken men reeled about the streets until carefully stowed away by their friends in a tent or stall in the tavern stable.

"If the inebriate had not yet polled his vote, his whilom friends would be more solicitous in the attention bestowed upon him. It not infrequently happened that the indifferent voter would purposely play into the hands of both parties. It was a golden opportunity for free lunches and whisky, and the longer he deferred the fateful hour when he was to announce to the returning officer the candidate of his choice the more difficult it was for him to choose. In his dilemma he would seek his solace in a little more whisky, and, in the end, perhaps vote for the wrong man. If unhappily he did make such a mistake, his political guardians never failed to call his attention to the error in a manner not likely to be soon forgotten. Such incidents were thereafter associated in the mind of the offended with the unpleasant recollections of the village pump or the nearest creek."[38]

Public holidays were infrequent in pioneer days, but there were more occasions when both townsmen and farmers would call it a day and hold a celebration in honour of

[38]Herrington: *Pioneer Life on the Bay of Quinté* (Lennox and Addington Historical Society, *Papers and Records*, Vol. VI, pp. 20-21).

some notable event. Among the most usual opportunities in war time for such festivities were the reports of victories over the enemy,—even if the news did arrive three or four months after the event!

Even in "the backwoods" any excuse for a celebration was promptly seized. Samuel Strickland describes an impromptu holiday in 1830 among the employees of the Canada Company near Goderich, then "far in the bush". The occasion was about two months after the death of George IV and the accession of William IV, a newspaper having just been received from the Old Country with the news. The squire read the proclamation to the assemblage, which included "everyone within ten miles"; then nine British cheers were given, the National Anthem was sung, "accompanied by the Goderich band composed of two fiddles and a tambourine", and everyone drank his Majesty's health from a pail of whisky with a tea-cup floating on the surface, "even the fair sex, on this propitious occasion, not disdaining to moisten their pretty lips with the beverage".

After the party had eaten and drunk everything in sight the band struck up *The Wind Shakes the Barley*, and country dances, French fours, and Scotch reels alternated on the level meadow; while those who did not dance amused themselves in ball-playing, pitch-and-hustle, and a variety of old English games. Even the "Yankee" millwright waxed enthusiastic: "I do declare", said he, "if this don't almost put me in mind of the 4th of July. Well, I vow if I don't feel quite loyal. Come, let us drink the old gentleman's health agin. I guess I feel as dry as a sand-bank after so much hollerin' ".[39]

Picnic parties, often combined with berrying or fishing, were more frequent when the hardships incident to the first years of settlement in the wilds were past. The experience of the Hon. William Hamilton Merritt, who, when a youth of sixteen, "went strawberrying with a nice party, lots of fine young girls, very delightful",[40] is typical of such activities. The "merry maple sugar making" was similarly an occasion of happiness among the young people, and

[39]Strickland, *op. cit.*, Vol. I, pp. 289-91.
[40]Journal of William Hamilton Merritt, July 8, 1809. (Coventry Papers, Public Archives of Canada.)

"sugar-eating bees" and other parties of a pleasant character welcomed the first signs of spring. In later years tea-meetings, fowl or oyster suppers, garden parties and strawberry festivals, usually in connection with church or school, were prominent events in every locality, and their popularity has remained undiminished to the present.

The pleasures of home life are, perhaps, better imagined than described. The evenings spent around the open fire, reading and sewing, cracking nuts or popping corn with the children, provided most satisfaction and enjoyment to those whose training and inclination enabled them to appreciate the better things of life. Among such people pleasures and amusements were undoubtedly most refined and of greatest permanence. A settler of education frequently spent most of his spare time writing letters to "the old folks at home", —letters which have so greatly enriched the annals of pioneer life in Canada. Many examples might also be given of the pleasure derived from the beautiful scenery, the luxuriant wild flowers, and the birds and animals, all so characteristic of the country. One settler was very enthusiastic about Canadian sunsets, and wrote in his diary:

"June 6, 1843,—Sunday—I witnessed on this evening a splendid and gorgeous sunset, far surpassing anything of the kind I had ever seen at home. Even a sunset in Italy, as a commissariat officer settled on a farm near me (who had served in that country) declared, could not be compared to it".[41]

Among those in whom the love of nature was a source of infinite pleasure none rank higher in their contribution to the literature of pioneer life than the Strickland sisters, Mrs. Catharine Traill and Mrs. Susanna Moodie. Settled near Lakefield at the foot of Katchawanoonk Lake, they were in the beautiful Kawartha Lakes district. Mrs. Moodie describes a long-anticipated trip northward to Stoney Lake in the summer of 1835. They started out early one beautiful morning and paddled up the Katchawanoonk to Young's Point, where dwelt the first Youngs, hunters and millers. Two of the sons were to conduct the Moodies through Clear Lake to Stoney Lake, long the jealously-guarded paradise of Handsome Jack and his Indian tribe.

[41] Quoted in *Letters from Canada*, 10th Edition, 1862, p. 26.

After a banquet at the Youngs, which for variety of game, fish and pies would have done credit to the famous epicure, Samuel Pepys, the party of six set out. Two beautiful new birch bark canoes had just been purchased from the Indians, and in these the expedition was soon approaching Sandy Point, then a ridge extending half way across Clear Lake. A stop was made here to pick some of the beautiful flowers which grew in profusion; then the canoes rounded the point and entered Stoney Lake, the first sight of which called forth exclamations of delight from Mrs. Moodie:

"Oh! what a magnificent scene of wild and lonely grandeur burst upon us as we swept round the little peninsula, and the whole majesty of Stoney Lake broke upon us at once, another Lake of the Thousand Isles in miniature, and in the heart of the wilderness! Imagine a large sheet of water, some twenty-five miles in length, taken up by islands of every size and shape, from the lofty naked rock of red granite to the rounded hill covered with oak trees to its summit, while others were level with the waters, and of a rich emerald green, only fringed with a growth of aquatic shrubs and flowers. Never did my eye rest on a more lovely or beautiful scene. Not a vestige of man or his works was there. The setting sun that cast such a gorgeous flood of light upon this exquisite panorama, bringing out some of these lofty islands in strong relief, and casting others into intense shade, shed no cheery beam upon church spire or cottage. We beheld the landscape, savage and grand in its primeval beauty".[42]

[42]Susanna Moodie: *Roughing It in the Bush*. 1852. Edition of 1923, pp. 320-337.

CHAPTER X

AMUSEMENT AND SOCIAL LIFE IN THE TOWNS

"Had I but plenty of money, money enough and to spare,
The house for me no doubt, were a house in the city-square;
Ah, such a life, such a life, as one leads at the window there!

Something to see by Bacchus, something to hear, at least!
There, the whole day long, one's life is a perfect feast;
While up at a villa one lives, I maintain it, no more than a beast.

Ere you open your eyes in the city, the blessed church bells begin:
No sooner the bells leave off than the diligence rattles in:
You get the pick of the news, and it costs you never a pin.

Bang-whang-whang goes the drum, *tootle-te-tootle* the fife.
Oh, a day in the city-square, there is no such pleasure in life!"

ROBERT BROWNING: *Up at a Villa—Down in the City*.

WITH the exception of the settlements along the Detroit, where the French predominated, and a few "backwoods" villages where American influence early made itself felt, the social life of the towns of Upper Canada during the first half century after the creation of the province was patterned after that of English towns of the same period. This was largely a result of the influence of the official class and the military, for the first towns, if they can be dignified by that appellation, were primarily garrison towns. Before entering upon a description of the social life of these first centres of population it is essential to describe their birth and early development.

When the Province of Upper Canada was established in 1791 the chief inhabitants were a few thousand United Empire Loyalists who had settled, during the preceding seven years, along the shores of the St. Lawrence, the Bay of Quinté, the head of Lake Ontario, and the Niagara and Detroit Rivers. The settlement at Detroit had at that time about 2,000 inhabitants, mostly French, and it was the largest town in the province. When it was surrendered to the United States in 1796 its population decreased from 2,200 to 500 owing to the exodus of British and French Loyalists to the other side of the Detroit, where they could remain under British rule. Fort Malden (Amherstburg) was thereupon established to replace Detroit for military purposes, while Sandwich was laid out to accommodate many of the civilians.

Kingston, Niagara and York had each a share in the early administration of the government of Upper Canada, and each was a garrison town. While, however, Kingston and Niagara had been military and naval posts for many years, the town of York was not founded until 1793. In 1794 Kingston had a population of 345, while a lesser number of people lived at Niagara and York, the garrison comprising most of the inhabitants in every case. The growth of these settlements was very slow for many years, York increasing from 336 in 1801 to 577 in 1809, and having a population of only 1,240 in 1820.

By 1823 the population of Upper Canada had increased to about 130,000, but the largest town was Kingston with 2,336 inhabitants. At the end of the first quarter of the century the chief towns and villages of Upper Canada were Cornwall, Prescott, Brockville and Gananoque on the St. Lawrence; Perth and Richmond in the Ottawa Valley; Kingston, Bath, Napanee and Hallowell (Picton) in the Bay of Quinté district; Belleville, Cobourg, Port Hope and York along the shores of Lake Ontario; Hamilton, Dundas and Ancaster at the head of the lake; Grimsby, St. Catharines, Niagara, Queenston, Chippawa and Fort Erie in the Niagara district; St. Thomas, Vittoria, Burford, Woodstock and Shade's Mills (Galt) in the inland districts northward from Lake Erie; and Chatham, Sandwich and Amherstburg in the west. Many of these settlements were very small "backwoods" villages, but they were centres of trade for large areas surrounding them, and in most cases had post offices to add to their importance. The present large cities of Ottawa and London, and many a smaller one, had not even been founded in 1825.

The turning-point in the growth of population occurred in the late twenties, when immigration on a large scale resulted in a great development of the towns. York, for example, comprised only 1,817 people in 1827, but by 1833 it had a population of 6,094, and was to become the city of Toronto in the following year. In 1837 Cobourg had a population of 1,653, while thirteen years earlier it had num-

THE CITY HALL AT BROADWAY AND PARK ROW, NEW YORK
CITY, 1837

The New York bus of a century ago may be seen in the foreground

From *London Interiors.* 1842

THE STOCK EXCHANGE, LONDON, ENGLAND, IN 1840

These reproductions of steel engravings illustrate contemporary
conditions in New York and London

From the *Illustrated London News*, April 4, 1868

MR. AND MRS. DISRAELI'S ASSEMBLY AT THE NEW FOREIGN
OFFICE, LONDON, 1868

Reproduced by Courtesy of Miss Ivy Romain, who appears at the lower right.

FANCY DRESS BALL IN AID OF THE PROTESTANT ORPHANS'
HOME, TORONTO

The old Music Hall, Adelaide and Church Streets, April 19, 1870

bered only about 100; Brockville had 1,130 inhabitants in
1830, and Brantford was surveyed into village lots during
the same year. St. Thomas, London and Bytown (Ottawa)
were rapidly becoming thriving towns. An exception to
the general development was provided by the slow growth
of the western villages, Chatham, Amherstburg, Sandwich
and Richmond (Windsor), none of which had a population
of more than a few hundred until the late forties.

In describing the social life of the towns, York will
serve as an example of the development of the official and
garrison towns, of which Kingston and Niagara were the
chief others; and Cobourg will provide an illustration of the
growth of social life in settlements of lesser rank. What
was taking place in York and Cobourg may be presumed to
have been characteristic, with local variations, of the other
towns along "the front"; while social life in the later-
settled "backwoods" villages was similar, due allowance
being made for their remoteness and comparative inac-
cessibility. Many other towns will, however, be mentioned
from time to time.

At Kingston, Niagara and York, and to a lesser extent
at Amherstburg, the presence of government officials,
officers of the army and navy, and other "gentlemen", gave
a higher tone to social life than was usually to be found
elsewhere during the early period of settlement. The
amusements of that day depended largely upon individual
effort, or upon arrangements made by small groups of social
equals. Both women and men were fond of visiting their
friends and associates, and such calls, especially on New
Year's Day, were of a much more formal nature than visits
in the rural districts, where the elements of spontaneity
and surprise predominated in the interchange of civilities.

Class distinctions were very rigid in early days, and
the fashionable society of these first towns was restricted
to a comparatively small section of the population. The
military and civilians alike were fond of horse-racing and
field sports, fishing and sailing, football and cricket in
summer, and of skating and carrioling in winter; while
at all seasons dancing, chess, whist, wine and conversation
served to while away the time.

Mrs. Simcoe gives some account of these activities in

her diary. While at Niagara she wrote: "We play at whist
every evening. Colonel Simcoe is so occupied during the
day with business that it is a relaxation. I have not lost
one rubber since the 28th of November. We usually play
four every evening."[1] Two weeks later she notes: "Mrs.
Macaulay gave me an account of a subscription ball she was
at, which is to be held in the town of Niagara every fortnight during the winter. There were fourteen couples, a
great display of gauze, feathers and velvet, the room
lighted by wax candles, and there was a supper as well as
tea."[2] In 1796 she refers to a ball at her house where "we
danced eighteen couple and sat down to supper seventy-
six".[3] Military bands supplied the music at these official
social functions, and at all fashionable balls or "assemblies"
in the garrison towns full evening or military dress was
worn.

The first notice with reference to public dances in York
occurs in the *Gazette* of December 8, 1798, where it is
announced that a meeting of "the gentlemen of the town
and the garrison" will be held at Miles' Hotel to arrange
for the York assemblies.[4] The earliest of these events
of which we have an intimate account took place at Frank's
Hotel in 1814. The original manuscript of the arrangements informs us that "at a meeting of the gentlemen of
York, subscribers to the assemblies, Stephen Jarvis and
George Ridout, Esquires, were appointed managers for the
season, the sum to be paid by each subscriber to be three
pounds, Halifax currency. . . . First dance on St. Andrew's night, dancing to begin at half-past eight o'clock.
The dresses worn by the ladies are called "chaste and
elegant"; while a private letter gives us the interesting
information that "one lady of great loveliness" wore black
lace over an underskirt of crimson, with an artificial rose
in her waist and hair.[5] A few prominent merchants usually
joined the government officials and the officers of the garrison in these dances.

A notable ball took place at Niagara in 1807, on the

[1]*Diary of Mrs. John Graves Simcoe*, December 31, 1792.
[2]*Ibid.*, January 15, 1793.   [3]*Ibid.*, June 4, 1796.
[4]York *Upper Canada Gazette*, December 8, 1798.
[5]See John Ross Robertson: *Landmarks of Toronto.* 1894-1914. Vol. I,
   p. 498.

evening of the King's Birthday, June 4th. It provided a
fitting climax to the annual militia parade-day, and appears
to have been arranged on a grander scale than any held
previously in Upper Canada. The *Gazette* contained a
full account of it:

"His Excellency Lieut.-Governor Gore, having previously announced his intention of celebrating his Majesty's
birthday at this place, arrived with Mrs. Gore and suite
early on Tuesday morning.

"On Wednesday, the 3rd, a numerous and splendid
assemblage of ladies from various and distant parts of
the district were presented to Mrs. Gore, who received them
with all that ease and politeness which inspires confidence,
and for which she is so universally distinguished and admired.

"The ball commenced at 8 o'clock in the Council House,
which was fitted up and lighted in an elegant manner,
with an orchestra of the charming band of the 41st Regiment. A temporary building was also erected, eighty feet
in length and of sufficient width for two sets of tables to
accommodate 200 persons at supper, and the building was
connected with the dancing-room by a covered way.

"Mrs. Gore and the Honourable Robert Hamilton led off
the first dance, and about fifty couple of spirited dancers
occupied the floor till one o'clock, when they retired into
the supper-room where a most sumptuous entertainment,
served up with true English elegance, was provided. Everything rare and good was found on the hospitable board, and
the wines of Champagne and Burgundy served to recruit
the exhausted spirits and called for a renewal of the dance,
which was kept up till after daylight, when the company
separated, highly satisfied with their princely entertainment.

"On the whole the birthday was celebrated with a splendour and magnificence hitherto unknown in this country."[6]

People frequently travelled long distances to be present
at the social gatherings of the *élite*. Mrs. Anna Jameson
wrote on May 20, 1837: "Last night a ball at the govern-
ment-house, to which people came from a distance of fifty—
a hundred—two hundred miles—which is nothing to signify

[6]*York Gazette*, June 13, 1807.

here. There were very pretty girls, and very nice dancing". The wealthier classes usually insisted on the best of music at their assemblies, and if the Paul Whiteman or Vincent Lopez of the day was not available the deficiency was quickly noticed; Mrs. Jameson, for example, referring to the same ball, observed that "we had all too much reason to lament the loss of the band of the 66th Regiment, which left us a few weeks ago—to my sorrow".[7]

It was not easy to be up-to-the-minute in dance steps when square and fancy dancing was in vogue. Quadrilles and schottisches were usual at the fashionable balls at Government House on such occasions as the opening of legislature; while dancing schools endeavoured in addition to insure proficiency in "Zodiac's New Pantomime, Scotch Sling, Children's Hornpipes, the 6th and 4th Hanoverian Waltzes, De la Cour Minuet walked in six corners, and Country Dances".[8]

In some localities the character of the inhabitants, apart altogether from the influence of the officers of the garrison or the officials of the government, was the factor which led to the development of a gay and refined social life. In Cobourg, for example, sleighing parties, afternoon teas and informal dances were prominent in the early twenties among a number of aristocratic families of half-pay officers and other "genteel" settlers. A few years later the gentlemen settlers in the Newcastle District were holding "Bachelor's Balls" in Cobourg and Peterborough, and the select society in which they moved was said to be "the most brilliant and polished in Canada".[9]

Even backwoodsmen like John Langton and Thomas Need arrayed themselves in full dress and drove thirty or forty miles to attend these dances. In 1833 Need travelled from Peterborough to Cobourg by sleigh to attend a ball,

[7]Anna Jameson: *Winter Studies and Summer Rambles in Canada.* 1838. Vol. I, p. 292. One of the most celebrated fancy-dress balls in the early days of York was one held in 1827 in the assembly room of Frank's Hotel; this was given jointly by John Galt, Commissioner of the the Canada Company, and Lady Mary Willis, wife of Mr. Justice Willis. A full description of the event may be found in Henry Scadding: *Toronto of Old.* 1873. pp. 111-12.

[8]Kingston *Upper Canada Herald,* August 2, 1825.

[9]Patrick Shirreff: *A Tour through North America.* 1835. p. 123.

and was "amply repaid for the trouble by a lively dance, good music, and excellent supper. The ladies of Upper Canada, like their sisters of the Northern States, are strikingly handsome in early youth, and pleasing and natural in their manners: about thirty couple of dancers assembled, who kept up the ball until nearly daylight".[10] In February, 1836, he wrote in his journal: "On the 29th, (being leap year), I mounted my sleigh and drove along the new road, to assist at a ball given by the bachelors of the district at Peterborough. 'A ball in the Bush!' I think I hear my fair partners of former days exclaim; but let me assure them that the bachelors of our district are not at all to be despised, and that the 'rank and fashion' of the neighbourhood comprised nearly 200 persons."[11]

A similar social life flourished at other points where aristocratic settlers were to be found in sufficient numbers. Near Woodstock Mrs. Jameson found the society "particularly good; several gentlemen of family, superior education, and large capital, (among whom is the brother of an English and the son of an Irish peer, a colonel and a major in the army), have made very extensive purchases of land and their estates are in flourishing progress".[12] She observed, however, an unfortunate lack of social intercourse in many other parts of Upper Canada, a condition which bore most heavily upon the women. Referring to London she noted that "here, as everywhere else, I find the women of the better class lamenting over the want of all society, except of the lowest grade in manners and morals. For those who have recently emigrated, and are settled more in the interior, there is absolutely no social intercourse whatever".[13]

The wayside tavern and the town inn were centres of the social life of the community to an extent which is hard to realise in modern times. The inn, like the mill, formed the nucleus around which developed many a village; and not infrequently the tavern-keeper was the best-known and most popular man in the district. The first church services and circuses were held at taverns, as well as dances, ban-

---

[10]Thomas Need: *Six Years in the Bush*. 1838. p. 47.
[11]*Ibid.*, p. 116.
[12]Jameson, *op. cit.*, Vol. II, p. 124.
[13]*Ibid.*, Vol. II, pp. 146-8.

quets, and the meetings of Agricultural Societies, lodges
and other social organisations. Those who, like Sir John
Falstaff, enjoyed taking their ease at their inn had plenty
of choice in a day of taverns. In addition to the usual
pleasures of eating, drinking and smoking, there was evident a spirit of conviviality in many a hostelry. The roaring
logs of the winter fireplace added zest to the discussion
of clergy reserves, bad roads, and European news three
months old.

A type of amusement in which many an early traveller
participated was the pleasure created in stage-coach hos-
telries when the guests gathered around the open fire in
the living-room and related their experiences of travel and
adventure. Mine host of the inn was always ready to develop any subject of interest, for the hotel-keeper was in
close touch with everything that affected the life of the
community, and was first informed of the news from distant parts. Much of this sociability and entertainment disappeared when coaching days came to an end, and the importance of the inn was still further diminished by the
speedy travel made possible by the motor-car; but, though
the growth of centres of population has removed the intimate touch between host and guest, the hotel remains
much more than "a house of public entertainment",[14] for
it is the meeting-place of conventions, clubs and banquets,
and the social centre for balls, bridges and receptions.

Lodges and fraternal societies played a very important
part in early social life, especially after settlements had
grown into thriving communities. The first Masonic Lodge
in Canada was formed among the members of the garrison
at Halifax in 1749, and the first in Upper Canada at Niagara
in 1793. Among other fraternal organisations were the
Saints and the Orangemen, a celebration of the latter
association being recorded in the press of York in 1822.[15]

The National Societies of St. Patrick, St. George and St.

[14]A "house of entertainment" was an inn without a tavern license.
The difference was more imaginary than real, however, for
Joseph Pickering observed (*Inquiries of an Emigrant*, November 4, 1826) that one was served whisky with his meals, but
the law was superficially observed by charging only for the
food, though the price was always made high enough to include the drink!
[15]*York Gazette*, July 18, 1822.

Andrew were long important in the social life of the towns. These organisations date from the early years of the province, for they were prominent in Niagara in the seventeen-nineties. A St. Andrew's Dinner, for example, was held there on November 30, 1799, the Hon. Robert Hamilton entertaining thirty Scotchmen and a few of other nationalities on that occasion. A report of the event says that it was considered that "no dinner on any occasion has been given in the Canadas equal to Mr. Hamilton's".[16] In some instances the Societies were early established but were intermittent in their activities, so that it is not always easy to trace their inauguration. After the first quarter of the nineteenth century the organisations were more common. In the early twenties there was a St. George's Society in York, while in the thirties and forties some or all of the national societies were to be found in Cobourg, Bytown, Kingston, and numerous other towns. At first all meetings were held in taverns, but in later days many societies had club-rooms of their own.

It was natural that such organisations should be formed at a time when many of the inhabitants of the province had come but recently from the Old Land. The feeling of nationality was strong, and the memories of former days amid very different surroundings were fondly treasured. The English, Irish and Scottish societies were at the height of their popularity in the late fifties and early sixties, when many of the first settlers of importance were still living, and before the growth of national feeling in Canada had received a strong impetus as a result of the Fenian Raids and the Confederation movement. A description of the activities of the societies in Cobourg during this period may be assumed to be characteristic of the organisations.

On April 23, 1864, the members of the St. George's Society combined the celebration of St. George's Day with that of the 300th anniversary of the birth of Shakespeare. An outdoor demonstration during the day was prevented by heavy rains, but at 7 p.m. about 150 men, including representatives of the other national societies, sat down to a dinner of which it is said in the press that "the Roast Beef of Old England occupied prominent places on the table,

[16]Niagara *Canada Constellation*, December 7, 1799.

which was loaded with all that the eye could fancy or the palate suggest". No less than twelve toasts were proposed by the chairman and each was responded to by one or more speakers. Between toasts many a good old song was sung, among them *The Fine Old English Gentleman, When I a-Courting Went, Old King Cole,* and *The Laird o' Cockpen.* As midnight approached, the proceedings waxed Shakespearian when the Principal of the Grammar School gave an excellent characterisation of Sir John Falstaff, choosing the ever-popular humorous scenes from the second act of the first part of Shakespeare's greatest historical play, *King Henry the Fourth.* The meeting was thus concluded in great merriment, and the happy company departed for their homes with reluctance.[17]

The St. Andrew's Society similarly celebrated the anniversary of its patron saint on November the 30th of each year. In 1862 a grand dinner was held in Cobourg, and the speech-making and singing thereafter occupied several hours, among the most popular songs being *The Scottish Thistle, Wha wad na fecht for Charlie, The Miller of Fife, Scotland Yet,* and the inevitable *Laird o'Cockpen.* After the last regular toast the President left the chair, and the party continued the round of toast, speech, song and chorus until the wee sma' hours o' morn.[18]

A particularly elaborate procession was characteristic of the St. Patrick's Day celebration. Headed by the Chief Marshall, the Union Jack and a brass band, the members, adorned with their gay regalia, paraded the streets of the town on March 17, 1862, carrying the insignia of the order, flags, battle-axes and wands. They proceeded to church, where the priest delivered an address on the life of St. Patrick; whereupon the members paraded back to the Globe Hotel and listened to speeches by the officials of the Society, after which the proceedings came to a close with cheers for Auld Ireland, Canada, and the Queen. The *Cobourg Sentinel* comments upon "the respectable and orderly manner" in which the celebration was conducted: "Nothing but good feeling, sobriety, order and decorum reigned throughout the whole day's proceedings, and Irishmen in this

[17]See the *Cobourg Sentinel*, April 30, 1864.
[18]*Ibid.*, December 6, 1862.

neighbourhood may long remember and feel proud of the manner in which St Patrick's Day was celebrated in Cobourg in 1862."[19]

It was usual for inhabitants of the rural districts to join their brethren in the towns in the activities of the national societies. Meetings were usually held once a month, and on special occasions balls and picnics were arranged which added not a little to the social life of the community. While the feeling of nationality remained very strong it was not unusual for fights and brawls to result from these activities, though such regrettable occurrences were more characteristic of events of a more partisan nature, such as Orangemen's "walks". In the seventies and eighties, however, so cordial were their relations that it was customary in Cobourg for the members of the three national societies to join in honouring each patron saint in turn by marching in a body to the church named by the Society directly concerned in the anniversary.

The national societies have continued to the present in some towns, the St. George's Society of Toronto, for example, having celebrated the anniversary in 1932 by holding the 98th annual dinner. But the survivals, if the same in name, are more in the nature of a "high festival of once a year", and have retained but little of the spirit of their predecessors of the later pioneer period; for the sense of original nationality decreased after the passing of the first generations, and there gradually developed a national feeling distinctly Canadian. There was, too, another circumstance which, though much less important, influenced in varying degrees all organisations in which banquets formed a prominent part: this was the changing attitude towards the free use of wines and liquors. As drinking in public came to be considered a vice rather than an accepted custom some men lost interest in such gatherings; for, whatever may be one's opinion concerning the use of intoxicants, there is no doubt that their effect at such meetings was to induce conviviality and create merriment, even if it was somewhat artificial, and, if judged by modern standards, not infrequently lacking in refinement.

Perhaps the most important mutual-benefit organisation

[19]*Ibid.*, March 22, 1862.

was that of the fire-fighters. At first everyone in the community was expected to join in such activities,—in fact it
was his own interest to do so in a day when wooden buildings predominated, and when many a settlement was almost obliterated by fire. As fire brigades were soon to become prominent in the life of the town, some account of
their development will not be out of place here. A regulation was in force in York in 1800 requiring that each householder must have a ladder leading from the ground to the
roof of his house, and another placed on the roof as an
approach to the chimney.[20] In December, 1802, Governor
Russell presented a fire engine to the town, and as an ex-
pression of their gratitude the citizens built a firehall by
subscription.   In the eighteen-twenties it was the law in
York that each householder must keep two leathern buckets
hanging in a conspicuous place in front of his home. The
only bell in the town was in St. James' Church, and upon an
alarm of fire a double row of citizens was formed from the
burning building to the Bay, or the nearest cistern or
pump, and along one line passed buckets of water, while the
empties returned along the other.   Among regulations
adopted in York was one stating that fire wardens should
have "a white handkerchief on the left arm, above the
elbow, as a distinguishing badge of authority", and anyone
who did not obey their orders might be fined from twenty
to forty shillings.[21]

In 1826 the first fire department was organised in York,
and among the members of this purely voluntary association were "some of the most respectable merchants and
tradesmen of the town".   There were Fire-engine and
Hook-and-Ladder companies, each with a full quota of
officers.[22] In a similar manner fire-fighters' organisations
developed in other localities, and in many instances remained entirely voluntary societies until almost the end
of the century. The members carried out their duties without remuneration, the social activities of the company being the chief attraction, though in some towns fire-fighters
were exempt from poll tax, from militia duty in peace time,

[20]Ladders may be seen on the roofs of the houses of the garrison
    at York in the illustration facing page 105.
[21]York *U. E. Loyalist*, January 26, 1827.
[22][W. L. Mackenzie's] *New Almanac for the Canadian True Blues.*
    1834. p. 11.

ENGINE OF THE TORONTO FIRE BRIGADE, 1837

Effectively used in December, 1837, when Peter Matthews' rebels set fire to the Don Bridge

John Ross Robertson Collection   From an Old Print

ROSSIN HOUSE FIRE, TORONTO, NOVEMBER, 1862

A centre of social life for a century; 1833—British Coffee House; 1855-7—Rossin House, rebuilt in 1863; 1909—Prince George Hotel

FIREMEN'S ARCH IN COBOURG IN THE SEVENTIES

A Fire-Fighters' Meet—Rochester, Port Hope, Belleville and Oshawa

COBOURG FIREMEN AND PARADE MACHINE IN THE SEVENTIES

Volunteer fire brigades long played an important part in social life. In the rear is Victoria Hall, opened in 1860 by the Prince of Wales

and from serving in the capacity of constable, juryman, or in any other office.

There was a spirit of camaraderie in the firemen's organisations that led to much wholesome rivalry between the companies of a brigade, and to competitions sometimes even international in scope. The Cobourg firemen, for example, frequently travelled to Kingston, Peterborough, Brantford and Rochester to engage in meets with other brigades, and to enjoy a social "good time" with them. In one town at least a certain spirit of bravado developed within the firemen's organisations, for it is more than hinted that some of the many incendiary fires in Cobourg in the sixties and seventies were started by firemen to provide excitement and to enable one company, which knew of the certainty of the fire before it occurred, to arrive upon the scene before its rivals.[23] It appears, however, that such activities were restricted to old, unused buildings; nor does the questionable conduct of individuals in any way detract from the public spirit and self-sacrifice which was characteristic of fire-fighters in Cobourg as elsewhere.

There was an annual festival and parade-day for the firemen of Cobourg, when the entire brigade of some 250 men marched in full uniform, and each company was inspected by the municipal council and received the cheers of its admiring friends. Fire engines and other equipment were polished to perfection for the occasion, and companies sometimes even had parade machines valued at $1500 or more, and without practical utility apart from the admiration which their display engendered! A grand supper and ball concluded the festival, and it was for many citizens the social event of the season. Among other activities of firemen's organisations were smaller dances, social evenings, picnics, and friendly calls upon the fire-fighters of neighbouring towns; there were occasions, too, when a minstrel show or some other theatrical venture would be undertaken by the members of the brigade.

The amusement and social intercourse based upon firemen's organisations came to an end with changing con-

[23]See E. C. Guillet: *Cobourg*, in the *Cobourg Sentinel-Star*, August 14, 1930. For many valuable reminiscences with reference to the history of Cobourg the writer is indebted to Postmaster Andrew Hewson.

ditions. As fire-fighting apparatus developed in efficiency, and centres of population increased in size, a more permanently-reliable force of firemen became necessary. In most towns and villages the fire department now receives some remuneration, and has lost most of its voluntary character; while in the cities fire-fighting has become a full-time occupation second to none in importance among civic employees.

Upper Canada had many citizens of the calibre of John Evelyn, the English diarist of the seventeenth century, who wrote on December 2, 1673, after a day of benevolent and charitable activities: "It was one of the best daies I ever spent in my life." Among associations of a philanthropic nature was the Stranger's Friend Society, established in York in 1822 for the reception and relief of immigrants. Citizens of Cobourg, Kingston and other ports frequently welcomed new arrivals, and provided supplies, paid hospital expenses, and in many other ways brightened what was often a very sad time. Of a similar nature were religious organisations such as the Society for Promoting Christian Knowledge, and the British and Foreign Bible Society, which had numerous branches in Upper Canada. A little over a century ago the first Temperance Societies began to be a strong force for good, and in the eighteen-thirties there was a parent organisation in Toronto called the Upper Canada Temperance Society.

Prominent among associations which aimed at mutual improvement was the Mechanics' Institute. Joseph Bates, who had had experience in such societies in London, England, appears to have established the first in Upper Canada at York in 1831. Four years later this organisation was granted £200 by the government to aid in the establishment of a library and the conduct of educational classes and weekly lectures. In York a membership fee of 5s. per year was charged, and many men of importance gave their time to provide an opportunity for improvement among "the middle classes, working men and intelligent mechanics",[24] who, in a day of social exclusiveness, had little chance to develop intellectually and culturally.

It was frequently difficult to maintain interest in the Institutes. When Mrs. Jameson visited Toronto in 1837 she

[24]*Cobourg Sentinel*, January 17, 1863.

found that there was a commercial news-room, but that
this was "absolutely the only place of assembly or amusement, except the taverns and low drinking-houses. An
attempt has been made to found a Mechanics' Institute and
a literary club; but as yet they create little interest, and are
very ill supported".[25] In later years, however, the Institute
in Toronto was more successful, and, in addition to its regular activities, there were occasional exhibitions of fine and
decorative arts, designing, fancywork, and other crafts.
In 1883 the Toronto Mechanics' Institute came to an end,
its building on Church Street becoming a public library.

Mechanics' Institutes became very numerous in Upper
Canada in the fifties and sixties, even small villages frequently having organisations. It was found in many localities that the societies languished from the lack of support
of those whom they were formed to benefit; but upon the
whole they were for half a century a very valuable contribution towards the provision of a broader life for tradesmen and labourers. They were conducted under the direction of officers chosen from among those in the community
—frequently the leaders in business and professional life—
who interested themselves in the organisation. The Institutes were eventually supplanted in their library facilities through the operation of the Free Libraries Act of
1882; while their social and recreational activities were
undertaken by the Canadian Institute, and, later, by the
Young Men's Christian Association.

Many of the public libraries of the province have consequently grown out of the library of the local Mechanics'
Institute. There were a few, however, of earlier origin.
The first in Upper Canada was established at Niagara in
1800, and was supported by private subscription. A few
of the wealthier early inhabitants had private libraries,
and frequently allowed their books to pass around among
their friends. In the early thirties there were good public
libraries at Niagara, York, Kingston and Cobourg.

Among other associations of an educational nature were
literary, debating and oratorical societies. One of the
earliest of these organisations was formed in 1831 at York
by Archdeacon Strachan; a few years later similar societies

[25]Jameson, *op. cit.*, Vol. I, pp. 273-4.

were in operation in many other towns. All such associations provided social intercourse and relieved the monotony of life, as well as developing the individual; they were, too, a means of creating a democratic feeling of social and political equality.

At the time of the opening of the War of 1812, when feeling against the United States was running high, the Loyal and Patriotic Society was formed in York, and grants of money were made to many whose services merited reward. Medals were struck in London to be given out to those worthy of them, but so difficult was the task of selection that the Society came to an end before any were distributed, and the medals were all destroyed! The British Constitutional Society was another ephemeral organisation of early times, as was also the Upper Canada Agricultural and Commercial Society, which held meetings in York previous to 1808 when it was dissolved from lack of support. Thirty-three years later Sir Richard Bonnycastle visited Toronto and learned that there had been "various attempts to get up respectable races, to establish a theatre, and a winter assembly for dancing", but without much success; he also states that a national Literary and Philosophical Society was organised with difficulty, but lasted only about a year.[26]

While learned societies received but scant support, the advancement of music was no greater. In 1837 Mrs. Jameson found that Archdeacon Strachan was collecting subscriptions to provide a £1000 organ for St. James' Church in Toronto, and that "an intelligent musician" had trained a good choir; but she learned that the conductor had received so little encouragement "that he is at this moment preparing to go to the United States".[27]

In the thirties and forties the first brass bands began to be organised among the citizens of some of the more progressive towns. These developed in imitation of the regimental bands in the garrison towns, and provided an important outlet for musical ability. The National Societies, and other organisations which frequently held parades, usually aided in the financial support of the town band. As

[26]Sir Richard Bonnycastle: *The Canadas in 1841.* 1842. Vol. I, p. 168.
[27]Jameson, *op. cit.,* Vol. I, p. 274.

time passed, interest in higher types of music increased, and concerts in which famous musicians supplied the entertainment were occasionally held in the larger towns.

There were many progressive citizens interested in agriculture and horticulture. Under the auspices of Agricultural Societies local exhibitions were early held in almost every settled part of Upper Canada. Queenston had a fair previous to 1800, and there were others during the first quarter of the new century, especially after the War of 1812. The legislation of 1820 aiding the societies financially proved a great impetus to the establishment of fairs and exhibitions, and they were held twice a year, during the early twenties or before, at York, Cobourg and Port Hope. Horse-races and ploughing matches were early characteristic of the fairs, of which that in the autumn was the more important because the crops were then ready for exhibition. In some cases the fair of the county society was held alternately in the chief villages, and there were also others sponsored by township or village agricultural societies.

In 1846 the Agricultural Association of Upper Canada was formed, and the first Provincial Exhibition was held in Toronto the same year. During the next twelve years the fair alternated among the chief towns of the province, being held on two occasions in Hamilton, Cobourg, Toronto and Kingston, while Niagara, Brockville, London and Brantford were the locale of the exhibition once each. The attendance of the Lieutenant-Governor added social prestige to the Provincial Exhibition, and he was the *raison d'être* of numerous fashionable events, which usually included a levee after a triumphal procession through the streets in the carriages of the aristocracy.

At the middle of the century and afterwards, Horticultural Societies were formed in many towns, and the exhibitions which they held provided an incentive to the introduction and proper culture of flowers and fruit. In Cobourg it was customary to close the exhibition with a reception and promenade in Victoria Hall. In later years Horticultural Societies usually co-operated with the agricultural organisations in holding a combined fall fair, an event which still thrives in many centres of population throughout the province.

Private schools and colleges were an important factor in elevating and broadening the social life of some towns. Upper Canada College in York, and Upper Canada Academy, later Victoria College, in Cobourg, are examples of schools which developed with the towns in which they were established. Through the agency of public lectures, receptions, conversaziones and balls they permeated the intellectual and social life of the district.

A prominent feature in such schools was the Annual Examination and Exhibition, an event in some measure similar to the modern Commencement which has recently become usual in public as well as private schools. The Public Examination of the Upper Canada Academy in April, 1840, occupied three days, and attracted some spectators from a distance, though many who would have attended were unable to do so because of the bad roads. The attendance was largest in the evenings, and particularly on the last evening. The examination of each day opened with prayer and sacred music, and "the exercises were agreeably and judiciously interspersed and diversified with music, vocal and instrumental, by the Preceptress and some of the young ladies, and with declamation and dialogues by some of the male students". During the day, classes were examined in the subjects of study; while essays and speeches somewhat more generally interesting filled the evening session. Among the "original compositions" read by young ladies was one considered very appropriate at the time, "The Pernicious Effects of Novel Reading", which, no doubt, induced many in the audience to read novels.

The third day of the Examination was known as the Annual Exhibition, and "before the hour of commencement the chapel was crowded to excess, and great difficulty was experienced in conducting the young ladies from the entrance to the seats assigned to them. Nothing was to be seen but a mass of moving heads, and fears were entertained that order could not be preserved, which, however, was happily not the case". During this session there were no less than twenty addresses, dialogues, declamations or orations on subjects of every type and variety; some spoke in English, while others showed their ability in Latin, Greek, French or Hebrew. A Valedictory Address by a clever student, and a concluding speech by the Principal, formed a fitting climax to such a display of erudition.[28]

It may be assumed that few people attended the Exhibitions of schools unless they were directly interested in students in attendance; and, even though family pride was gratified by their evident progress in education, yet the lengthy and learned examination must have been, upon the whole, a monotonous proceeding to a large majority of the audience.

Lectures, dramatic readings and the display of oratorical ability were popular forms of entertainment in many localities.   Such events were frequently arranged under the auspices of churches, literary societies or colleges.   The Literary Association of Victoria College sponsored the appearance in Cobourg in 1864 of Vandenhoff, advertised as "the celebrated dramatic reader and entertainer".   Tickets for this "rare treat" were only 25 cents, and the front seats were reserved "for ladies and the gentlemen accompanying them".[29]   In 1863 J. H. Siddons, professor of elocution, and his daughter, Fanny Kemble Siddons, were brought to Cobourg by the Mechanics' Institute, and gave two performances consisting of readings, songs and music. Such was the popularity of this well-known theatrical family that some of the citizens organised a complimentary concert and reception in their honour.

Among college activities of a non-academic nature were public receptions or *soirées,* attended chiefly by the intellectually and socially *élite.*   Accompanying the Annual Convocation of Victoria College in 1863 was an event new to Cobourg—a conversazione.   This proved very popular, and it was consequently repeated in 1864 and succeeding years. A press account of the event says that it was "not very much like the model evening parties with which we are acquainted, for it apparently partakes of them all to some extent, and makes up in the variety of the scene what is wanting in life and enthusiasm".   The Quadrille Band was

[28]See Letter of the Rev. John Manly in the *Christian Guardian,* April 29, 1840; or Nathanael Burwash: *History of Victoria College.* 1927. pp. 48-53.   In Henry Scadding: *Toronto of Old.* 1873. pp. 157-9, may be found the details of similar proceedings at the 1819 examinations of the York Grammar School.
[29]*Cobourg World,* November 25, 1864.

in attendance and "performed some beautiful pieces, including polkas, waltzes, galops and orchestral selections, very agreeable to listen to. . . . The ladies turned out in all the gay plumage this season affords, their gorgeous opera cloaks and brilliant flowing costumes lending an elfin charm to the scene, which became more varied and intensified as they glided along the spacious avenues allotted for promenading. The beauty, fashion and intelligence of our locality were better represented than ever we remember to have witnessed before".

Those who had been accustomed to the dance found the promenade a little aggravating. The editor of the *Cobourg Sentinel* noted that "when we glanced along the extended lines of beaming countenances and sparkling eyes which filled Victoria Hall on Wednesday evening we were reminded of the remark of a traveller, 'that Cobourg could boast of more beautiful women than any town he had visited in Canada' "; but while the music was found to be "enlivening to march to when a blooming nymph is safely leaning on each arm", yet it was "most decidedly tantalising to those who are accustomed to use the swelling melodies for livelier purposes". Delectable refreshments, including oranges, a luxury at that period, and almonds, raisins, candies and "cupid's messengers", were served to the guests, and a soda fountain was liberally patronised. The evening's entertainment closed with songs and recitations, and the whole affair was considered "one of the richest and one of the pleasantest that it has been our fortune in many years to witness".[30]

One of the first sports to be developed in Upper Canada was horse-racing, which, with sailing and fishing, formed the chief diversion of the garrisons at Kingston, Niagara, Detroit, Amherstburg and York during the first years of the existence of the province. The first race-track was probably that opened at Niagara in the early seventeen-nineties, and "the Sport of Kings" quickly spread everywhere. The following announcement of a meet at Niagara in 1797 illustrates the chief characteristics of town races:

---

[30]*Cobourg Sentinel*, May 14, 1864. This interesting account and several others quoted from the *Sentinel* were written by Daniel McAllister.

"Niagara Races—Will be run over the new course on the plains of Newark (West Niagara) on the 6th day of July next, a purse of twenty guineas; on the 7th one of ten guineas, and on the 8th the entrance money, be it more or less. The best of three heats, twice round to a heat, making one mile, more or less. Free for any mare, horse or gelding, carrying not less than 150 lbs., which shall be entered with either of the stewards on or before Monday, the 3rd of July, together with the dress of riders, as no one will be permittted to ride unless dressed in a short round jacket; caps not being to be had, a black handkerchief must be worn as a substitute.

"No person will be allowed to enter horse, mare or gelding without first becoming a subscriber, and the sum of four dollars, being the entrance money, must at the time of entering be paid in hand.

"The races will begin at 11 o'clock a.m. of each day, and it is requested that no dogs be brought on to the course."[31]

One of the earliest race-courses at York was laid out before the War of 1812, at the commencement of the peninsula leading to what is now the island. This was a straight track, and its location was chosen largely because the peninsula was a popular resort for those who enjoyed the pleasures of walking, riding and driving; particularly did the military engage in these pursuits so characteristic of English watering-places. The importance attached both to the race-course and the other facilities for pleasure on the peninsula may be seen from the attempt to build by private subscription in 1822-23 two bridges over the Great and Little Don. Though these causeways were partially constructed, there was not money enough to complete them until 1835, and then only with the aid of a subsidy from the military chest, made available through the interest of the Lieutenant-Governor, Sir John Colborne. Their opening was an occasion of gratulation no less than that in modern Ontario when a stretch of paved highway is officially inaugurated; but in this instance the old-world pomp and ceremonial was reminiscent of a lord mayor's installation.

In towns like Kingston, Cobourg, York and Niagara the "gentlemen" of the district formed steeplechase and other

[31]Niagara *Upper Canada Gazette*, June 28, 1797.

racing clubs of a semi-private nature. Cobourg, for example, had three race-courses during the predominance of the turf. Many of the members of these clubs followed the way of life of English gentlemen, having fine estates and large stables of horses specially bred for the hunt and the race-track. Some men, like the Hon. George S. Boulton of Cobourg, had private driveways constructed through their extensive estates, and there the members of the family drove in their carriages or rode horseback in no less style than the nobility in London's exclusive Rotten Row.

Tandem and carriole clubs were other organisations dependent upon horses, the membership of these societies being largely restricted to officers. The Toronto Tandem Club was organised in the winter of 1839-40, and the activities included weekly drives in sleighs and cutters to the Peacock Inn or some other favourite resort, where gay dinners not infrequently drew forth poetical effusions from the more gifted members.[32]

In the so-called backwoods settlements, like Richmond, Perth and Bytown, horse-races were much less aristocratic events, and commonly resulted in fights and brawls; while in all parts of the province gambling and drunkenness were characteristic of such sporting activities. There were races of all varieties and conditions, but they were usually restricted to native horses, which the meets aided greatly in developing. In the pioneer period the gambling element, which has always been pre-eminent in horse-racing, was productive of a great deal of evil; men had then little actual cash to wager, but bets of 10,000 feet of lumber, barrels of pork or flour, and even of land grants and homes, were quite usual.

During the winter months horse-racing on the ice was early a popular sport in all parts of the province. A man still living recalls his participation in many a race on the Bay of Quinté, at Trenton and Belleville, on Lakes Scugog and Simcoe, and in the vicinity of Port Hope and Peterborough. Valuable purses were awarded at these meets, long characteristic of the Canadian winter season.[33]

[32]See Robertson, *op. cit.*, Vol. II, pp. 1040-48.
[33]See the reminiscences of Monroe Lawson, Brighton, in E. C. Guillet: *Cobourg*, in the *Cobourg Sentinel-Star*, June 25, 1931.

W. H. Bartlett

COBOURG, 1840

The building flying a flag is the Customs House. In the background old Victoria College stands out prominently; and at the right is the first Anglican Church

From the *Illustrated London News*, May 9, 1868

FUNERAL PROCESSION OF THE HON. D'ARCY McGEE, MONTREAL, 1868

CRICKET MATCH AT TORONTO, SEPTEMBER 2ND AND 3RD, 1872

The Cricket Grounds were situated just south of College Street, west of University Avenue. This match was between "twelve of the Gentlemen of England and twenty-two of the Toronto Club"

"THE FASTEST IN THE WORLD"
PROFESSIONAL HOCKEY—CHICAGO BLACK HAWKS VS. TORONTO MAPLE LEAFS

13,500 fans at the Maple Leaf Gardens, Toronto, November 12, 1931. Similar ceremonies are usual at the opening of the baseball season.

Among the earliest outdoor games to be played in Upper Canada were lacrosse, bandyball, football, cricket and curling. Lacrosse originated among the Indians, but it was not prominent in the days of early settlement. Bandyball had some of the charactertistics of both tennis and hockey. Football and bandyball were commonly played by those who did not aspire to social heights, while cricket was particularly the game of the English middle and upper classes, and curling that of Scottish settlers. Some of the first clubs were formed among officers resident in the older towns. In the late thirties there were cricket clubs in Toronto, Hamilton, Ancaster, Brantford, Woodstock, Guelph, Cobourg and Kingston, and probably in other towns. Curling soon ceased to be a monopoly of the Scotch, and there were clubs during the same period in Toronto, Fergus, Galt, Guelph, Niagara and Kingston, as well as in certain townships. Cricket gradually decreased in importance and is now played in Canada chiefly at preparatory schools where the cultivation of an English attitude is considered desirable.

Inter-club games, particularly in cricket and curling, were sometimes played in the thirties and forties, though the difficulties of transportation placed such competitions in the category of a half week's holiday. It took three days, for example, for the curlers of Toronto to engage in a competition with the Hamilton club; and when the Cobourg Cricket Club visited Bowmanville in 1846 to play a friendly game it was most convenient to travel the day before on the steamboat *America*, though the distance was only twenty-five miles.

Football, bandyball and tennis were usually played more informally, and seldom resulted in the formation of clubs in the early period. In later days Association football (soccer) was an organised sport in urban centres, as well as in most townships; but, except among "Old Countrymen" in the towns, the game has been largely replaced by baseball or by rugby football. Quoits and other hurling games were early popular, especially in the rural districts, but golf and lawn bowling had not been introduced, much less such ephemeral sports as miniature golf and box lacrosse. Baseball was first played in Canada in the sixties, when it was introduced from the United States. The rules of this sport differed in some respects from the baseball of today. It was a real "he-man's" game at its inception, for no gloves were used; but, (possibly because men become more effeminate as life grows easier), the old game is being to some extent replaced by softball, in which our "emancipated" women join—though often with more enthusiasm than grace.

Toronto and Kingston were among the earliest towns to have Yacht Clubs, and during the early sixties Cobourg and other ports joined in the competitions, which were notable sporting events. The regattas frequently lasted two days or longer, and a few enterprising citizens who invested money in yachting were responsible for the sailing races, which attracted entries from many Lake Ontario ports. A ball usually provided an enjoyable culmination to the races, which were very fashionable occasions, quite different from the canoe regattas which, from the days of early settlement, had been held along the Ottawa and at some of the "back lakes" settlements.

Among indoor games whist, chess and billiards had their devotees. Some hotels in the towns had billiard tables, and matches for cash prizes were occasionally held. Chess clubs frequently competed against one another, one match between Cobourg and Port Hope in 1864 being carried on by telegraph, then only seventeen years old and still something of a novelty.

Special occasions which provided amusement for both urban and rural population—for people came from far and near to be present—were elections, militia parades and public holidays. Elections usually lasted a week unless one candidate retired before the time was up. William Lyon Mackenzie describes an election at Niagara Falls as attracting people of all nationalities, plus "poetical as well as most prosaical phizes, horsemen and footmen, fiddlers and dancers, honourables and reverends, captains and colonels, beaux and belles, wagons and tilburies, coaches and chaises, gigs and carts; in short, Europe, Asia, Africa and America had there each its representative among the loyal subjects and servants of our good King George, the

fourth of that name".[34] The opening and closing days drew
particularly large crowds, most people coming to receive
free liquor and to enjoy themselves, rather than for the
purpose of voting. Drunken brawls frequently occurred,
and at the end of the voting an outburst of enthusiasm led
to parades, horse-play of one type or another, and fighting
between the partisans of the victor and the vanquished.

In later years such celebrations gradually became somewhat more genteel, though no less enthusiastic. In 1861
the news of victory in a provincial election led to a
celebration in Cobourg which included a torchlight procession led by the town band. A newspaper states that
"conspicuous in the front ranks of the procession was a
coffin borne by four individuals and supposed to contain
the remains of the defeated leader of the opposition party,
on either side of which, in large letters, appeared the in-
scription, 'Brown Politically Dead'. Finally the procession
arrived at a point below the town, where preparations had
been made for a bonfire. The coffin was placed upon the pile,
the match was struck, and the town soon became illuminated by the flame. During the night large quantities of
fireworks were sent hissing through the air." The editor
is pleased to say in closing, however, that "all passed off
without any serious disturbance, much to the credit of the
party in honour of the defeat of the great political leader
of which the demonstration was got up".[35]

The militia parades provided a holiday usually observed
in the rural districts as in the towns. All men from sixteen
to sixty-five years of age were enrolled in the militia and
many of them took part in the proceedings on parade-day,
which consisted of a little drill and a good deal of horse-
racing and drinking. June the 4th, the birthday of George
III, was celebrated in this manner long after his death,
and in later years Victoria's birthday, May 24th, superseded it. In the larger towns where there was a garrison of
regulars it was usual to have a review of them also; but
in every case the military manoeuvres ended in a *feu de joie*.

The militia parade grew out of the establishment of

[34]W. L. Mackenzie: *Sketches of Canada and the United States*. 1833.
    p. 89.
[35]*Cobourg Sentinel*, July 13, 1861.

the Upper Canadian militia, for it was obviously necessary that some pretence at the training of the citizens should be made. There appears, for example, in the *Niagara Herald* of May 23, 1801, a notice inserted by Samuel Street, Deputy-Lieutenant of the County of Lincoln, that the militia will meet at Chippawa Bridge on June the 4th, and that "all quakers, menonists or tunkers" must attend, bring certificates of exemption and pay the exemption fee, "or expect to be proceeded against as the law in such case directs". In the same issue the *Herald* announces that "it is intended to make the 4th of June a day of rejoicing in this county, as well for the added years as for the recovered health of His Majesty. It is said that after the review at Queenston, there will be premiums on the best shots among the armed companies; that there will be a horse-race in the afternoon, and that other plans are in forwardness for promoting the amusements of the day".[36]

In most cases the militia parades were ludicrous in appearance and more or less useless in accomplishment. Some men came to them in partial uniform and with some sort of arms, but the general effect led to such descriptions as "a parti-coloured and curiously-equipped regiment", and "a laughter-stirring spectacle".[37] Joseph Pickering describes in his journal "training-day" as the occasion "when the militia meet at appointed stations, near home, throughout the province, to be trained, some with guns and some without. I need not say that they learn but little when the reader is informed this is the only day in the year they meet, and then not half of them perhaps, and nearly one-half of the officers know as little of military exercises as themselves; it is merely a frolic for the youngsters".[38] Another writer emphasises the ludicrous appearance of the militia:

"One might have imagined that each man of them kept his own tailor. . . . As far as we could discern, not one garment was kin to another, they were as distinct as the countenances of the wearers; and the *chapeaux* that defended their craniums from the sun, too, of every discordant

[36]*Niagara Herald,* May 23, 1801.
[37]Need, *op. cit.,* p. 12.
[38]Joseph Pickering: *Inquiries of an Emigrant.* 1831. June 4, 1826.

variety. Lastly, the weapons that dangled from the fists of the doughty heroes would have been still more difficult to classify: guns, whips, bludgeons, hoes, umbrellas, canes, sticks."[39]

Most of the participants came not to drill but for the day's outing, and they were usually impatient for the commencement of the horse-races and other holiday activities. In the larger towns a ball provided a fitting close to the day's festivities. In the capital the presence of the governor and the garrison added interest and dignity to the celebration of the King's birthday. At York in 1799 "the Queen's Rangers fired three volleys, the militia assembled on the beach, and a Royal Salute of 21 guns was fired by the Royal Artillery. At night the Government Buildings were superbly illuminated, at which place his Honour the President gave a splendid ball and supper".[40]

The events of parade-day at Niagara in 1807 included a reception by Lieutenant-Governor Gore:

"On the morning of the birthday the militia began to make their appearance at an early hour, and about 12 o'clock 1,000 formed in a line on the plains for the review of his Excellency, who expressed the highest satisfaction at their conduct and appearance.

"Previously to seeing the militia, his Excellency on horseback, attended by his aide-de-camp, Lieut. Loring of the 49th Regiment, appeared on the garrison parade during the royal salute in honour of the day, and at two o'clock held a levee at the commanding officers' quarters, where the officers of the militia and other gentlemen from distant parts of the district, not before introduced, were presented."[41]

After the middle of the century the militia was frequently important in social life all the year round. The celebration of the Queen's birthday, May 24th, was often carried out in more style than had been usual on earlier parade-days. In 1861, for example, the streets of Cobourg "presented a very military appearance as the cavalry and rifles, with their red and green uniforms, passed through

[39]David Wilkie: *Sketches of a Summer Trip to New York and the Canadas*. 1837. pp. 158-9.
[40]York *Upper Canada Gazette* June 8, 1799.
[41]*York Gazette*, June 13, 1807.

to join their comrades at the several stations assigned for their meeting. . . . At eleven o'clock the town was enlivened by the soul-stirring strains of Professor Chalaupka's unrivalled Cobourg Brass Band, which marched from their band-room to the armoury of the rifles, and escorted them to Perry's Common, where they were joined by the cavalry under the command of Colonel Boulton, and both joined in a grand *feu de joie* in honour of Her Majesty's birthday".[42]

It was usual on such occasions to close the day's festivities with a ball. Among other activities connected with the militia were picnics, and rifle matches with units in neighbouring towns; while the young ladies of seventy years ago were not as mid-Victorian as one might have presumed, for in Cobourg a number of them actually took a course of twenty-four lessons in military manoeuvres, and are said to have performed the various evolutions with credit.

An interesting holiday celebration occurred in Toronto on April 2, 1840, in honour of Queen Victoria's marriage. A peculiar account of the event says that "one ox roasted whole . . . was brought into the centre of the Market Square in Procession. . . . Every person, Man, Woman and Child who intended to partake of this banquet was requested to come cleanly attired, each with a 'Knife, Fork and Plate'. The City was beautifully illuminated from 8 o'clock to 11. There was also a display of Fire Works and Balloons".[43]

Whenever royalty or the highest officials of the country honoured communities with a visit, the occasion was always a memorable one. The progress through Canada in 1860 of the Prince of Wales, later Edward VII, was punctuated by a series of enthusiastic receptions and balls wherever he went, marred only by a few partisan demonstrations arising out of the strong religious prejudices of the times. Triumphal arches were everywhere erected, and the inhabitants lost no opportunity to show the popular prince everything of interest along his route. The celebrated Blondin performed in his presence unparalleled feats on a tight-rope at Niagara Falls; at Ottawa they ran a special

[42]*Cobourg Sentinel*, May 25, 1861.
[43]Toronto *Mirror*, April 3, 1840.

G. H. Andrews

GRAND CANOE RECEPTION ON THE ST. LAWRENCE TO THE PRINCE OF WALES

Given by Sir George Simpson of the Hudson's Bay Company when the Prince visited Dorval, August 29, 1860

G. H. Andrews

From the *Illustrated London News*, October 13, 1860

HIS ROYAL HIGHNESS ESCORTED TO MONTREAL BY A FLEET OF LAKE AND UP-RIVER STEAMERS

E. C. Reed

KING AND JORDAN STREETS, TORONTO, 1818-1933

The magnificent 33-storey Canadian Bank of Commerce Head Office, the highest building in the British Empire, stands on the site of the first Methodist Church in Toronto, a primitive frame meeting-house which in 1834 became (*horribile dictu!*) the Theatre Royal.

excursion for him down a timber slide; while at Cobourg he must needs be given a trip on the pet enterprise of the citizens—the Cobourg and Peterborough Railway—though the trestle bridge over Rice Lake was too unsafe to allow His Royal Highness to cross by that means. Ballroom dancing received a great impetus by the visit of this devotee of Terpsichore, and many of the social belles of Canada West were thrilled by a dance with the future king.

An occasion which sometimes assumed the characteristics of a holiday and resulted in a large gathering of people was a public execution,—fortunately comparatively rare. Many people were then of the opinion of Dr. Samuel Johnson: "Sir, executions are intended to draw spectators. If they do not draw spectators they don't answer their purpose. . . . The age is running mad after innovation. . . . The old method was most satisfactory to all parties; the public was gratified by a procession; the criminal was supported by it. Why is all this to be swept away?"[44]

When Dr. W. H. King was hanged at Cobourg in June, 1859, many people travelled all night to be present, and 10,000 persons, including some 500 women, saw the murderer pay the penalty; even schools were closed because of the general exodus towards the place of execution. Such an event was always expected to produce a speech from the murderer, warning his hearers to avoid the pitfalls which had brought him to the gallows; and this execution ran true to form, for the Doctor, though insisting upon his innocence up to the last day, finally confessed his guilt and admitted that his punishment was deserved. The huge crowd which witnessed the "sad spectacle" are said to have "preserved the utmost good order during the whole time. . . . . All dispersed quietly and went to their respective homes, and the unfortunate Dr., I hope, went home to heaven".[45] Interest in the morbid has, of course, always been a prominent characteristic of human nature. The dead man's spiritual adviser, the Rev. Vanderburg, had a congregation of 1,500 to hear him preach on the following Sun-

[44]James Boswell: *Life of Dr. Samuel Johnson.* 1791. Everyman's
    Library, Vol. II, p. 447.
[45][Alexander Stewart]: *The Life and Trial of William H. King,*
    M.D., for Poisoning His Wife at Brighton. 1859. p. 53.

day in his small rural church at Codrington; and no less than three books were published concerning the life and death of Dr. King.

In particular instances the exploitation of natural attractions as amusement centres was early evident. The vicinity of Niagara Falls was commercialised by the establishment not only of hotels and mills but refreshment booths and a variety of amusements of the type usually associated with beaches and pleasure resorts. The tavern-keepers and concession-owners arranged spectacles from time to time to attract crowds. In 1827 and 1829 old schooners, with animals as enforced passengers, were sent down the river to amuse large crowds of the curious who had assembled, though the boats broke up before they reached the Falls; and in later years many people attained notoriety or death by daring attempts to go over the Falls, swim the rapids, or cross the river on a tight-rope. Barnet's Museum of stuffed birds and animals, and the Camera Obscura, which beautifully reflected the Falls, were among the amusements of nearly a century ago which were worthy of a visit.

The development of commercialised picnic-grounds began in York over one hundred years ago. The Island was early noted as a pleasure resort, and was approached by canoe or horse-boat. A notice in Mackenzie's *Almanac* for 1834 refers to an hotel there for the convenience of picnic parties:

"Horse-boat to the Island. A boat propelled by four horses runs every day from the Steamboat Wharves to the Starch Factory on the peninsula or island across the Bay— her trips regulated to suit public convenience. Fare to and from the island, 7½d. A hotel has been opened on the island to accommodate sportsmen, parties of pleasure, etc."[46]

By 1850 the Island had developed greatly as a pleasure resort, and contained some of the amusements which have long characterised the beaches and other public playgrounds. Under the head "Cheap Pleasure", L. J. Privat advertises his horse-boat service across the Bay. The

[46][W. L. Mackenzie's] *New Almanack for the Canadian True Blues.* 1834. p. 15.

steam ferry *Victoria* succeeded its more primitive fore-runner in 1851, but the reference in the advertisement to pasturage for horses and cattle shows how close to rural life Toronto was at that period:

"That Safe and Convenient Horse-Boat, the *Peninsula Packet* will leave Mr. Maitland's Wharf, foot of Church Street, every day at ten o'clock a.m., 12, 2, 4, and 6 p.m., for the Peninsula Hotel. Returning at 11 a.m., 1, 3, 5 and 7 p.m. precisely. Fare to and from, 7½d. Family Season Tickets $4 each. Swings and Merry-go-round, etc., for the amusement of Children. Dinners, Lunches, Teas, etc., to be had at the shortest notice. Good pasture for Horses and other cattle, which can be conveyed over by the first boat —not later."[47]

In many towns where there was no such beauty-spot to be developed as a centre of recreation, picnics and similar gatherings were commonly held in pleasant groves. The first park in many a town grew out of the "common" where it had long been customary to hold the militia parades, cricket and football matches, and other similar activities of town life.

It was nearly half a century after the arrival of the first settlers before commercialised theatrical exhibitions were to be found in Upper Canada. Writing just previous to 1820 Robert Gourlay found that "the country is too young for regular theatric entertainments and those deli-cacies and refinements of luxury which are the usual at-tendants of wealth. Dissipation, with her fascinating train of expenses 'and vices, has made but little progress on the shores of the lakes".[48] Among the earliest dramatic efforts were occasional plays produced by the officers of the gar-risons at York, Kingston and Niagara; in these the female parts were usually taken by men. As a general rule only comedies were attempted, Goldsmith's *She Stoops to Con-quer* being among the number. The first theatrical per-formances by professionals were introduced by American companies in the eighteen-twenties. Two plays were usually produced for one evening's entertainment, a rather

[47]Advertisement quoted in Robertson, *op. cit.*, Vol. II, p. 884.
[48]Robert Gourlay: *A Statistical Account of Upper Canada.* 1822. Vol. I, p. 250.

serious play being followed by a boisterous comedy, with perhaps a little vaudeville during the intermission.

The course of development of theatres in York may be taken as typical of that in the other towns of Upper Canada. The first theatre in the town was the ballroom of Frank's Hotel; there, in the early twenties, travelling companies presented such plays as *Pizzaro; Barbarossa, or the Siege of Algiers; Ali Baba, or the Forty Thieves; The Lady of the Lake;* and *The Miller and His Men.* A small stage, few dramatic effects, and little or no scenery were characteristic of this as of all other early theatres in Upper Canada. In 1824 a local club, the Canadian Amateurs, was giving occasional dramatic performances in the Little Theatre, located in the rear of Frank's Hotel. After its use for religious purposes was discontinued in the early thirties, the Wesleyan Chapel on King Street was used as a theatre. In 1834 it was given the name Theatre Royal and the first entertainment was *A Panorama of the Burning of Moscow.* The early theatres of York usually charged half a crown for good seats, and 1s. 3d. for those in the rear.

It is, of course, impossible to gauge the value of any entertainment from the producers' announcements; nor can a press report of it always be accepted as unbiased criticism. The fact that most of the players "hailed from" the United States prejudiced the chances of a fair reception at the hands of a considerable number of people, among whom the editor of the *British Colonist* appears to have been one of the most pronounced in his views. With obvious dislike he records a visit to the Theatre Royal in 1839, when "a party of strolling players from Yankee-land" were performing. He says that "the performance commenced with what was styled in the bills 'The much-admired farce of Nature and Philosophy', on the youth who never saw a woman. . . . Both the farce and the actors of it are altogether too contemptible for criticism". A Scotch song was "brutally murdered" by Mrs. Lennox. This was followed "by an attempt to act the opera of *The Maid of Cashmere,* and it was but an attempt. Miss Ince danced tolerably well, and that is all that can be said in favour of the performance. By this time our patience was quite exhausted; we left, and immediately set to write this notice,

lest by delay we might so far forget what we had witnessed
as to do injustice afterwards to any of the company by de-
tracting from their just merits as players. . . . There is
no reason why such a miserable catchpenny as that at
present in operation should be tolerated. The municipal
authorities should interfere and abate the nuisance".[49]

In spite of such scathing criticism, however, it is probable that this company was no worse than the average of
the day; and it is likely that many unprejudiced patrons
enjoyed the entertainment provided. The spread of the
drama into other parts of Upper Canada depended largely
upon the growth of communities, and their accessibility;
amateur productions were frequently to be found first, and
performances of travelling companies later.

Several organisations of minstrels were playing in
Canada West in the early sixties, among them being
Christy's and Sharpley's; a similar performance was given
by Kelly's Theatrical Troupe. Some minstrel shows had a
repertoire of "stock" plays, particularly of the more emotional and humorous types, and many of them had brass
bands. With its light program of vaudeville and burlesque,
broad comedy and sentimental melodrama, the minstrel
show is a type of entertainment which has retained its
popularity with the average amusement-seeker, for it does
not require the same capabilities and attention that are
necessary for the proper appreciation of the higher operatic
and dramatic performances.

In addition to the minstrel shows there were circuses
and various types of travelling exhibitions to interest those
who found dramatic performances and educational lectures
not to their liking. Some of these shows, notably the
circuses, not only travelled from town to town, but were
also presented at or near rural taverns, the proprietors of
which usually acted as agents of the organisations insofar
as the advance sale of tickets was concerned. The circus,
usually of American origin, was among the first commercialised amusements to tour Upper Canada. As early as the
eighteen-twenties travelling manageries found their way
into all but the most remote sections of the province, and

[49]Toronto *British Colonist*, September 4, 1839.

were consequently almost as well-known to the farmer as to the dweller in the towns.

In the fifties and sixties Van Amburgh's "collection of the animal kingdom" was among the most popular of the organisations which travelled the province. When circus performances were given they frequently offended the sensibilities of the more refined, so Van Amburgh advertised that, as there was no such entertainment accompanying his show, "it will afford an opportunity to the most religious of gratifying their curiosity in seeing with their eyes some of the wonders of the animal creation". The admission charged for afternoon and evening exhibitions was 25 cents for adults and 15 cents for children, and it is announced that the show "will form a feast to the naturalist, and an opportunity to the Christian philosopher to contemplate the Wisdom and Power of the Supreme Being in the creation of animated nature".[50]

As early as 1827 York had a resident circus under the management of Besnard and Black. This was held in the barn of Dr. Forest's Hotel on King Street, east of Sherbourne. There was no menagerie connected with it, the entertainment consisting of "riding and feats of horsemanship, trapeze and horizontal bar performances, and tricks of juggling". Mrs. Besnard was the favourite of the circusgoers of that early period, and her "tossing of balls and knives was one of the principal features of the show".[51]

The regular amusements available in Toronto in the late fifties were closely associated with saloons, two of the more pretentious of which were the Terrapin, (formerly the St. Nicholas, and situated on King Street near the site of the present King Edward Hotel), and the Apollo Saloon and Concert Room on the same street. In describing the attractions of these places of entertainment a contemporary publication introduces the subject by noting that "we believe there is no city of its size on the continent which is pestered with so many saloons and taverns; and, if the morals and habits of our people were to be judged by this criterion, the stranger would form a very unfavourable and unjust opinion".

[50]*Cobourg Sentinel*, July 6, 1861.
[51]Robertson, *op. cit.*, Vol. I, p. 479.

The Apollo Saloon appears to have staged nightly a show which may be called the forerunner of the night club, though it was available upon much more reasonable terms. The price of admission was only twelve and one-half cents, and from his modest investment the patron was entitled to "a smoke or a drink", as well as to witness a "performance of negro minstrelsy, comic and sentimental singing, etc". The actors, Mr. Burgess and Mr. Den Thompson, are described as "inimitable in their way, ... the one as a negro performer, and the other as a 'broth of a boy' from the Emerald Isle". Visitors to the Provincial Exhibition of 1858 are assured that "the place is well worthy of a visit".

The same authority describes for us Toronto's theatre of that period—the Royal Lyceum—which, "although small, and, since the hard times commenced, has not met with the encouragement its management merited, is an exceedingly pleasant resort". The manager, Mr. Nickinson, was himself "a first-rate actor", and he was ably assisted by others "equally good in their line", notably Mr. Petrie, Mr. Marlowe, Mr. Lee, Mrs. Marlowe and Miss Frost. The "general run of pieces" were well presented by this stock company, and we are glad to learn that "the performances are always characterised by morality and good breeding".[52]

Shows featuring midgets and monstrosities were not in early days confined to fall fairs and exhibitions. The 1863 variety of Tom Thumb visited Cobourg, accompanied by "his beautiful little wife, the fascinating Queen of Beauty, and Commodore Nutt, the $30,000 Nutt, (so called because he received that amount from P. T. Barnum for three years' service), and Elfin Minnie Warren, the smallest lady of her age ever seen—all four weighing but 100 pounds". As an extra attraction it is announced that Tom Thumb's wife "will wear the identical wedding costume as worn at Grace Church on February 10, 1863, when $60 was offered for a ticket to the wedding; here the same thing can be seen for a trifle". Before the show commenced there was—as has

---

[52]These Toronto amusements of 1858 are described in the *Descriptive Catalogue of the Provincial Exhibition, 1858*. Second Edition, 1858, p. 79.

long been customary with circuses and minstrel shows—a
street parade.[53]

Previous to the days of motion pictures there were
numerous attempts to give graphical representations of
popular subjects, usually with an accompanying lecture, or
with music on the tambourine or some sort of "musical
machine". There were figures in wax as well as illustra-
tions of other kinds. Large numbers of pictures illustra-
tive of Bunyan's *Pilgrim's Progress* comprised one entertainment, while others consisted of panoramas of Biblical
themes, the Holy Land, and kindred subjects. On one
occasion in the early sixties a panorama of the *Bible* was
exhibited for six nights in Cobourg, and may be presumed
to have visited all parts of the province.

Another performance, "sure to inculcate a high moral
tendency and to warn every young man, and older one, too,
who has commenced to tamper with the intoxicating glass",
was Verey's Zographicon, consisting of a lecture, accompanied by 150 views from *The Pilgrim's Progress,* and
Arthur's *Ten Nights in a Bar Room.* The allegorical representations and striking scenes were given with "full and
very often touching and vivid explanations", and were of
a character "calculated to give an elevated tone to the
morals of the community".[54]

It was early considered—and it still holds true—that
concerts, lectures and shows were more attractive to
patrons if they were advertised as from London or New
York. Friend's Panorama of the British Isles was heralded
as "direct from St. James' Hall, London, England", and the
art work is described as "a moving panorama painted by
Mr. Friend himself on over 50,000 feet of canvas". The
exhibitor is referred to as "the celebrated artist, vocalist,
musician and entertainer", who "will sing melodies, accompanying himself on different instruments, including a
Grand Euphonium Piano".[55] Performances and lectures of
this kind may be assumed to have been neither better nor
worse than those of today; the best of them must have

[53]*Cobourg Sentinel,* October 17, 1863.
[54]*Cobourg World,* November 25, 1864.
[55]*Cobourg Sentinel,* May 14, 1864 .

contributed greatly to the education and enjoyment of those who attended.

It has always been characteristic of showmanship to advertise productions in a most bombastic and exaggerated manner. To this was added in the pioneer period, and later, an evident intention of attracting people to performances by announcing them in huge, almost unpronounceable words; possibly this was a recommendation in a day when education was not so generally diffused. We find, for example, the Papyrotamia, or gallery of paper cuttings, which was shown in Meighan's Ball Room, York, in 1827; and in later years a magician advertised his show as "The Grand Thaumaturgic Psychomanteum", and himself as "the celebrated artist and arch-magician, Professor Anderson, known throughout the civilised Globe as the Wizard of the North, and an Illusionist, Physicist, Thaumatist and Traveller", whose "Soirés de Prestidigitation constitute the most marvellous entertainment in which, at any time, the attempt has been made to blend the highest science with the most genial amusement".[56]

The same high-sounding names were still further developed in the advertisements of circuses and menageries of the sixties. J. B. Lent's travelling show visited Cobourg in 1862 under the name "Hippozoonamadon", which was described as "the largest exhibition in the world", a combination of three circuses, a hippopotamus and elephant exhibition, and an aquarium. A word large enough to frighten the most learned savant is used to describe a part of the Hippozoonamadon—the Athleolympimantheum—in which Mlle. Ariane Felecia from Paris formed the main attraction, for she is described as "the most beautiful, graceful, daring and dashing equestrienne in the world". Numerous other features, including the Grand Opera Band, were offered as a part of the Hippozoonamadon—and all for twenty-five cents![57]

In the folowing year J. B. Lent came around again, probably with the same show; but he had been able to invent for it a new name—Equescurriculum. In addition to the "unparalleled combination of three circuses" there was "a troop of acting bears, the educated sacred Indian bull, leap-

[56]*Ibid.*, October 11, 1862.   [57]*Ibid.*, July 5, 1862.

ing buffaloes and performing dogs and monkeys". The whole formed "a magnificent phalanx of exhibitions—perfection in every detail"; and, as before,—all for twenty-five cents.[58]

Times have changed, however. We still have magicians and circuses, vaudeville and burlesque, comedies and tragedies, romances and melodramas; we have revived the comic opera of Gay, and Gilbert and Sullivan, and developed the typically American musical comedy and girl-and-music show; and in addition to all these we have the radio and the talking motion picture. But something has gone out of town life: Hippozoonamadons, Equescurriculums, Thaumaturgic Psychomanteums and Athleolympimantheums have departed from our midst forever!

[58]*Ibid.*, July 25, 1863.

CHAPTER XI

PIONEER SPORTS—CURLING

"When Winter muffles up his cloak,
And binds the mire like a rock,
Then to the loch the Curlers flock
Wi' gleesome speed."
ROBERT BURNS.[1]

THE ancient Scottish sport of curling, or channel-stane as it was long called, is very closely connected with pioneer life in Canada. In the history of the early settlement of our country there is but little reference to organised sport, but among the first games played in both urban and rural districts was curling.

An authority on the development of the game in Scotland writes that "the early history of curling is involved in such obscurity that the time even of antiquarians might be better employed in eating beef and greens, or in playing the game, than in endeavouring to discover its origin." The game is certainly of great antiquity, for references to curling (and to golf as well) are found in a book published in 1638; while in the 1695 edition of Camden's *Britannia* the Isle of Copinsha, in the Orkney group, is described as containing "in great plenty excellent stones for the game called curling".[2] The stones that were early used were irregular in size and shape. Some of these have been recovered from the bottom of "lochs" and mill-dams; one is dated 1551, and is eleven inches long, ten inches broad and five inches thick.

The game should be considered the national sport of Scotland if the enthusiasm of the players is any criterion. We find many a sentiment written in the following strain:

"I've played at quoitin' mony a day,
And maybe I may da'et again,
But still unto myself I say
This is no the channel-stane.

[1]Robert Burns: *Tam Samson's Elegy.*
[2]See John Kerr: *The History of Curling.* 1890. p. 88.

Oh for a channel-stane!
The fell guid game the channel-stane;
There's no game that e'er I saw
Can match auld Scotland's channel-stane."[3]

The Scottish curler always finds it difficult to appreciate
the Englishman's enthusiasm for cricket:

"Old England may her cricket boast,
    Her wickets, bats, and a' that;
And proudly her Eleven toast,
    Wi' right good will and a' that.
For a' that, and a' that,
    It's but bairns' play for a' that;
The channel-stane on icy plain
    Is king o' games for a' that."

In the last stanza of the same poem the writer strikes
a philosophical note in referring to death as the last curling
match:

"And when the score o' life is made,
    As made it will for a' that;
When hin-han death's last shot is played,
    And time's a hog, and a' that,
For a' that, and a' that,
    Our besom friends for a' that,
We hope to meet, each rink complete,
    Round Higher Tee for a' that."[4]

The first *Annual* of the Ontario branch of the Royal
Caledonian Curling Club, issued in 1876, contains a long account of the "Great Gathering" of the Grand Caledonian
Curling Club at Kilmarnock, Scotland, on October 22, 1841,
when over 150 "brithers a'" met under the presidency of
Lord Eglinton. The dinner in the town hall was laid out in
unusual splendour. Speech followed toast for several hours,
and songs of a lively nature were interspersed to add zest
and induce merriment. One man was present who had
curled as early as 1784; while another notability was

[3]James Hogg ("the Ettrick Shepherd"), quoted in John Macnair:
    The Channel-Stane, or Sweepings frae the Rinks. 1883-5. Vol. I,
    p. 52.
[4]H. Shanks: *Curling Song.* See Macnair, *op. cit.,* Vol. III, pp. 75-7.

Thomas Samson, the son of the Tam Samson whom the
beloved Rabbie Burns complimented as a curler in the lines

> "He was the king o' a' the core
> To gaird, or draw, or wick a bore,
> Or up the rink like Jehu roar
>   In time o' need;
> But noo he lags on death's hog-score—
> Tam Samson's deid!"[5]

Throughout the centuries that the game has been played
in Scotland it has always been noted for its democratic
tendencies. An early encyclopaedia states that "peers, peasants, clergymen, farmers, country gentlemen, tradesmen and
artisans all meet hilariously and familiarly for the occasion".[6] In Canada, too, "the spruce tailor, the burly stone-
mason, the active weaver, the quiet-thinking minister, the
humble voter, and the M. P. are all on a level. The grand
test is who curls best."[7] The sense of good sportsmanship,
alike in victory and defeat, has been equally prominent
wherever curling has been played, for, in the words of the
poet,

> "It's a slippery game for a' that;
> We're ne'er afraid to meet on ice
> The best o' folks for a' that."[8]

Curling began in Canada at Quebec in the last years of
the eighteenth century, though the first organised club was
instituted in Montreal in 1807. Among the earliest curlers
were Scotch officers of the garrisons, who relieved the
monotony of military life by engaging in the game. Matches
were played on the St. Lawrence River, and there is record
of a game in 1807, on the river below Montreal, as late as
April 11th. Among the rules of the first club, which contained twenty members, was that it should meet "at Gillis's
on Wednesday every fortnight at 4 o'clock to dine on salt
beef and greens; . . . . and the club dinner and wines shall

[5]Robert Burns: *Tam Samson's Elegy*.
[6]*Chambers' Encyclopaedia*. 1860-68. Vol. III, p. 368.
[7]William Roper: *A Canadian Plea for Curling*. Reprinted from the
    Guelph *Mercury* in the 1876 *Annual* of the Ontario Curling
    Association, p. 82.
[8]Shanks, *ibid*.

not exceed 7s. 6d. a head".[9]   During the War of 1812 the members of the club did not meet as frequently as before.

In later years matches occurred between the curlers of Montreal and Quebec, half of the players of each club proceeding to the other and playing the match the same day, so that no news which might affect the result could be obtained at either city,—for these mighty tussles were of great importance to the participants.

In 1835 a notable match between the two cities (perhaps the first inter-club match in Canada) was played on neutral ice at Three Rivers. The Montreal players left the city on January 7th and 8th, some in the stage and some in their own conveyances, the first of them arriving at Three Rivers about noon on the 9th. The roads were very bad as there had been a heavy snow. At Three Rivers there was difficulty in finding ice, and the curlers had to make use of a very uneven piece at the mouth of the Black River. Two rinks a side engaged in the match, and when it was over the score stood: Quebec 31, Montreal 23.

At the grand dinner afterwards there was no haggis, nor was there "good, nor even tolerable whisky to be had at Three Rivers";[10] but these deficiencies were in some degree made up by nine roast turkeys and excellent champagne, though the latter appeared to some to be very much out of place at a Scotchmen's dinner. The eight Montrealers, who had been defeated, paid £3 2s. 6d. each for the dinner and about the same amount for transportation, so it is no wonder that victory in these matches was so desirable!

The records of the Montreal Club state that in 1837-38 "there was no club dinner because of the insurrection"; but in spite of the Rebellion there was considerable curling "on a new artificial rink made of wood and put up under cover in the St. Ann suburb, near the Lachine Canal".[11] This was probably the first closed rink in Canada.

French-Canadians did not know what to think of these activities of the Scotchmen upon the ice. One of them, a farmer near Quebec who had just seen the game for the first time, related excitedly to his neighbour: "Today I saw a band of Scotchmen, who were throwing large balls of iron

[9]Quoted in Kerr, *op. cit.*, p. 324.
[10]Colonel Dyde quoted in Macnair, *op. cit.*, Vol. IV, p. 80.
[11]Macnair, *op. cit.*, Vol. IV, p. 81.

SKATING IN THE RINK

Though undoubtedly a little *risqué*, the ladies are enjoying the sport

THE TORONTO RED JACKETS ON TORONTO BAY, 1873

T. McGaw is at the "hack", having just delivered his stone. J. Grey and D. Walker are the sweepers, the former with his broom in the air. Captain Perry is the skip with one knee on the ice. It is a good "end", for all the stones are "in the house".

CURLING ON THE DON RIVER, 1860

CURLING IN HIGH PARK, TORONTO, 1860

These companion sketches were made by the same artist, whose name
is unknown. The Rennies were the leaders of a group who enjoyed
the "roarin' game" on Grenadier Pond.

like tea-kettles on the ice, after which they cried 'Soop! soop!', and then laughed like fools. I really believe they ARE fools."[12]

The introduction of curling into Upper Canada followed closely upon the settlement of Scotchmen in the various parts of the province, though it was not long before teams of non-Scotch, sometimes referred to as "Barbarians", were enthusiastically engaged in the game. The first club in the province was probably that formed at Kingston in 1820. As early as 1829 curling was enjoyed on the Don River, though the first Toronto club was not organised until the winter of 1836-37. The Humber River, Grenadier Pond in High Park, and the Bay were also used by Toronto curlers in later years.

Several of the pioneer clubs of the province were formed in the "Huron Tract", which was being settled by the Canada Company in the eighteen-thirties. The earliest of these clubs was at Fergus, Wellington County, in 1834, the gloom of the first winter being dispelled by the introduction of the game. The Hon. Adam Fergusson was the founder of this Scottish settlement in the Township of Nicholl, and he was the organiser and first President of the Fergus Club. Similar associations were instituted at Galt and Guelph in 1838, but there had been curling on Altrieve Lake, near Galt, a year or two earlier. Among other early clubs in Upper Canada were those at Perth, West Flamborough, Niagara, Scarborough, Newmarket, Dundas and Milton.

In playing the game various substitutes have been made for the granite stones always used in Scotland, and now invariably in use in Ontario. In the early days of curling at Fergus, Galt and Guelph, blocks of hardwood, usually maple or beech, were employed; at Fergus they were sometimes loaded with lead in order that they might be approximately equal in weight. Iron handles were inserted into these blocks.

In Quebec and Montreal bell-shaped irons weighing from sixty-five to eighty pounds were commonly used, and this tended to lessen the intercourse between the curlers of Canada East and Canada West. The origin of the use of

[12]*Ibid.*, Vol. I, pp. 73-4.

irons is said to have been the metal-rimmed hubs of the gun-carriages, into which handles were inserted. These primitive "stones" were used by the officers of the garrison, who soon had a blacksmith imitate them. It was found that the intense cold sometimes cracked granite stones, so the use of irons was continued; but at present both types are found in Quebec. The use of irons was general also among the early curlers at the village of Dundas in Upper Canada.

When the game was introduced in Niagara, in 1836, one gentleman was generous enough to import from Scotland sufficient granite stones for the use of all the members of the club. In Toronto and vicinity stones were always used, some being imported from Scotland, while others "were made by the stone-cutter to the club, from blocks of excellent quality picked up by him on the land in the vicinity".[13] At the Oshawa Curling Club may still be seen a number of these roughly-hewn curling stones, a curiosity reminiscent of other times.

To keep the ice free from dirt and snow during the game brooms are used. In Scotland they were made of the Scotch broom as a general rule, though occasionally birch twigs or heather were substituted. In Canada corn brooms were in common use, but the early curlers near Scarborough, who had emigrated from Lanarkshire, imported stocks of genuine Scotch broom, which under their cultivation soon became popular.

The rules of curling have changed but little through the centuries, the important matter being to get one's stone nearest the "tee", and to keep it there until the "end" has been played. The length of games has changed considerably, however. In Scotland, where the continuance of the curling season was very precarious, it was customary to play all day, a lunch of bread, cheese and whisky being taken to the loch to stave off the pangs of hunger. In Canada, too, many an early curler is said to have set out the night before and travelled all night on "Shank's mare", curled all the next day, and returned home thereafter. Some clubs played three-hour matches, while in the early Toronto Club (now Toronto Victorias) a certain number of

[13]James Bicket: *The Canadian Curler's Manual.* 1840. p. 11.

shots, as 7, 13, 21, or more usually 31, signified the end of a game. The "points game", consisting of a series of difficult shots, was long popular, and the individuals making the best scores were awarded Caledonian medals by the Canadian branch of the Grand Caledonian Curling Club.

It is interesting to know that the Rebellion of 1837 had its effect upon curling. It was usual among Toronto curlers at that time to have the players "fall in" in the order in which they were to play, and "number off" from right to left. In those trying days, "when military terms and ideas were infused into every department of life", it was considered that a man who played in the wrong order was fit neither for a soldier nor a curler![14]

Owing partly to the customs of the times, and partly to the country in which the game originated, whisky-drinking during matches was early prominent and long persisted. In fact a writer observed in 1875 that "many people are under the impression that whisky and curling go hand in hand. This was the case at one time, but I rejoice to say that bottles of whisky at the head of each rink during play is now the exception and not the rule."[15] An interesting example in picture form of this change in sentiment is found in the first *Annuals* of the Ontario Curling Association. In the 1876 *Annual,* and for a year or two following, appeared an engraving of the famous Red Jackets playing a match on Toronto Bay. The game is being contested with much spirit, some of which, however, was obtained from time to time from a basket of bottles which are in plain view at one end of the rink. As temperance sentiment grew stronger the presence of the whisky evidently caused uneasiness in the minds of many, for in the 1879 *Annual* the same engraving appears, but with the addition of a black cloth which has been discreetly drawn over the bottles, giving the basket a most innocent appearance!

Difficulties of transportation made inter-club matches infrequent during the first half of the century. When the Toronto Club arranged to play a match with the Hamilton Thistles in the early fifties it took three days to do so,— one to travel the forty miles by sleigh, another to play the match, and a third for the return home. In spite of these

[14]*Ibid.,* p. 21 fn.   [15]Roper, *op. cit.,* p. 82.

difficulties it was customary to hold an annual "bonspiel", the word being derived from the Danish *bondespil,* meaning "a rustic game". On February 12, 1839, a bonspiel was held on the Don River, Toronto, and twenty-four curlers from outside points measured their skill against a similar number from the city. The governors of Canada have usually taken an active interest in the game, and at this match the spectators included the Governor-General, Lord Sydenham, and the Lieutenant-Governor of Upper Canada, Sir George Arthur.

The completion of the Grand Trunk Railway from Montreal to Toronto in 1856, and the building of the Great Western Railway in the Lake Erie region, made possible the largely-attended annual bonspiels which are still so popular among curlers. In 1858 Burlington Bay was the location of the event, while the following year East played West on the Don River.

Another interesting occasion in the fifties was a tussle at Quebec between Scottish and "Barbarians". An account of the match describes "the host of ladies and gentlemen, and many gay equipages", the "bursts of merriment", and the "snatches of broad Scotch" as the curlers coaxed on an important stone with honied expressions, as though their lives depended on the issue of the game. In the background arose the fortress of old Stadacona, where the target practice of the artillery "seemed as if it were a royal salute to the curlers". Many "fair admirers" witnessed the match in spite of a biting north-west wind.[16]

It was quite usual in the early days to play under severe weather conditions, perhaps exposed to a heavy snow drift, and with the thermometer below zero. On January 8, 1864, four curlers had their ears frozen during a match at Port Hope with the curlers of Cobourg. A contemporary account of the event says: "The game commenced at noon, with an interruption of twenty minutes for lunch; the time set was 4.15 p.m., and although the day turned out one of the most severe that we have had this winter, the 'roarin' game' was kept up with much spirit, notwithstanding four of the players suffered severely from Jack Frost playing tricks with their ears."[17]

[16]See Kerr, *op. cit.,* p. 326.
[17]*Cobourg Sentinel,* January 15, 1864.

On February 10th the Port Hope curlers played a return match at Cobourg, on the ice of the Victoria Skating Rink at the Factory Creek. Play commenced at noon and continued until 5 p.m.; but at two o'clock John Butler called the players from the ice and served refreshments, "which we can speak of with much credit to his good lady, for the excellent cup of coffee and other good things which we received at her hands." At the end of the match the participants were served a sumptuous dinner at the North American Hotel; after which President Ward of the Port Hope Club presented the "Broom", with colours attached, to the Cobourg curlers, as a token of victory.[18] This trophy, like the modern silver cup or tankard, was retained as long as the holders could successfully defend it on the ice.

Just as the tiresome but necessary "shovel exercise" had been one of the main reasons for the formation of clubs, in order that "the time which was formerly wasted in preparations that may be performed by labourers is now spent in the game,"[19] so, in the same way, the uncertain weather conditions led, in the early seventies, to the building of closed rinks, which soon became common throughout the province. One of the last and most notable of open-air bonspiels was held on Burlington Bay in 1875. No less than 360 curlers were present for the East *versus* West match, and the only prize awarded was a gold medal to the Chatham Club for having the highest average score. This bonspiel followed almost immediately upon the organisation of the Ontario branch of the Royal Caledonian Club, formed chiefly because the eastern Canadian clubs were so far away and used irons in place of stones. A description of this bonspiel in the first Ontario Curling Association *Annual* (1876) notes that: "the Bay presented a most lively and festive appearance. Crowds of spectators, including many of the fair sex, on foot and in sleighs, covered the Bay during the contest."[20]

A famous Canadian team in the sixties and seventies was the "Red Jackets" of the Toronto Club. The team obtained its name at the International Bonspiel at Buffalo in 1865, when twenty-three rinks of Canadians defeated the American curlers by 658 shots to 478. At the height

[18]*Ibid.*, February 13, 1864.   [19]Bicket, *op. cit.*, pp. 36-7.
[20]A full account of the event is found in the 1876 *Annual*, pp. 86-95.

of their effectiveness the Red Jackets consisted of T. Mc-Gaw, lead; Major Gray, second; D. Walker, third; and Captain Charles Perry, skip. The Ontario Curling Association *Annual* for 1886 says: "They continued to play together in the same positions for about ten years (1868-1878), during which time they travelled many thousands of miles on curling excursions, and played against select rinks from many of the strongest clubs in Canada and the United States, and won seventy-five matches in succession before they met their first defeat; a record, we may well believe, without a parallel."[21] During the heyday of this team there was another, the "Callants" of Montreal, which was almost as famous for the skill of its members. A remarkable feature in connection with this team was that the combined ages of the four members amounted to 287 years. These veterans of the besom and the stane challenged any club to a friendly game. The challenge was accepted nine times and on each occasion the Callants were victorious.

An interesting event in the annals of Canadian curling occurred on December 11, 1876, when the first curling match in the province of Manitoba took place in Winnipeg. In this match the old Scottish custom of playing for oatmeal to be distributed among the poor of the parish was imitated. After the game the prize, a barrel of meal, was presented to the Winnipeg General Hospital. In more recent years Manitoba curlers have repeatedly proven themselves the best in the Dominion in many a competition open to the outstanding teams of the various provinces.

All of the winters of earlier times were not "old-fashioned", for we find that the winter of 1875-76 was as mild as that of 1931-32, and drew forth a

CURLER'S LAMENT ABOUT THE WINTER OF 1876

Oh! Canada, adopted mither!
You've kept us in a dreary-swither,
Have ye forgot us a'thegither?
    Ye're sair to blame
For sendin' sic saft southern weather
    For curlers' game.

[21]Obituary notice of Captain Charles Perry, 1886 *Annual*, pp. 97-8.

December cam and ga'ed awa',
And scarcely brought a frost ava;
January's been a'e continued thaw
        Just much the same,—
Contrary quite to Nature's law,
        With scarce a game.
            *   *   *   *

Oh! cheerful frost, we'd welcome thee,—
Each curler's voice shouts loud with glee.
We'd gladly gather round the tee
        And ne'er gang hame;
We'd play as long as we could see,
        Grand roarin' game![22]

To keep abreast of the times an increasing number of modern curling clubs use artificial ice, which provides facilities for the game during five or six months of the year, irrespective of weather conditions. But many an old club —like the Toronto Victorias—has proud memories of the days of open-air curling, and the old times are recalled whenever we hear George S. Lyon sing *My Wild Irish Rose*, or Henry Wright thunder out—with the help of his fellow-curlers—*Jock McGraw*. Such joviality represents the good-comradeship inspired by the game; for in earlier times the devotees of the sport met at the festive board after the match and dined on the proverbial curler's fare; whereupon all joined in the

CURLERS' SONG AFTER THE BEEF AND GREENS
    (Air—*Willie Brewed a Peck o' Maut.*)

Now, brothers in the roaring game,
        Come, join a curling stave with me,
As if your soul were in the stane,
        And heaven itself were near the tee.

Chorus:- Then soop, soop, soop! soop, soop, soop!
        And draw the creepin' stane a wee;
    The ice may thaw, the day may snaw,
        But aye we're merry round the tee.

[22]1877 *Annual*, pp. 105-6. The poem was signed "W. (Toronto)".

Then hand around the neeshin' horn
The wintry evenings quickly fa';
Wha lose today may win the morn—
Thou roarin' game, hip hip hurrah![23]

[23]1876 *Annual*, pp. 109-110.